ARABIA AND THE GULF: FROM TRADITIONAL SOCIETY TO MODERN STATES

Professor M.A. Shaban

ARABIA AND THE GULF: FROM TRADITIONAL SOCIETY TO MODERN STATES

Essays
in Honour of
M.A. Shaban's 60th Birthday
(16th November 1986)

Edited
by
IAN RICHARD NETTON

BARNES & NOBLE BOOKS
Totowa, New Jersey

first published in the USA 1986 by
Barnes & Noble Books
81 Adams Drive
Totowa, New Jersey, 07512
Printed in Great Britain

Library of Congress Cataloging-in-Publication Data

Arabia and the Gulf.
Includes index.
1. Arabian Peninsula. 2. Persian Gulf Region.
I. Netton, Ian Richard.
DS204.A68 1986 953 86-14148
ISBN 0-389-20658-X

By the Same Author

Middle East Materials in United Kingdom and Irish Libraries: A Directory (1983)

Muslim Neoplatonists: An Introduction to the Thought of the Brethren of Purity (Ikhwān al-Ṣafā') (1982)

Contents

List of Tables, Figures and Maps

Tables

Figures

Maps

Preface

Professor Muhammad Abdulhayy Shaban was born on 16 November 1926 in the Egyptian village of Nikla al-'Inab which lies between Cairo and Alexandria, in the Province of al-Buhayra. He received an important part of his early education from his father who was Professor of Qur'anic Exegesis at the Azhar University in Cairo. He was blind and from an early age Shaban used to read to him so that he could prepare his lectures. Fifteen years of such training gave Shaban a good grasp of the most difficult kind of Arabic, and stimulated many serious discussions about profound theological questions. Because of this experience he acquired a deep understanding of the thinking of Muslim theologians. But it was a military career which Shaban pursued first. The academic within him was yet to emerge. After training at the Military Academy, he joined the army, rising to the rank of Captain and becoming a friend of General Neguib. His army career took him to Palestine where, briefly, in 1948 he became 'unofficial' Governor of Gaza. Shaban left Palestine in 1949, left the army also and entered the new University of 'Ayn Shams in Cairo in 1950. He graduated in 1954 with a First Class BA Honours degree in Oriental Languages (Arabic, Persian and Turkish). In March of the same year he sided with Neguib against Nasser and, as Vice-President of 'Ayn Shams Students' Union, Shaban led the Universities in opposition to Nasser.

On 13 November 1954, 5,000 students were arrested. Shaban was not among those so detained but he was called in by the government and given the choice of government service or prison. He decided to pursue his studies at Harvard for which purpose, in December 1954, the Egyptian Government awarded him a scholarship. Shaban had been helped in his decision to go to Harvard by the persuasive counsels of Professor Jim Kritzeck who, in August 1954, had advised Shaban to study in the United States and even sat down and personally typed his letter of application to the Head of the Middle East Center, Harvard. The answer which had been received was: Come in February 1955!

Shaban's time at Harvard and in the United States was both a personally happy and an intellectually stimulating one. On 16 November 1957 he met for the first time his dear wife Bessie, a Scottish lady who was working in a senior post in the Widener Library, Harvard, as a Supervisor Cataloguer. Their son Timmy (Neil Tamim) was born in Boston on

29 August 1962. While studying at Harvard, Shaban worked as a Teaching Assistant in Arabic and Persian, in the Center of Middle Eastern Studies from 1955 to 1960. He graduated with his Master's degree from Harvard in 1956 and received his PhD in History and Middle Eastern Studies in 1960 from the same university for a thesis entitled 'The Social and Political Background of the 'Abbāsid Revolution in Khurāsān'.

The thesis was supervised by the famous Professor Sir Hamilton Gibb to whom Shaban later dedicated his first book, *The 'Abbāsid Revolution*, which was based on his doctoral thesis. Shaban in future years always spoke of Gibb with respect: he admired, in particular, his knowledge of sources, describing Gibb as 'the undisputed master' in the art of their use, and also Gibb's ability to read through work quickly.

After graduating with his doctorate, Shaban held a number of short-term posts: he was, successively, Instructor in Persian in the Department of Near Eastern Languages at the University of California, Berkeley (1960–61); Cultural Attaché at the UAR Embassy, Washington (with special permission to reside in Cambridge, Mass., to pursue further research under Professor Sir Hamilton Gibb at Harvard, as a Research Associate (1961–64)); and Visiting Professor of Islamic History at the University of Riyadh in Saudi Arabia (1964–65).

Shaban then moved to Britain and from 1965 to 1966 he was a Lecturer in Arabic and Islamic Studies in the Department of Arabic Studies of the University of St Andrews. Though he found that the Department at that time lacked some of the intellectual excitement of Harvard, he was enchanted by Scotland as a region. However, after only one year there he moved south and took up another lecturing post in the School of Oriental and African Studies (SOAS), University of London, where he remained until 1971. The present editor of this volume had the good fortune, as an undergraduate at SOAS during the period 1968–72, to come under Shaban's influence and recalls many happy hours spent learning Islamic History under his guidance and inspired tuition.

In 1971 Shaban's academic travels finally came to an end in the University where he was to obtain his chair. He was appointed a Lecturer at the University of Exeter in the Department of Theology. A Readership was swiftly bestowed in 1974 and in 1979 M.A. Shaban was appointed to a Personal Chair in Arabic and Islamic Studies in the now independent Department of Arabic and Islamic Studies. The years up to his retirement in 1985/6 were years of difficulty but nevertheless growth: difficulty, because of the shortages of money and staff for any new University Department in the late 1970s and early 1980s; growth because, despite the difficulties, Professor Shaban turned himself into a fund-raiser *par excellence* for the Department, the related Centre for Arab Gulf Studies founded by him in 1978, and the University of Exeter as a whole. This was in addition to his heavy scholarly, teaching and administrative commitments as Head of the Department of Arabic and Islamic Studies and Director of the Centre for Arab Gulf Studies.

The foundation of the latter two entities ranks as one half of Shaban's achievement: the other half, of course, is the fruit of his scholarly excellence and wide-ranging knowledge of Arabic sources. Apart from his articles, this fruit is contained, principally, in his three books: *The 'Abbāsid Revolution*, (Cambridge University Press, 1970; reprinted in hardcover and paperback, 1979, and also translated into Arabic, French and Malay); *Islamic History: A New Interpretation 1: AD 600–750 (AH 132)*, (Cambridge University Press, 1971; reprinted in hardcover and paperback, 1976 and subsequently; also translated into Arabic, Spanish and Hebrew); and *Islamic History: A New Interpretation 2: AD 750–1055 (AH 132–448)*, (Cambridge University Press, 1976; reprinted in hardcover and paperback, 1978 and subsequently; also translated into Arabic, Spanish and Hebrew). In all these volumes Shaban did not hesitate to espouse bold and often excitingly controversial views, many of which have now been accepted by his fellow historians. Indeed, the first volume on *The 'Abbāsid Revolution* has already, and deservedly, become a classic in the field and is widely used by both researchers and undergraduates. The verdict on the subsequent two volumes of Islamic History was perhaps most neatly summed up by the reviewer in the *Times Literary Supplement* (4 February 1972, p. 130) who contrasted *Islamic History: A New Interpretation 1* with the recently published *Cambridge History of Islam* (2 vols., C.U.P., 1970). He wrote:

> That the state of Islamic studies is healthier than *The Cambridge History of Islam* might suggest is demonstrated by M.A. Shaban, an Egyptian scholar who has recently come to the front rank of Islamic historians . . . this is a period [i.e. AD 600–750] that has been well worked over in the past, and this careful and scholarly work [*Islamic History: A New Interpretation 1*] is an object lesson in what can be done with familiar source material.

Shaban has strong views about how Islamic history should be researched and taught; scholars should take a *new* look at everything, all the sources primary and secondary, and he is not afraid to submit his own work to critical examination. It is the hope of the editor of this *Festschrift* that he will indeed find something new in the essays collected here. They are diverse in their range and no attempt has been made by the editor to impose a uniform style on the way in which they have been written: some are light and journalistic in flavour, some are the result of many years spent working in the Middle East, and yet others are the deeply researched products of scholarly reflection on some of the manifold problems and, indeed, delights thrown up by Islamic Studies. The authors' views (and mistakes!) are also their own and no attempt has been made by the editor to harmonise conflicting views. What the essays try to do, for the most part, is to contribute to the principal theme of the book: the transition of the Arabian Gulf from a traditional society to modern states. To this end, the volume is divided into two parts: the first provides some historical background for the second which surveys the political, social, cultural and economic evolution of the Gulf. These essays also mirror, in a very real sense, the great breadth of Shaban's own interests: a medievalist historian by training, he became head of both the Department of Arabic and Islamic Studies *and* the Centre for Arab Gulf Studies at the University of Exeter. He was capable of supervising doctorates as much within the field of medieval Islamic philosophy (for example, the editor's own thesis on the Ikhwān al-Ṣafā' accepted by the University of Exeter in 1976)[1] as within that of modern history (for example, the thesis written by H.H. Shaykh Sulṭān Muḥammad al-Qāsimī, Ruler of Sharjah, entitled 'Arab "Piracy" and the East India Company Encroachment in the Gulf 1797–1820' accepted by the University of Exeter in 1985).[2]

It will be seen that one of the essays, that by R. Hitchcock entitled 'Hispano-Arabic Historiography: The Legacy of J.A. Conde', does not fit very readily into the general theme of the book delineated above. However, it has been included, firstly, because it provides a kind of intermezzo between the two sections of the book, showing how orientalists (and one in particular) have, over the years, used Arabic sources; and secondly, because it reflects the research preoccupations of M.A. Shaban himself since the completion of his second volume of *Islamic History*, and his insistence on the need for continual care in the evaluation of source material.

It is the deep hope of the editor that these essays will provide a small indication of the enormous affection and esteem in which Professor M.A. Shaban is held by all the contributors and all his colleagues and friends who wish him and Bessie a happy and fruitful retirement.

Ian Richard Netton
University of Exeter

Notes

1. Later published as *Muslim Neoplatonists: An Introduction to the Thought of the Brethren of Purity (Ikhwān al-Ṣafā')*, (Allen & Unwin, London, 1982).

2. Later published as *The Myth of Arab Piracy in the Gulf*, (Croom Helm, London, 1986).

Acknowledgements

I would like, first of all, to express my deep gratitude to the Secretary of the Department of Arabic and Islamic Studies, University of Exeter, Mrs Sheila Westcott, for her hard and careful work in producing the typescript of this book. I am grateful, too, to our sister department, the Centre for Arab Gulf Studies, University of Exeter, for agreeing to pay the typing costs. I would also like to acknowledge and thank the following: the Hakluyt Society for the reproduction of the map on p. 30; the United Nations Economic Commission for Western Asia, Beirut, for the reproduction of Tables 13.1 and 13.2 on pp. 192–3; OPEC for the reproduction of Tables 16.1, 16.2 and 16.4 on pp. 228–9 and 231; and the International Energy Agency for the reproduction of Table 16.3 on p. 230. Finally, I would like to thank most warmly my editors at Croom Helm, Peter Sowden and Alison McWilliam, for their care and courteous help at every stage in the production of this book.

Note on Transliteration

The scheme of transliteration for Arabic words used in this volume is an adapted form of the scheme which appears at the front of *EI*^{2} vol. 1,[1] with *qāf* being rendered as 'Q' rather than 'Ḳ' and *jīm* rendered as 'J' instead of 'Dj'. The transliteration of the few Persian and Turkish words which appear is the same as that in *The Cambridge History of Islam*,[2] e.g. Riżā for Reza. Common words and names in all three languages which have a well-known Anglicised form are written in that form, e.g. Mecca, Ayatollah Khomeini etc. (To a certain degree, the identification of what is well-known and what is not will be seen to be subjective.) Otherwise place names etc. are written with full diacriticals, though the initial 'al' may sometimes be dropped, e.g. Baṣra rather than Al-Baṣra. With the exception of major dynasty names like 'Abbāsid and Fāṭimid, diacriticals are omitted when the Arabic word is transliterated with an English ending, e.g. Wahhābī but Wahhabite. (But I prefer 'Saudi' which is a well-known English form.) When the transliteration of place names on figures and maps reproduced from other sources differs from the standard transliteration, or Anglicised form, used in this volume's text, the alternative word is placed in brackets in the text of the relevant essay, e.g. the Anglicised version Fujairah is written 'Fujairah (Fujayra)' in an essay where the latter form Fujayra appears on a table. Finally, the symbol * is used in J.R. Smart's article to indicate hypothetical forms which do not yet exist.

Notes

1. *The Encyclopaedia of Islam*, 2nd ed., ed. by H.A.R. Gibb, J.H. Kramers, E. Lévi-Provençal, J. Schacht *et al.*, (5 vols. cont., E.J. Brill/Luzac, Leiden/London, 1960), vol. 1, p. xiii.

2. *The Cambridge History of Islam*, ed. by P.M. Holt, A.K.S. Lambton and Bernard Lewis, (2 vols., Cambridge: Cambridge University Press, 1970).

Abbreviations

AH	Anno Hegirae
ANM	Arab Nationalist Movement
ARAMCO	Arabian American Oil Company
BAPCO	Bahrain Petroleum Company
CASOC	California Arabian Standard Oil Company
CENTO	Central Treaty Organisation
CPE	Centrally planned economy
DELCO	Delaware Electric Company
ECWA	Economic Commission for Western Asia, United Nations
EI^2	*Encyclopaedia of Islam*, second edition
FAO	Food and Agriculture Organisation
GCC	Gulf Co-operation Council
GDP	Gross domestic product
GNP	Gross national product
GSP	Government selling price
IBRD	International Bank for Reconstruction and Development (= World Bank)
IEA	International Energy Agency
IISS	International Institute for Strategic Studies
IMF	International Monetary Fund
KFAED	Kuwait's Fund for Arab Economic Development
MEED	Middle East Economic Digest
MEES	Middle East Economic Survey
MERI	Middle East Research Institute
MERIP	Middle East Research and Information Project
mn b/d	Million barrels a day
mtoe	Million tons of oil equivalent
NCW	Non-Communist world
NGL	Natural gas liquids
NLF	National Liberation Front
OAPEC	Organisation of Arab Petroleum Exporting Countries
OECD	Organisation of Economic Co-operation and Development
OPEC	Organisation of Petroleum Exporting Countries

PD(O)	Petroleum Development (Oman)
PDRY	People's Democratic Republic of Yemen
PFLOAG	Popular Front for the Liberation of Oman and the Arab Gulf
SA	Standard Arabic
SAVAK	Shah's secret police
SCC	State Consultative Council
UNECWA	United Nations Economic Commission for Western Asia
UNEF	United Nations Emergency Force
WHO	World Health Organisation
YAR	Yemen Arab Republic

PART ONE
THE ROOTS OF TRADITIONAL SOCIETY

1 Arabia Felix: Israelites, Jews and Christians

J.R. Porter

Israel

In the Old Testament, the word Arabia is used somewhat vaguely but it generally seems to include the Arabian peninsula proper, the territory east of the Gulf of 'Aqaba, Sinai and the Palestinian Arabah as far as the southern end of the Dead Sea, that is the Arabia Petraea and Arabia Deserta of the classical authorities, as well as their Arabia Felix. As might be expected, it is with the more northern parts of this whole area that the Israelites had closest contacts and it is on these that scholars who have dealt with Arabia and the Bible have mostly concentrated.[1] But there is considerable evidence that Arabia Felix, and not least its more southern parts, was well known to the Biblical authors and that they viewed it very much as did the classical authors, as a semi-mythical place, 'a land of fabulous wealth and luxury'[2] and particularly as 'the aromatic country'.[3] However, the Old Testament references are not without their problems and it is to some of the points of interest which arise from a number of them that we must now turn.

We may begin with two geographical texts, indicating Israel's knowledge of the world of which it formed part and its links with it. The first of these is particularly interesting because it appears to go back a long way. This is the passage Genesis II: 10–14, which now forms part of the Yahwistic document, usually dated *c.* 950 BC, but which is generally agreed to be an older piece of information which the author took up, originating in oral tradition, whose hazy and primitive notions of geography indicate its great age.[4] In verse 11 'all the land of Havilah' is mentioned as one of the four quarters of the world. Elsewhere in the Old Testament, Havilah denotes various areas in Arabia[5] but here the word has the definite article, probably meaning 'the land of sand'; the context shows that it must represent a considerable area and hence it would appear to denote the entire Arabian peninsula, Arabia Felix.[6] Noteworthy is the fact that this is the only one of the four quarters of the world of which a description is given, consisting of a list of its distinctive products — bdellium, 'a sweet-scented, golden, translucent resin from south Arabia',[7] onyx, found in the Yemen,[8] and especially gold, although the cognate word in Sabaean suggests that the Hebrew word here should rather be rendered 'frankincense', the most famous product of Arabia Felix. In any event, we have a list of the main exports from South Arabia as these were known to the Israelites[9] and the reason for their mention here would appear to be the result of trading links with the north, already long established when Genesis II: 10–14 was written down and for which this passage perhaps provides our earliest evidence.

That Havilah represents the whole Arabian peninsula is also suggested by the mention of the river which encircles it. It has often been noted that Pishon and Gihon (verses 11, 13), unlike the Tigris and Euphrates of verse 14, are not names of any known rivers but rather are both generic terms from roots meaning 'to spring up' and 'to bubble forth'. Above all, there is no great river in Arabia and certainly not one that could be said to encircle it. No doubt it is correct to speak here of 'mythical' and 'symbolic' geography[10] and to claim that the author's main purpose was to state that the fertility of the world, brought by its rivers, comes from the river in the garden of God.[11] Nevertheless, he is also clearly trying to give a description of real areas as these were known to him. Hence one may wonder whether Pishon may not be a river in the strict sense but rather that it means the sea which surrounds Arabia from the head of the Arab Gulf to the top of the Red Sea, especially if, as many scholars think, the author of Genesis II intended to locate Eden, whence Pishon originates, at the head of the Arab Gulf.[12] The Israelites knew little of the sea and perhaps did not distinguish too clearly between the waters of seas and rivers: certainly 'rivers' in Hebrew can sometimes plausibly mean 'ocean currents'.[13] If this view could be accepted, it would suggest that the circumnavigation of Arabia may have been known much earlier than has often been supposed, certainly long before the famous Skylax.[14] And would it be too bold to suggest that the other mysterious 'river', Gihon, which encircles all the land of Cush and, if this means Ethiopia, can hardly be the Nile,[15] is in fact the other side of the Red Sea and the part of the Indian Ocean bordering on Ethiopia?

Mention of Cush leads on to the second geographical passage we propose to consider, verses 6 and 7 of the so-called 'Table of the Nations' in Genesis X. This is part of the Priestly writing, probably to be dated *c.* 550 BC and, though it again rests to some extent on older traditions, it seems to reflect a picture of the world that became known to Israel from the seventh century BC onwards. Two related problems arise from these verses: first, 'the sons of Cush' are not places in Ethiopia or Nubia but in South Arabia and secondly, there appears to be a distinction drawn between *s^e^ba*, a son of Cush and *š^e^ba*, a son of Raamah, probably the South Arabian Ragmat mentioned in Minaean and Sabaean inscriptions.[16] No doubt these two names are identical in signification, as the Septuagint rightly understands, *s^e^ba* representing the correct Minaean and Sabaean form: but why was the distinction made? For it is not confined to the Priestly writer. Psalm LXXII: 10 differentiates between them[17] and in Isaiah XLIII: 3 *s^e^ba* is associated with countries in North Africa. We should therefore see this phenomenon as showing the Old Testament's desire to distinguish between two places having really the same name, one in Africa and one in Arabia, and this in turn reflects its awareness of the Sabaean colonisation of Ethiopia, 'which certainly took place no later than the 7th century BC and perhaps as early as the 10th century BC'.[18] Not all the other names in Genesis X: 7 may refer directly to Arabia: it has been suggested that Sabtah and Sabtecha may refer to foundations of the Ethiopian Pharaoh Shabaka, and perhaps also of his son Shabataka, at the end of the eighth and the beginning of the seventh century BC.[19] On the other hand, the mention of Raamah, Sheba and Dedan seems to mirror the great trade route from South Arabia to the north, for these names occur in Ezekiel XXVII: 22, together with their characteristic exports, 'choicest spices, every kind of precious stone and gold', in a passage which reproduces information from a number of important trading centres. Hence by this time we can see how significant the commerce with Arabia had become in Israel's economy, something which really developed with the introduction of the monarchy around the beginning of the first millennium, when the Hebrews first became an organised state and an important component of the ancient Near Eastern world.

This brings us next to the famous visit of the Queen of Sheba to King Solomon, narrated in I Kings X: 1–13, which has been described as 'the earliest evidence of commercial relations with Arabia',[20] as far as Israel is concerned. As it stands, the story no more than hints — though we shall see it does that — at commercial relations and it is still often dismissed as a mere legend.[21] However, compared with the fantastic accretions which gathered round the story of the visit in later Jewish, Islamic and Ethiopic tradition, the Biblical narrative must seem very sober and restrained. With Solomon the Israelite state first really 'arrived' on the political scene of the ancient Near East and ceremonial visits between royal houses, accompanied by the exchange of valuable presents, were a common occurrence there. Again, the ability of a sovereign to demonstrate his wisdom and knowledge to another was a valuable diplomatic tool. Hence there is nothing very improbable in the account of the meeting as we have it in the Old Testament.

Moreover, it seems likely that there were some negotiations between the Queen of Sheba and Solomon and that these resulted in some sort of trading agreement between them. This is suggested by the statement that Solomon 'gave the queen of Sheba all she desired, whatever she asked', which seems to imply that the queen had come with definite proposals which were eventually agreed. It may be worth noting that in the Ethiopic *Kebra Nagast* there occurs what one authority has described as a 'realistic story'[22] to the effect that the queen's visit was prompted by enthusiastic reports from the head of her caravans, who had already been engaged in large-scale trading operations with Solomon. Further, the episode of the Queen of Sheba is, in the Bible, immediately preceded by a mention of Solomon's trading enterprises in the Red Sea, I Kings IX: 26–28, and immediately followed by a note of his revenues, especially those from the Red Sea voyages, I Kings X: 22, while there is a rather odd interpolation in the narrative of the queen's visit, again concerning produce brought to Jerusalem from the south via the Red Sea, I Kings X: 11–12.[23] It appears likely that it was Solomon's initiative in thus moving into the area where trade in their products had previously been in the hands of the South Arabian kingdoms which led to the queen's visit. She and Solomon would have had interests in common. The South Arabian states sought for growth not through military expansion and territorial conquest, unlike the great monarchies of the ancient Near East, but through the expansion of their mercantile activities: Solomon, who fought no wars throughout his whole reign, clearly had the same policy. A trading agreement, bringing about further commercial development, would have been to the mutual benefit of both parties, a fact which accounts for the amicable relations between Solomon and the Queen of Sheba which the Biblical story underlines. Solomon controlled the King's Highway in Transjordan and also the route across southern Palestine to Gaza, the two arteries by which the luxury goods of Arabia were distributed to consumer nations. Thus, it is possible that the interview between the two monarchs 'resulted in a reciprocal agreement whereby Solomon's fleet was given access to African and Arabian ports controlled by the Queen of Sheba, while the security of the northern section of the caravan routes and points of distribution was guaranteed by Solomon'.[24]

So far, we have assumed that the queen ruled over a state in the far south of Arabia, in the region of the saba of the South Arabian inscriptions. But this identification has been questioned from two different sides.

On the one hand, it has been claimed that, while prominent queens are known from North Arabia, Sabaean inscriptions contain no mention of one: it has further often been alleged that the Sabaeans originally lived in northern Arabia[25] and that, perhaps as late as the eighth and seventh centuries BC, at least part of saba lay in this area and that it was from this northern Sheba that the queen came.[26] But this is to some extent an argument from silence, for there are no extant records which refer to any Sabaean ruler, male or female, before about 800 BC, long after Solomon's time. It would seem that the assumption of a northern saba rests on the mention of two Sabaean kings, Itiamara and Karibilu, in the annals of the Assyrian rulers Sargon II and Sennacherib respectively: it is asserted that those kings could not have ruled in the south of Arabia because of the great distance separating it from the centre of Assyrian power. But van Beek has pointed out that the Assyrian emperors do not claim to have conquered the territories of the Sabaean monarchs but only to have received tribute from them.[27] Kings ruling in the southern part of the peninsula might well have done this to protect the northern end of their trade routes, which Assyria at this period controlled. There is really no evidence for any Sabaean state in northern Arabia and no real reason to question the long established opinion that the Queen of Sheba came from the far south and this is supported by the fact that the gifts she brought with her, spices, gold and precious stones, I Kings X: 2, are the typical products of that region.

On the other hand, Edward Ullendorff is prepared at least to entertain the possibility that her home may have been in the horn of Africa, which might account for her prominence in later Ethiopian legend. The only evidence he produces is a claim that the reference to rich forests in I Kings X: 11–12 might possibly favour this assumption.[28] But these verses do not refer to the homeland of the Queen of Sheba but to a sea voyage undertaken on behalf of Solomon to Ophir, wherever that may have been. In any case, there are considerable forests in the Yemen,[29] where Ophir is likely to have been situated.[30] It is true that, at least in the historic period, as Ullendorff says, 'connexions between the two shores of the southern Red Sea have at all times been close',[31] but the movements were always from Arabia to Africa before the former came under the strong influence of Ethiopia at the beginning of the Christian era. Everything, then, would seem to point to a firm identification between the Old Testament Sheba in I Kings X and a state in the area of Sabaean domination in South Arabia.

In summary, it can be said that, while there were close ethnic connections between Israel and tribal elements in northern Arabia, which have often been studied,[32] the links with Arabia Felix known to the Old Testament were exclusively through the medium of trade. The main basis of this commerce was the export and import of myrrh and frankincense, in the production of which the South Arabian states had a virtual monopoly.[33] From the Old Testament, it is possible to glimpse what a significant part these must have played in the economy of ancient Israel. Frankincense comprised fifty per cent of the incense, Exodus XXX: 34–35, which was burned twice daily in the Temple, Exodus XXX: 7–8, and, before the centralisation of worship in Jerusalem, was used in numerous other sanctuaries as well; a clay stamp, with a South Arabian text, which can only be understood as evidence of the frankincense trade, was discovered at the great religious centre of Bethel.[34] In addition, incense was widely used by individuals in private houses, both on social occasions and at household shrines.[35] Some indication of the extent of its consumption can be gauged from the fact that, when Alexander the Great captured the important entrepôt of Gaza, he found about two tons of frankincense there.[36] Myrrh, along with other spices, was a principal ingredient in the holy oil used in worship: according to Exodus XX: 23, about 50 lb of these spices were used on a single occasion. Oil was also extensively employed for personal adornment and the Old Testament references make it clear that this too was heavily perfumed. To the spice trade must, as already noted, be added the commerce in gold and precious stones from South Arabia, while Joel III: 8 (Hebrew IV: 8), which refers to the people of Judah selling slaves 'to the Sabaeans, a nation far away', strongly suggests that the Israelites were involved in the great slave traffic with the far south of Arabia, which is also attested in at least one Sabaean inscription. All this evidence, which could easily be added to, indicates how accurate was the knowledge and how close the connections of the Biblical Israelites with the Arabia Felix of the first millennium BC.

Judaism

In considering the emergence of Jews and Judaism in Arabia we shall confine our attention solely to Arabia Felix, the Yemen, from which the name properly comes,[37] leaving aside the well-known Jewish tribes of the Ḥijāz. It is difficult to pinpoint the origins and causes of Jewish settlement in South Arabia and the development of Judaism there, because of the paucity of the sources. There are legends about Israelites returning with the Queen of Sheba: it has been suggested that Jews from the contingent sent by Herod the Great (37/34 BC–AD 4) to accompany the expedition of Aelius Gallus in 25–24 BC may have afterwards remained in the country and that others may have joined them as a result of Titus's conquest of Palestine in AD 70,[38] but there is no clear evidence for these proposals. It seems more plausible to think rather of settlements of Jewish merchants in Arabia Felix, in view of the extensive commercial relations previously surveyed. It would appear likely that the opinion of the Arabic genealogists that the South Arabians, Yemenites or Himyarites, were descended from 'Joktan' is the result of Jewish teaching, based on Genesis X: 26–30 and XXV: 3. The list of names in the former passage reveals a close knowledge of a fairly small area of south west Arabia and it is widely accepted that it details places with which the Israelites had trading links, perhaps as early as the time of Solomon.[39] Nor do we have to think of any large scale Jewish emigration into Arabia Felix for, judging from their names, most of the Jews there were rather Jewish converts or at least Judaised Arabians.

Our earliest direct witness to the existence of a Jewish community in South Arabia comes from the period of the Himyarite kingdom from c. 115 BC. It consists of some inscriptions, dating from the third century AD, found in the necropolis of Beth She'arim in Galilee, which from the second to the fourth centuries AD was the centre of Jewish life as the seat of the Sanhedrin. Pious Jews from all over the Near East had their bodies brought there to rest with those of the famous rabbis of that city. One section of the cemetery was labelled as the resting place of the Himyarites; there is a Greek epitaph there of a certain Menaḥem 'elder of the Himyarites' and in another monogram he is described as 'the Himyarite *qawl*', corresponding to the Arabic *qayl*.[40] Menaḥem's ethnic origin seems to be indicated here,[41] that is, he was a Judaised Arabian, and 'elder' and *qawl* are very likely to be understood as the same title from a Jewish and Arabian background respectively;[42] in other words, he was a leading figure of a Jewish community but also had an important, perhaps even an official, place in the Himyarite state and society. This evidence shows that by the third century AD there was already a wealthy and well-established Jewish group in South Arabia and hence it is reasonable to assume that its origin goes back considerably further, perhaps as early as the first Himyarite monarchs, who may well have encouraged Jewish settlement as part of a policy of mercantile development.

During the period of the second Himyarite kingdom, Judaism in the Yemen greatly increased in numbers and influence. According to the Christian writer Philostorgius, who provides the first mention in literature of South Arabian Jews, in the mid-fourth century AD they were powerful enough to prevent a Byzantine envoy from making any Christian converts. Some of the kings, such as Abu-Kariba, are supposed to have been converted to Judaism, but the accounts are late and legendary and probably based on no more than the fact that they caused several Jewish monotheistic inscriptions to be erected in their kingdom. But this in itself indicates a desire to win the support of the Jewish population and it is entirely credible that Abu-Kariba should have moved towards Judaism because of his designs on Yathrib where there were powerful Jewish tribes. However, the last Himyarite sovereign, the famous Dhū Nuwās (AD 517–525) was certainly a convert to Judaism and some Christian sources mention his contact with scribes of the famous Jewish academy at Tiberias. This coincided with the migration of a certain Mar Zutra, son of the exiliarch in Babylon, to head the Tiberian academy in AD 520, and it has been suggested that the move was part of an ambitious project on the part of Dhū Nuwās to create a 'Jewish West Arabia' with the support of Jews elsewhere in the Near East.[43] In any case, Dhū Nuwās was anxious for the aid of the Jews in his territory who, unlike the Christians there, posed no political threat, against the menace of the Christian powers of Byzantium and, especially, Ethiopia and their Christian supporters in Yemen.

It is interesting to speculate on the reasons for the great success and prestige of Judaism in Arabia Felix. If it is correct to see the Himyarite Jews, unlike their co-religionists in the Ḥijāz, as mainly merchants, their commercial success would have won them considerable influence. No doubt also the spread of Judaism there reflects the highly successful Jewish proselytising and apologetic of the last centuries BC, which was if anything intensified after the destruction of the Temple and the subsequent foundation of large and impressive Jewish academies in the Near East. But there was probably much in their religious background to predispose the Arabs to the Jewish religion. It has been noted, for instance, that the rite of circumcision had long been widespread among the pagan Arabs.[44] Again, a characteristic of the Himyarite Jewish religious inscriptions already mentioned[45] is their invariable designation of God as *Rahmanân*. This is certainly a South Arabian formula[46] but it is also an attribute of the deity in the Old Testament, as notably at Exodus XXXIV: 6, where the cognate Hebrew expression occurs, and so is clearly to be seen as an important link between the two religious systems. Not only circumcision, but other significant rites and taboos were common to both the South Arabian religious tradition and Judaism. There is a class of Sabaean inscriptions which take the form of a public confession of ritual sins.[47] One of these records a man's confession to the Sabaean god Dhū Samâwî, 'because he drew near to a woman during a period illicit to him and fondled a woman during her menses; and that he came together with a woman in childbed; and that he went without any purification; and that he touched women during their menses and did not wash himself; and that he moistened his clothes with ejections'.[48] The offences listed here are virtually identical with those found in the Jewish purity laws of Leviticus XV: 1–30, where attention may be directed especially to verses 13, 16–18, 19 and 24. Hence there was room for a considerable syncretism between elements of pre-Islamic South Arabian religion and later Judaism, which, together with the other factors already discussed, helped to bring about the rapid spread of the latter in the Himyarite kingdom.

Christianity

When we turn to consider the origin and development of Christianity in Arabia Felix, we are hardly better informed on this subject than we are in the case of Judaism. Most of the Christian sources are much later than the events they purport to describe, and they are often tendentious, confused or contradictory, with some clearly legendary elements. The same applies to the Arabic authorities, who in general seem only to have a somewhat vague knowledge of Christians and Christianity in this region. This is not to say that they contain no authentic historical evidences, as will be seen, but these are not easy to disentangle from the less trustworthy material and scholars still differ greatly over the weight to be attached to particular items.[49] The effect of the most recent studies is to suggest that, compared with the north and east of the peninsula, the Christian presence in South Arabia was spasmodic and superficial and limited to a small number of centres. Again, compared with neighbouring areas, the archaeological evidence for Christianity in the Yemen is very sparse — only two clearly Christian inscriptions, both as late as the sixth century AD and of Ethiopian provenance,[50] and the remains of two ancient churches.[51] It would seem to be the case that Christianity here, at least until a period in the sixth century, was much less widespread and deeply rooted than was Judaism.

Various reasons may be suggested to account for this. In the first place, Christianity in Arabia did not manifest a clear and unified system of belief and practice to the extent that Judaism did. Arabia was in touch, through its international contacts, with all the three forms of Christianity in the

Near East, Nestorian, Monophysite and Byzantine. As far as Arabia Felix is concerned, the earliest influence of the first appears to have come through missionaries from Ḥīra, where the Nestorians were strong,[52] but they also formed a powerful group in the Persian empire and their version of Christianity may well have profited during the Persian occupation of South Arabia after AD 575. Monophysitism was dominant in Syria, it spread from there to Arabia and there is evidence of contacts between Christians in the Yemen and the Monophysites of Syria;[53] but it was also the official faith of Ethiopia, which established colonies in South Arabia at various times, but particularly after the Ethiopian conquest of the region around AD 525. As will be seen, Christianity was used as a tool by the emperors at Constantinople to further their political ambitions in the south of Arabia, but the Sinai peninsula was a stronghold of Byzantine Christianity and it is likely that it also spread southwards from there, although it would appear that it was never as strong in Arabia Felix as the other two groups. These different versions of Christianity were generally in bitter dispute with one another and there can be little doubt that this gravely weakened the impact of Christianity in the region, for the Arabs were well aware of the conflicts between them, however imperfectly they may have grasped the subtle theological points at stake. In his account of the Christian delegation which came to Muḥammad from Najrān, Ibn Isḥāq notes that, 'although they were Christians of the Byzantine rite,[54] they differed among themselves in some points, saying He is God; and He is son of God; and He is the third person of the Trinity, which is the doctrine of Christianity':[55] this seems to be a confused and rudimentary attempt to list the distinctive tenets of Monophysitism, Nestorianism and orthodox Byzantine Christianity respectively. In any case, it reveals the considerable variety which could be found within a single Christian community in the Yemen.

Secondly, in this same account Ibn Isḥāq relates that the bishop of Najrān had been honoured by the kings of Byzantium, who had paid him a subsidy and given him servants. The promotion of Christianity in Arabia was furthered by the empire of Constantinople as part of its struggle with the Persian state over the South Arabian commerce, in seeking to check Persian expansion which threatened to close to Byzantium the lucrative sea and land routes from the Yemen. The first literary mention of Christianity in South Arabia is in the Ecclesiastical History of Philostorgius, who recounts that, around AD 356, the emperor Constantius sent a bishop Theophilus as an emissary to the Himyarite king, as a result of whose mission three churches were built at Ẓafār the capital, Aden and Hormuz on the Arab Gulf and the king was converted to Christianity.[56] Certainly Philostorgius considerably exaggerates the significance and effect of this mission. Like Constantius and Theophilus, he was a convinced Arian and wishes to give the impression that the earliest Arabian Christianity was Arian;[57] there is no evidence for any Himyarite Christian king, while the third church he lists seems to be a pure invention on his part since the Himyarite state never extended as far as the Arab Gulf. Nevertheless, the real motives behind the mission can be glimpsed in the account, for we are told that Theophilus's purpose was to obtain both liberty of worship and freedom to trade for the Byzantine merchants in South Arabia and that at Aden, where a church was founded, there was already an imperial trading post.[58] This, and similar interventions by later Byzantine rulers, inevitably meant that Christianity would appear as to some degree an alien importation to the Arabians, supported by the wealth and influence of a foreign power, as part of its commercial and political ambitions: by contrast, Judaism was much less exposed to such strictures. When the Qur'ān, however, castigates the wealth of both Christian monks and Jewish rabbis[59] — though this is not the whole story — we are perhaps made aware of a deep resentment against those who had been well endowed by the mercantile success of their co-religionists and by external subventions.

Thirdly, the fortunes of Christianity in Arabia Felix were intimately bound up with the relations between that area and the region of Ethiopia. As we have seen, these were of long standing but they came to assume particular significance from the middle of the fourth century AD, when a strong kingdom was established at Aksūm, whose monarchs henceforward tried to gain control of the seaborne trade through the Red Sea and laid claim to the Himyarite territories, which were by then in a weakened condition as a result of internal feuds and foreign intrigues. Monophysite Christianity from Egypt penetrated Ethiopia during this period and at some stage the dynasty embraced it, although, owing to the confused and legendary nature of the available sources, it is not easy to say when, but perhaps not before the beginning of the sixth century AD.[60] At any rate, there appear to have been a number of invasions from Ethiopia, with at least the tacit support of Byzantium, and the Christian communities became an important means of sustaining the Ethiopian presence and influence. Once more, religious, commercial and political concerns went hand in hand. It is probably for this reason that the famous Christian colony of Najrān achieved its great significance. It was on the caravan route to the north and had an annual fair of exceptional importance: it may be noted that one narrative of an Ethiopian invasion, of uncertain date, asserts that this was undertaken because the Himyarite ruler had attacked the Christian merchants passing through his lands,[61] and the Christian *sayyid* of Najrān around AD 522 seems to have been an agent of the Ethiopian government.[62]

Christianity paid the price for its close association with the politics of Ethiopia and Byzantium on the occasion of the revolt of Dhū Nuwās, which took place about this date, and when, for the first time in the shadowy events of South Arabian Christianity, we are on sure historical ground.[63] The revolt was very likely, in part at least, a nationalist uprising against Ethiopian domination and it is significant that it was directed, with great ferocity, against the Christians who were seen as the allies of the kingdom of Aksūm. The emperor Justin is said to have instigated the Ethiopian ruler to undertake, in revenge, a kind of religious crusade, although he probably needed little prompting, as a result of which Arabia Felix came firmly under his control. But this also meant the re-establishment of Christianity, which now appeared as a kind of state religion, under joint Ethiopian and Byzantine sponsorship.

We might therefore conclude that Christianity in South Arabia was very much a part of the chequered history of the Christian world, with its strongly political overtones, in the fifth and sixth centuries AD and that this was the main reason for its somewhat limited success in the area. But this should not be taken as the complete picture. Precisely because of its commercial contacts, considerable evangelisation in South Arabia seems to have been carried out by individual monks and ascetics, who followed the trade routes from Monophysite Syria[64] — the kind of people, such as Baḥīrā and others, with whom Muḥammad is said to have had friendly contacts when he travelled with the caravans.[65] According to Ibn Isḥāq, Christianity was brought to Najrān, later so richly and officially endowed, by an itinerant ascetic mason from Syria, a victim of the Arabian slave trade, who had been captured by a party of caravaneers and then sold in Najrān.[66] Certainly, the narrative is largely legendary, but the hero's name, Faymiyūn, is actually Greek, Phēmion, which may well indicate a genuine historical reminiscence of the fact that it was a simple man whose teaching and example first won Christian converts in that city.[67] Such people, marked out by their poverty, asceticism, piety and genuine concern for religion, rather than the higher clergy with their state and political involvement, were no doubt the ones who commended their faith to those like themselves. Encountering people of this kind was what led Muḥammad to his warm appreciation of Christianity, as contrasted with his attitude to Judaism, as being nearest to Islam 'because some of them are priests and monks, and they wax not proud' and in whose churches 'are men whom neither commerce nor trafficking diverts from the remembrance of God and to perform the prayer, and to pay the alms'.[68] In the same way, Muḥammad was alleged to have learned much of his message from two Christian slaves, probably of Ethiopian origin.[69] The nature of our sources means that we have only few and incidental notices of these humble and devout believers but it is perhaps significant that we only hear of them in Arabic material: they were the people who impressed the inhabitants of Arabia Felix and were the true source of the spread of Christianity among them.

Notes

These above few remarks about the period of Arabic history before the point where Professor Shaban's own specialist interests start are offered to him as a warm tribute from a colleague and in deep appreciation of all he has done for Arabic studies. *Ad multos annos!*

1. This is the case with the classic work on the subject, J.A. Montgomery, *Arabia and the Bible*, new edn. (Ktav Publishing House, New York, 1969).
2. P.K. Hitti, *History of the Arabs*, 10th edn. (Macmillan, London, 1982), p. 45.
3. Strabo, *The Geography*, Book XVI 4.25, ed. by H.L. Jones (Heinemann, London, 1930), p. 362f.
4. Cf. C. Westermann, *Genesis 1–11*, trans. J.J. Scullion (SPCK, London, 1984), p. 216.
5. Cf. Genesis X: 7, 29, XXV: 18; I Samuel XV: 7.
6. Cf. J. Simons, *The Geographical and Topographical Texts of the Old Testament* (E.J. Brill, Leiden, 1959), p. 40.
7. L. Köhler and W. Baumgartner, *Hebräisches und Aramäisches Lexikon zum Alten Testament*, 3rd edn. (E.J. Brill, Leiden, 1967), s.v. *b*^{e}*dōlah*, p. 106.
8. Cf. Pliny, *Natural History*, Book XXXVII 86–87, ed. by D.E. Eichholz (Heinemann, London, 1962), p. 232.
9. Cf. Ezekiel XXVII: 22, part of a list of regions, together with their commercial products, the names of which were preserved and handed down in trading centres.
10. Cf. M. Gorg, 'Ophir, Tarschisch und Atlantis. Einige Gedanken zur symbolischen Topographie', *Biblische Notizen*, vol. 15 (1981), pp. 76–86.
11. Cf. Westermann, *Genesis 1–11*, p. 216.
12. Cf. P.J. Achtemeier (ed.), *Harper's Bible Dictionary* (Harper & Row, San Francisco, 1985), p. 245, s.v. 'Eden'.
13. Cf. A.R. Johnson, *Sacral Kingship in Ancient Israel*, 2nd edn. (University of Wales Press, Cardiff, 1967), p. 27 n. 3, with reference to Psalm LXXXIX: 25 (Hebrew 26).
14. Cf. Montgomery, *Arabia*, p. 68f.
15. Cf. Westermann, *Genesis 1–11*, p. 218.
16. For the reference, cf. Montgomery, *Arabia*, p. 39 n. 7.
17. Hence in this verse the Septuagint also has to distinguish, rendering *s*^{e}*ba* as *'Arabōn*.
18. G.W. van Beek, 'Prolegomenon' in Montgomery, *Arabia*, p. XIV.
19. Cf. O. Procksch, *Die Genesis* (A. Deichertsche Verlagsbuchhandlung, Leipzig, 1913), p. 463; M.C. Astour, 'Sabtah and Sabteca: Ethiopian Pharaoh Names in Genesis 10', *Journal of Biblical Literature*, vol. LXXXIV (1956), pp. 422–5.
20. van Beek, in Montgomery, *Arabia*, p. XVII.

21. Cf. most recently, J.A. Soggin, *Storia d'Israele* (Paideia Editrice, Brescia, 1984), p. 130.

22. E. Ullendorff, *Ethiopia and the Bible* (Oxford University Press and the British Academy, London, 1968), p. 140.

23. Cf. J. Gray, *I & II Kings* (SCM Press, London, 1964), p. 238f.

24. van Beek in Montgomery, *Arabia*, p. XVIII.

25. Cf. Montgomery, *Arabia*, p. 59ff.

26. This has recently been maintained by A.K. Irvine, 'The Arabians and Ethiopians' in D.J. Wiseman (ed.), *Peoples of Old Testament Times* (Clarendon Press, Oxford, 1973), p. 299 and N. Groom, *Frankincense and Myrrh* (Longman, London and New York, 1981), p. 52ff.

27. Cf. van Beek in Montgomery, *Arabia*, p. XV.

28. Ullendorff, *Ethiopia and the Bible*, p. 134.

29. The Naval Intelligence Division volume, *Western Arabia and the Red Sea*, Geographical Handbook Series (Admiralty, Naval Intelligence Division, London, 1946), refers in the Yemen to a 'zone of tropical vegetation akin to the forests on the African side of the Red Sea'.

30. Cf. *The Biblical Archaeologist*, vol. 39 (1976), p. 85.

31. Ullendorff, *Ethiopia and the Bible*, p. 134.

32. Cf. most recently, E.A. Speiser, 'Man, Ethnic Divisions of', *The Interpreter's Dictionary of the Bible* (Abingdon Press, New York and Nashville, 1962), vol. III, pp. 235–42.

33. Cf. now N. Groom, *Frankincense, passim*.

34. Cf. G.W. van Beek and A. Jamme, 'An Inscribed South Arabian Clay Stamp from Bethel', *Bulletin of the American Schools of Oriental Research*, vol. 151 (1958), pp. 9–16; 'The South Arabian Clay Stamp from Bethel Again', *Bulletin of the American Schools of Oriental Research*, vol. 163 (1961), pp. 15–18.

35. Cf. the illustration to the article on 'Incense' in *Harper's Bible Dictionary*, pp. 420–1.

36. Cf. Plutarch, *Life of Alexander* XXX: *Plutarchi Vitae Parallelae*, ed. C. Sintenis, (Teubner, Leipzig, 1881), p. 307.

37. Cf. Montgomery, *Arabia*, p. 114 n.1.

38. Cf. *Encyclopaedia Judaica* (Encyclopaedia Judaica, Jerusalem, 1971), vol. 3, p. 235. In any case, it is rash to assume that Herod's mercenaries would have been Jews. Cf. D. Braund, 'Four Notes on the Herods', *Classical Quarterly*, vol. 33 (i) (1983), p. 239f.

39. Cf. Procksch, *Die Genesis*, p. 82.

40. For these inscriptions see conveniently G. Ryckmans, 'Le *qayl* en Arabie Méridionale Préislamique' in D.W. Thomas and W.D. McHardy (eds.), *Hebrew and Semitic Studies presented to Godfrey Rolles Driver* (Clarendon Press, Oxford, 1963), p. 151ff.

41. Ibid., p. 152.

42. Cf. M.I. Ben-Zvi, 'Les Origines de l'Etablissement des Tribus d'Israël en Arabie', *Le Muséon*, vol. LXXIV (1961), p. 161.

43. Cf. W. Caskel, *Entdeckungen in Arabien* (Westdeutscher Verlag, Cologne, 1954), pp. 14–26.

44. Cf. S. Dubnov, *History of the Jews* (Thomas Yoseloff, New York and London, 1968), vol. 2, p. 309.

45. For these cf. A. Jamme, 'La Religion Sud-Arabe Préislamique' in M. Brillant and R. Aigrain (eds.), *Histoire des Religions*, (Bloud et Gay, Paris, n.d.), vol. 4, p. 275ff.

46. Several Sabaean inscriptions associate the name with deities of the South Arabian pantheon, cf. C. Hechaïmé, *Louis Cheikho et son Livre* (Dār al-Mashriq, Beirut, 1967), p. 177.

47. Cf. G. Ryckmans, 'La Confession Publique des Péchés en Arabie Méridionale Préislamique', *Le Muséon*, vol. LVIII (1945), pp. 1–14.

48. Translation from J.B. Pritchard (ed.), *The Ancient Near East: Supplementary Texts and Pictures Relating to the Old Testament* (Princeton University Press, Princeton, New Jersey, 1969), p. 229.

49. For a thorough and judicious discussion of the sources, cf. C. Hechaïmé, *Louis Cheikho*, pp. 51–122.

50. Ibid., p. 55.

51. Cf. L. Cheikho, *Le Christianisme et la Littérature Chrétienne en Arabie avant l'Islam*, (3 vols., Imprimerie Catholique, Beirut, 1913–1923), pp. 64, 334, 345, 355, 441.

52. Cf. D.L. O'Leary, *Arabia before Muhammad* (AMS Press, New York, 1973), p. 141.

53. Jacob of Sarug (AD 451–521), Bishop of Osrhoene, sent Monophysite treatises and letters to encourage the Christians of Najrān who were suffering from the hostility of the Jews there.

54. Cf. A. Guillaume, *The Life of Muhammad* (Oxford University Press, London, 1955), p. 271: Ibn Isḥāq actually has 'the religion of the king', i.e. the emperor at Constantinople.

55. Ibid., p. 271.

56. Cf. Philostorgius, *Kirchengeschichte*, Book III 4–6, 3rd edn., ed. by J. Bidez (Akademie Verlag, Berlin, 1981), pp. 32–6.

57. Cf. Cheikho, *Le Christianisme*, p. 56.

58. *to Rōmaikon emporion*, Philostorgius, *Kirchengeschichte*, p. 34.

59. Cf. *Sūra* IX: 34–5.

60. The story of the conversion of the Ethiopian king is given by the Monophysite historian, John Malalas, writing in the latter half of the sixth century AD. He places it in the reign of Justinian (AD 527–565) but it has been held that it must have taken place in the fifth century, cf. L. Duchesne, *L'Église au VIe Siècle* (E. de Boccard, Paris, 1925), p. 287, n.1. However, Malalas's account seems very like a variant version of the Ethiopian invasion at the time of Dhū Nuwās, so his date may well be approximately correct.

61. Cf. Duchesne, ibid., p. 287.

62. Cf. O'Leary, *Arabia*, p. 145. For fuller details of Christianity in Najrān, cf. J.S. Trimingham, *Christianity among the Arabs in Pre-Islamic Times* (Longman/Librairie du Liban, London & New York, 1979), p. 294ff.

63. The basic text is a contemporary letter from Simeon of Beit-Arsham, bishop of Seleucia, who was the ambassador of the emperor Justin (AD 518–527) to the Arabic king of Ḥīra and obtained his information from a letter to that king from the Himyarite ruler. The evidence is described and assessed by Duchesne, *L'Église*, p. 289, n.1.

64. Cf. the role of Syria and its merchants in Ibn Isḥāq's narrative of Salmān, Guillaume, *Life*, p. 95ff.

65. Cf. G. Parrinder, *Jesus in the Qur'ān* (Sheldon Press, London, 1976), p. 164.

66. Cf. Guillaume, *Life*, pp. 14–16.

67. Cf. A. Fliche and V. Martin, *Histoire de L'Église* (Bloud and Gay, Paris, 1945), vol. 4, p. 524.

68. *Sūra* V: 85; XXIV: 36–37, trans. by A.J. Arberry, *The Koran Interpreted* (Oxford University Press, Oxford, 1983), pp. 113 and 357.

69. Cf. Parrinder, *Jesus*, p. 160.

2 The Desert and the Sown in Eastern Arabian History

Hugh Kennedy

One of M.A. Shaban's most important contributions to the study of early Islamic history has been the emphasis he placed on trade and trade routes.[1] He saw that trade was the most important factor in creating political units in early Arabia. In tribute to him, this essay is an attempt to illustrate something of the interaction between nomad, farmer and merchant in early Islamic Arabia.

The history of Arabia is notoriously difficult to write. Whereas the chronologies of other areas of the Muslim world are well established and the hand-books give numerous details of the succession of Caliphs, governors, generals and rebels who ruled the cities of the Fertile Crescent and the highlands of Iran, the history of much of Arabia escapes us. The chronologies of pre-Islamic history in the area are extremely vague; attempts to assign dates to the *Ayyām al-'Arab* run immediately into the difficulty that the bedouin world from which they sprang had neither interest in nor means of recording long time-scales. Anthropologists[2] suggest that the bedouin genealogical memory reliably extends no more than five generations back and beyond that all is legend and indefinite tradition. The endlessly repeated rhythms of bedouin life do not really give much scope for the working out of a picture of the gradual evolution, even progress, of the Muslim community embodied in such authors as al-Ṭabarī or Ibn al-Athīr. Any record of bedouin history over an extended timespan is necessarily the record of outsiders' impressions and comments, and is often only incidental details, mentioned in passing in the discussion of more important matters.

The major historical changes in early Islamic Arabia were the result not of bedouin activity, nor indeed of the doings of the people of the oases and cities, but rather of the interaction between the two. By far the most significant and the best known of these was, of course, the original Islamic conquests. The most recent commentator on these, Fred Donner in his masterly work *The Early Islamic Conquests*, stresses the way in which the conquests were set in motion by the settled people of the Ḥijāz, notably the citizens of Mecca and Ṭā'if.[3] But it must also be said that, without the military capabilities and numbers of the bedouin, the elite of the Ḥijāz could never have become a world power.

The Islamic conquests were not, however, the only example of this interaction between the people of the desert and the sown, nor was the Ḥijāz the only area where settled people were numerous enough to generate this movement. This paper will concentrate on two other areas and two other movements, Yamāma in the time of Musaylima, and Ḥasā (then called Bahrain) under the Qarāmiṭa (usually known in western works as the Carmathians) in the fourth century AH/ninth century AD.

Yamāma,[4] today the name of a small and unimportant settlement on the eastern slopes of the Jabal Ṭuwayq, was, in early Islamic times, the name applied to a large area of central Arabia immediately to the south of modern Riyadh, including not only the district of Kharj but many of the surrounding settlements as well. The springs which emerge from the Jabal Ṭuwayq mean that this is an area of permanent settlement, of palm-trees and cereal production. It was one of the areas which had formed the heart of the pre-Islamic kingdom of Kinda, whose rulers had, in the fifth and early sixth centuries, controlled much of the trade of central Arabia. The recent excavations at Qaryat al-Fā'w[5] have shown that there were important urban settlements in the area in pre-Islamic times. Islamic geographers make it clear that the land was wealthy; Qudāma b. Ja'far[6] says that Yamāma and Bahrain produced a revenue of 510,000 *dīnārs* per year, much more than the 300,000 of Oman and only slightly less than the 600,000 of Yemen. Nāṣir-i Khusraw, the Persian traveller of the mid-fifth/eleventh century speaks of the flourishing markets of the town of Ḥajar.[7] By the time of Muḥammad, however, the dominant tribe in the area were the Banū Ḥanīfa, whose name is still preserved in the *wādī* of that name to the south of Riyadh. In many ways, the Ḥanīfa of Yamāma were similar to the Quraysh of Mecca. Until his death in 630 the Christian king of the district, Hawdha b. 'Alī al-Ḥanafī, had acted as an organiser for Persian commerce in central Arabia, just as Quraysh attempted to control the trade of the Ḥijāz. With the collapse of the Persian empire under the invasion of Heraclius, Hawdha, like other Persian protégés in eastern Arabia, was obliged to stand on his own feet and it was natural that Yamāma, like Mecca, would seek to control the trade of the area for its own advantage. Yamāma was like Mecca in another way as well; it seems that it had a *ḥaram* or sanctuary, probably at Ḥajar, which is said by the early Islamic geographers to have been the fortified *qaṣaba* of the area but whose location is now entirely lost. It is possible that this ḥaram, like that at Mecca and the South Arabian *hawṭas* described by Serjeant,[8] formed the nucleus of the trading network. Like the Quraysh, the guardians of the ḥaram at Yamāma had commercial relations with the bedouin tridesmen who accepted the status of the holy place, notably the important north Arabian tribes of Asad and Tamīm. It is noteworthy that Tamīm, a large and very loosely-knit tribe, also had close relations with the Meccan ḥaram; the two centres were certainly in competition, a competition which was sharpened by the collapse of Persian influence.

It is not surprising, therefore, that Yamāma, like Mecca, produced a Prophet. The Muslim sources naturally stress that this Prophet, Musaylima, was an imitator of Muḥammad, trying unsuccessfully to emulate the true Prophet's success. Western scholars have sometimes doubted this and suggested that Musaylima's career may have been independent of and even previous to Muḥammad's but there are reasons for thinking that the Muslim tradition is correct. It is unlikely that a self-styled Prophet could have come to dominate Yamāma in the lifetime of the Christian king Hawdha b. 'Alī who died, as we have seen, in 630, long after the beginning of Muḥammad's mission. Until 630 Muḥammad was only ruler of Medina, struggling with the Quraysh for control in the Ḥijāz. Only after the conquest of Mecca and the subsequent victory over the Hawāzin at Ḥunayn was Muḥammad effectively leader of the Qurayshite area of influence and it would seem likely that it was at this time, after the death of Hawdha, that Musaylima began to assert his status as a Prophet.

The differences between him and Muḥammad are well known; it seems that Musaylima was content to divide authority with Muḥammad and possibly with other would-be holy leaders, like the Prophetess Sajāḥ of Tamīm. This would accord well with the traditional practice; if there could be a ḥaram in Ḥajar as well as a ḥaram in Mecca, it was only reasonable that both these could have their own Prophet, a vision of the future quite unacceptable to Muḥammad. The Prophet of Yamāma was defeated and killed in the *Ridda* wars and has gone down in Muslim tradition as the arch-imposter. The reasons for his failure are difficult to pinpoint. The single-minded and uncompromising policies of Muḥammad, his successors and the Quraysh elite made them more determined and ruthless. Their determination had economic as well as religious roots. Mecca produced no food and was not self-sufficient. The Quraysh had to trade or die. Furthermore they thought it necessary to dominate the trade with Iraq as well as that with Syria, precluding any natural division with their central Arabian rivals. The position of Yamāma was rather different. As has been pointed out, it was an area of agricultural as well as commercial wealth, and seems to have been self-sufficient in foodstuffs, even exporting wheat to the Ḥijāz on occasion. For the people of Yamāma trade was a luxury, the icing on the economic cake, so to speak, and though desirable it was not essential and compromises could be made. For the Quraysh trade was their life-blood and compromise was impossible; it could not be shared since it was their whole and only cake. The settled peoples of the Ḥijāz were united in their determination to control Arabia; the Ḥanīfa of Yamāma seem to have been divided. The resistance to Muslim conquest seems to have come from the settled people; the nomad sections of the tribe, and their nomad allies like the Tamīm, were much more ready to accept Muslim rule which did not really threaten their position. Whatever the reasons for his eventual failure, Musaylima's movement seems to have had certain clearly defined characteristics; the leadership came from the settled peoples of the oases who used their guardianship of the ḥaram to assert their influence over the nomads who acknowledged its status. In Musaylima they produced a Prophet to provide a cutting edge to the leadership, a cutting edge which seemed to be demanded by the success of Muḥammad. The attempt to mobilise the bedouin was only partly successful and the movement was destroyed by their more aggressive and determined rivals.

Musaylima was the most famous of the 'false prophets' of Arabia. He was also the last to exercise any real power. After the triumph of Islam, it was very difficult for rival new Prophets to exert any influence and most who did claim this status were, like the poet al-Mutanabbī, the object of ridicule rather than fear. This did not mean, however, that the settled people of Arabia no longer tried to control the bedouin or that they ceased to use religious leadership as a means of doing so. How this pattern was adapted to the new Islamic order can be seen in the history of the Qarāmiṭa of Bahrain who mobilised the military energies of the bedouin in the name of an Ismā'īlī claimant to the leadership of the Islamic community.

In early Islamic times, the term Bahrain applied not only to the island now called Bahrain but then known as Uwāl, but also to the mainland area opposite, roughly the modern Ḥasā province of Saudi Arabia.[9] The main settlements were in the Ḥasā oasis, notably at Hajar (not to be confused with the Ḥajar of Yamāma) which was a fortified town described by Yāqūt as the capital (*qā'ida*) of the province, and at Juwāthā', where Lorimer's *Gazetteer*[10] notes the ruins of an old mosque, and at Qaṭīf near the coast, a sort of second capital. By the time of Nāṣir-i Khusraw, writing in the mid-fifth/eleventh century at the end of the Qarmaṭī rule, the name Bahrain was applied, as now, to the island. Commentators stress the wealth of its agriculture and the remoteness of its situation:

'No ruler of Baṣra', says Nāṣir-i Khusraw,[11] not entirely accurately, 'has ever dreamed of attacking it'. Even Yamāma to the west, a province to which Bahrain was often aligned for administrative purposes, was several days' journey across the Dahnā' sands, a journey which was, again according to Nāṣir-i Khusraw, impossible in the summer. Visitors also make it clear that much of the wealth of Bahrain derived from taxes on trade, both shipping in the Gulf and overland caravans between Iraq and the Ḥijāz.

The history of the rise of the Qarmaṭī state in Bahrain once again illustrates the importance of the interaction of the peoples of the desert and the sown in Arabian history.[12] This essay is not concerned primarily with the ideological aspects of the Qarmaṭī movement but rather with its political objectives and the reasons for its military success. The Islamic conquest had not, of course, emptied the Arabian desert of all its bedouin inhabitants. What it had done was to provide an opportunity for all those who were discontented with their lot and who sought greater opportunities elsewhere. These opportunities did not cease with the end of the main conquests either. There remained areas of the Muslim world where there were still opportunities for military service and the acquisition of wealth; 'Uqaylīs on the Byzantine frontier, and Sulamīs in Armenia and on the shores of Lake Van could find outlets for their martial energies. Any historian of Arabia must be struck by the peaceful state of the area in the later Umayyad and early 'Abbāsid periods, and such peace must have been the result of gradual but sustained emigration. When the *Darb* Zubayda was constructed for the *ḥajj* from Iraq in early 'Abbāsid times, the provision of a water supply rather than protection from the bedouin was the main concern of the builders. The military 'reforms' of al-Mu'taṣim (833–842) and the development of the Turkish armies of Sāmarrā changed this; Arabs were dropped from the *dīwān*, which meant that subsidies were no longer paid to them. At the same time, opportunities on the frontier declined; when Mūsā b. Bughā undertook campaigns on the Byzantine frontier in the mid-third/ninth century we can be reasonably certain that it was his own Turkish followers who benefited, not the Arabs who had traditionally been involved in the *jihād*. Ironically, perhaps, the 'Abbāsid Caliphs even began to recruit Armenians to replace those Arabs they had recently removed from the armed forces.

All this might seem remote from the affairs of north-east Arabia but there is a connection, for it was precisely among those Qaysite tribes who had played so important a role on the Byzantine frontier, the 'Uqayl and Kilāb especially, that the Qarāmiṭa found their main bedouin supporters. Even before the arrival of the first Qarmaṭī propagandists, the ḥajj had been attacked and pillaged by the bedouin.[13] No doubt this was partly due to the weakness of the 'Abbāsid government, but probably more to bedouin anger at a system which effectively excluded them. The bedoun life-style is not, in effect, self-sufficient except in rare cases, and the bedouin needed to have some way of making an income with which to buy food, arms and occasional luxuries. If they were denied the opportunity of military service, government subsidies and control over trade, they had no option but to resort to violence and there was very little that any government before the twentieth century could do to restrain them. Nor did religious considerations mean that the annual ḥajj was immune from their depredations, not because they were notably anti-religious but rather because the ḥajj was perhaps the major economic event, as well as the major religious occasion, in the Arabian year.

It was against this background of increased bedouin discontent that the Qarāmiṭa first came to the oases of Bahrain.

The movement had begun among the settled agricultural peasantry of the Sawād of Iraq. It was from here that the eponymous Ḥamdān Qarmaṭ, who gave his name to the movement, was drawn and from here that his successors in the religious leadership, Zikrawayh and his sons, originated. But it soon began to attract recruits among the bedouin and others in north-east Arabia and the Syrian desert. From 886–7 Abū Sa'īd al-Jannābī had begun the mission in Bahrain. He found followers in two groups, the merchants of the Gulf sea-routes and the bedouin of the hinterland. Among the merchants, Abū Sa'īd made a valuable and lasting partnership with one al-Ḥasan b. Sanbar and for several generations the descendants of Abū Sa'īd and the descendants of al-Ḥasan ruled the community in apparent partnership and harmony. But equally important were the links Abū Sa'īd formed with the bedouin of the area, notably the Kilāb and 'Uqayl, the most important tribes in the area who came to form the military strength of the movement. In 972 Ibn Ḥawqal[14] was given a description of the elite of the Qarmaṭī state which included, besides the families of Abū Sa'īd al-Jannābī and al-Ḥasan b. Sanbar, 'Alī b. Aḥmad al-Ḥārithī in charge of justice, Thawr b. Thawr al-Kilābī as army commander, and the veteran, highly esteemed 'Alī b. 'Uthmān al-Kilābī (120 years old, they said) as *Ṣāḥib al-barīd*; the bedouin element was clearly very important and it is not surprising that Qarmaṭī policies reflected the interests of the bedouin. With this military support, the Qarāmiṭa began a series of attacks on Baṣra and other areas of central Iraq and on the ḥajj, taking pilgrims from Iraq to Mecca, activities which naturally brought them into contact with the 'Abbāsid government.

It is worth considering at this stage what the motives were for the aggression of the Qarāmiṭa and what the objectives of the movement were. At first sight it might appear obvious that they wished to conquer the Islamic world in the name of an Ismā'īlī *imām* and introduce a truly Islamic millennium. This would naturally have brought them into headlong conflict with the 'Abbāsids. But while some of the religious leaders may have aspired to these objectives, it seems that many of their followers had much more limited aims. Rather than wanting to conquer the Muslim world, they wished to have free access to Baṣra and the other ports of the Gulf, notably the developing port of Sīrāf on the Iranian shore, to secure the right to 'protect' the ḥajj and the payments that would result from that, and to receive payment and military salaries from the 'Abbāsid government as the Arab tribesmen of the area had done many years before. These demands were not in themselves unreasonable and it is clear that some elements in the 'Abbāsid government were prepared to compromise with them from an early stage. When these demands were met, if only in part, then the Qarāmiṭa could, and did, live at peace with their neighbours despite the different ideologies they espoused.

It has already been explained how the merchant al-Ḥasan b. Sanbar was involved in the movement from the beginning. This concern for maritime commerce becomes apparent in the negotiations which were begun by Abū Sa'īd's son, Sa'īd, with the 'Abbāsid authorities soon after his succession in 913, when the Qarāmiṭa were granted the right to free trade in Sīrāf. Later references suggest that the participation of the Qarāmiṭa in trade became more passive. Ibn Ḥawqal visited the area and with his keen interest in economic affairs and revenues he gives a full description of its financial situation. He explains how the island of Uwāl (modern Bahrain) was the point at which vessels were required to pay taxes to the Qarmaṭī authorities, showing clearly that they taxed maritime trade but not that they participated in it. In the next century, Nāṣir-i Khusraw tells of another source of income from the Gulf, the pearl fisheries, half of whose products were reserved for the Qarmaṭī leadership.[15]

If our evidence on maritime trade is disappointingly thin, we are much better informed about the relationship between the Qarāmiṭa and the land-based caravan trade. From the beginning of the movement, the Qarāmiṭa had used their military power to attack or control the caravan trade of the Arabian and Syrian desert. Al-Ṭabarī describes[16] how the Qarāmiṭa began their operations in the Syrian desert when they led the Banū Kalb, the most important tribe in the area, to cut the route between Kūfa and Damascus via Tadmur (Palmyra), preventing both messengers and traders from using it. In Bahrain, the Qarāmiṭa soon began to attack the ḥajj, as the Ṭayy and other bedouin had been doing for some years, but, with their greater numbers and superior organisation, they were able to prevent the pilgrimage going at all. In 922 and 923 the ḥajj was pillaged and many of the pilgrims slaughtered. The next year the authorities seem to have learned their lesson and the ḥajj was allowed to proceed after paying a substantial subsidy to the Qarāmiṭa. Relations between the 'Abbāsid authorities and the Qarāmiṭa seem to have broken down again after that.

There were two distinct points of view in Baghdad as to how the 'rebels' should be approached. One, espoused by the *wazīr* 'Alī b. 'Īsā and his group, believed that the Qarāmiṭa should be approached by peaceful means, and that they should be paid subsidies and given trading rights. If they were to be opposed militarily, it should be done by subsidising the tribes of the Kūfan desert, notably the Banū Asad, who were themselves threatened by the 'Uqayl and Kilāb who supported the Qarāmiṭa, and would have an interest in resisting them. The other party was represented by Ibn al-Furāt and his followers. As in other aspects, Ibn al-Furāt was reluctant to compromise the dignity of the 'Abbāsid government and unable to make the concession which the more flexible 'Alī b. 'Īsā saw as necessary. He refused to authorise subsidies and attempted to use the troops of his Iranian ally, Ibn Abī'l-Sāj, to oppose them, with disastrous results. Many of the difficulties which the 'Abbāsids had with the Qarāmiṭa at this time can be seen as a result of the constant changes in government in Baghdad during the disastrous reign of al-Muqtadir (908–932), which meant that there was no real continuity of policy. At one moment the Qarāmiṭa were encouraged to believe that subsidies would be forthcoming and that they would receive payment for allowing the free passage of the ḥajj; at the next moment, under a new administration, these benefits were refused and they were obliged to take violent action to have them restored. It is easy to see the conflict from the point of view of the 'Abbāsids who might regard the Qarāmiṭa as unpredictable and violent; the Qarāmiṭa might equally regard the 'Abbāsids as inconsistent and unreasonable. It is in this context that we should view the attack on the ḥajj in 317/930 and the carrying off of the Black Stone from the Ka'ba and its removal to the Qarmaṭī capital at Hajar. There is no evidence that the Qarāmiṭa disapproved of the Black Stone or the pilgrimage on religious grounds, though the formal observance of Islamic ritual formed no part of their own religious practice. The explanation is rather that, as has already been pointed out, the ḥajj was the most important economic event in Arabia, and the Black Stone was the key to the ḥajj; without it, the ḥajj could not take place. It is possible, but unlikely, that the Qarāmiṭa hoped to divert the ḥajj to Hajar but more probable that they were simply serving notice on the Muslim community that the ḥajj would not take place unless they were given a share in the benefits. The Black Stone was taken, not because it was the key to the religious life of the Muslim community but because it was the key to the commerce of Arabia.

The Black Stone was returned at the instigation of the Fāṭimid Caliph, then still based in Tunisia, in 951. Ibn Ḥawqal's account of the Qarāmiṭa state dates from shortly after this and shows that the Qarāmiṭa played a central role in the commerce of Arabia: 'Bahrain' he writes, referring to the entire area, both mainland and island, 'is endowed with a variety of revenues, tithes, all sorts of indirect taxes, tolls and the dues levied on their arrival on caravans coming from the area of Baṣra and Kūfa on the way to Mecca',[17] and it was these taxes on trade, along with those on the agricultural produce of the area, which accounted for the wealth and prosperity of the Qarāmiṭa. This prosperity in turn accounts for the comparative quiescence of the movement; once they had secured control of Arabian commerce, there was no longer any point in attacking the caravans or the lands from which they came.

Earlier in this essay, it was pointed out that one of the main reasons for bedouin discontent in the third/ninth century was the fact that they were excluded from military service and the subsidies which resulted from that, and it is clear that the Qarāmiṭa movement sought to change this. Given the fact that the Qarāmiṭa were believed to be opposed to the 'Abbāsid Caliphate and everything it stood for on religious grounds, it is remarkable how early we find Qarmaṭīs taking service with the 'Abbāsids. In 932, only three years after the abduction of the Black Stone, Qarmaṭīs were serving in the 'Abbāsid armies. The decay of 'Abbāsid government in the next two decades meant that their services were further in demand. We find them in the army of Ibn Rā'iq, the first *Amīr al-umarā'* who effectively ended the secular power of the 'Abbāsid Caliphs, and they seem to have had especially close relations with the Barīdī family, the tax farmers of Baṣra and southern Iraq, born perhaps of a common interest in the commerce of the area. The pattern seems to have continued under the early Būyids; Qarmaṭīs served under Mu'izz al-Dawla, and when the Qarāmiṭā began their final assault on Syria from 969 onwards, they acknowledged the authority of the 'Abbāsid Caliph and his Būyid protector. Here again Qarmaṭī policy seems to have been directed not by religious considerations but by the priorities of the bedouin, the need to find employment in regular armies. As with the trade, so with military service; when the Qarāmiṭa had access to employment opportunities in the Būyid armies, they had no interest in attacking the Būyid state. Ibn Ḥawqal reports that in his day senior members of the movement lived in Baṣra and Kūfa, both under Būyid rule.[18] They also served in the armies of the Ḥamdānids of Aleppo and it seems that they were paid at least in part in iron, unobtainable in Bahrain but vital for the manufacture of weapons.

It is in this light that we should see the dramatic rupture between the Qarāmiṭa and their fellow Ismā'īlīs, the Fāṭimids. The quarrel was essentially about Damascus and other Syrian cities. Under the Ikhshīdids, whose rule preceded that of the Fāṭimids in Syria and Egypt, the government had paid substantial tribute to the Qarāmiṭa of Bahrain. Whether this was in exchange for military service or simply a subsidy to keep them peaceful is not clear but it seems to have been important for the recipients. The Fāṭimids refused to pay this tribute and this in turn led to violent Qarmaṭī attacks on Syria and then on Egypt itself. The aggression only ceased with a new agreement to pay subsidies to Bahrain, and the increasing weakness of the movement in the fifth/eleventh century, and the growing disenchantment of their bedouin supporters which followed, meant that the Qarāmiṭa were unable to exert such pressure again and that their activities were increasingly confined to Bahrain itself.

The histories of the two movements examined in this essay have features in common, features which run through the history of Arabia in the pre-modern period. Both the brief flourishing of Musaylima's rule in Yamāma and the much more sustained rule of the Qarāmiṭa in Bahrain were the result of the people from the settled areas of Arabia providing the religious leadership which united, at least for a time, the neighbouring bedouin in a common purpose under their control. In both cases as well, the control of trade routes played an important part in the politics of movement. At the beginning it was pointed out how difficult it is to talk of the history of Arabia in the pre-modern period. In both of these examples, however, it is clear that the history is the result of the interaction between the people of the desert and the people of the sown under religious leadership. Without the people of the settled lands, the history of the bedouin is simply the endlessly repeated cycles of the pastoral life; without the bedouin, to provide military support, the people of the oases of Arabia are restricted to their own affairs and their own limited horizons. Only when these two groups came together could the people of Arabia exert an influence beyond the confines of their normal lives, and the agent which brought them together was religious leadership. Parallels with the early Islamic *umma* and the Wahhābī movement are numerous and obvious. Perhaps an examination of the two lesser enterprises discussed in this essay throws light on these larger concerns.

Notes

1. See, for example, M.A. Shaban, *Islamic History: A New Interpretation 1: AD 600--750 (AH 132)* (Cambridge University Press, Cambridge, 1971), pp. 3–15.

2. For recent anthropological work on the bedouin see W. Lancaster, *The Rwala Bedouin Revisited*, (Cambridge University Press, Cambridge, 1981) and D.P. Cole, *Nomads of the Nomads: the Āl Murrah Bedouin of the Empty Quarter* (Aldine Publishing Co., Chicago, 1975).

3. F.M. Donner, *The Early Islamic Conquests* (Princeton University Press, Princeton, New Jersey, 1984).

4. For accounts of Yamāma in more recent times, see J.G. Lorimer, *Gazetteer of the Persian Gulf, 'Omān and Central Arabia* (6 vols., Superintendent Government Printing, India, Calcutta, 1908–1915), vol. II, p. 1025 and H.St.J. Philby, *The Heart of Arabia* (Constable, London, 1922) vol. 2, pp. 20–34. For a recent, and extremely illuminating, discussion of Musaylima, see D.F. Eickelman, 'Musaylima: an Approach to the Social Anthropology of Seventh Century Arabia', *Journal of the Economic and Social History of the Orient*, vol. 10 (1967), pp. 17–52. I am indebted to M.A. Shaban for this reference.

5. See A.R. Al-Ansary, *Qaryat al-Fau: a Portrait of Pre-Islamic Civilisation in Saudi Arabia* (Distributed by Croom Helm, London, 1982).

6. Qudāma b. Ja'far, *Kitāb al-Kharāj*, ed. M.J. de Goeje (E.J. Brill, Leiden, 1889), pp. 249, 251.

7. Nāṣir-i Khusraw, *Sefer Nameh*, trans. C. Schefer (Publications de l'École des Langues Orientales Vivantes IIe Série, Vol. 1, Paris, 1881), pp. 223–4.

8. R.B. Serjeant, '*Ḥaram* and *Ḥawṭah*, the Sacred Enclave in Arabia' in A. Badawi (ed.), *Mélanges Taha Husain* (Dār al-Ma'ārif, Cairo, 1962), pp. 41–58.

9. Lorimer, *Gazetteer*, vol. II, pp. 642–57, 1535, 1543.

10. Lorimer, *Gazetteer*, vol. II, p. 648.

11. Nāṣir-i Khusraw, *Sefer-Nameh*, p. 225.

12. The fullest discussion of the Qarāmiṭa remains M.J. de Goeje, *Mémoire sur les Carmathes* (E.J. Brill, Leiden, 1886). Recent works have tended to concentrate on the religious side of their activities; for further bibliography see W. Madelung, art. 'Ḳarmaṭī', EI^{2}, vol. 4, pp. 660–5. There is a useful compilation of Arabic sources in S. Zakkār, *Tārīkh Akhbār al-Qarāmiṭa*, 2nd edn. (Dār Ḥarrān, Damascus, 1982). The following relevant thesis was supervised by M.A. Shaban: Faizah Ismail Akbar Hussain, 'The Qarāmiṭa', unpublished PhD Thesis, University of Exeter, 1984.

13. Muḥammad b. Jarīr al-Ṭabarī, *Tārīkh al-Rusul wa'l Mulūk*, ed. M.J. de Goeje *et al.* (15 vols., E.J. Brill, Leiden, 1879–1901), vol. 13, p. 2183.

14. Ibn Ḥawqal, *Kitāb Ṣūrat al-Arḍ*, trans. J.H. Kramers and G. Wiet (2 vols., Maisonneuve et Larose, Paris, 1964), vol. 1, pp. 25–6.

15. Ibn Ḥawqal, *Ṣūrat al-Arḍ*, vol. 1, p. 24; Nāṣir-i Khusraw, *Sefer Nameh*, p. 230.

16. al-Ṭabarī, *Tārīkh*, vol. 13, pp. 2217–20.

17. Ibn Ḥawqal, *Ṣūrat al-Arḍ*, vol. 1, p. 24.

18. Ibid., p. 25.

3 Arabia and the Pilgrim Paradigm of Ibn Baṭṭūṭa: A Braudelian Approach[1]

Ian Richard Netton

The *Riḥla* of Ibn Baṭṭūṭa (AD 1304–1368/9 or 1377) has been tackled over the years by a multitude of scholars in a variety of different ways. Often, however, the various studies which have been published have concentrated — to use, loosely, a not inappropriate pair of Ismā'īlī terms – on a *ẓāhir* exposition of the text and its problems rather than on an analysis of a *bāṭin* structure. I do not, of course, mean that the *Riḥla* might have a secondary meaning but that it has been analysed, for example, more often as a straight travelogue,[2] a problematic chronology,[3] a vehicle or mirror of Muslim institutions[4] and a focus for stylistic comparison.[5] The translation of three-quarters of it into English by H.A.R. Gibb for the Hakluyt Society series has placed it — at least for English non-Arabists — firmly within that type of travel genre or tradition in which the Hakluyt Society has always specialised. The essence or *raison d'être* of the genre was epitomised in the early resolution adopted in 1846 explaining that the Society was to be formed 'for the purpose of printing, for distribution among its members, the most rare and valuable voyages, travels and geographical records, from an early period of exploratory enterprise to the circumnavigation of Dampier'.[6] The emphasis, in other words, was to be on the voyage and on the data which might have resulted from original exploration. Finally, to provide a last illustration, the *Riḥla* has been examined recently by the present writer in terms of myth and magic,[7] and it is upon the approach used then that I would like to base that employed in the present essay.

In my article 'Myth, Miracle and Magic in the *Riḥla* of Ibn Baṭṭūṭa' I put forward the proposition that Ibn Baṭṭūṭa used the *Riḥla* as a kind of frame story in a manner akin to the usage in *Kalīla wa Dimma* and the *Panchatantra*.[8] In other words, what was being stressed was the sheer *artificiality* of the art form employed by the author and/or his editor.[9] If we examine his *Riḥla* in these terms, we may go on to ask whether the whole is a frame for just a collection of disparate and, perhaps, unconnected places visited, episodes, interests, and prejudices,

Map No. 1

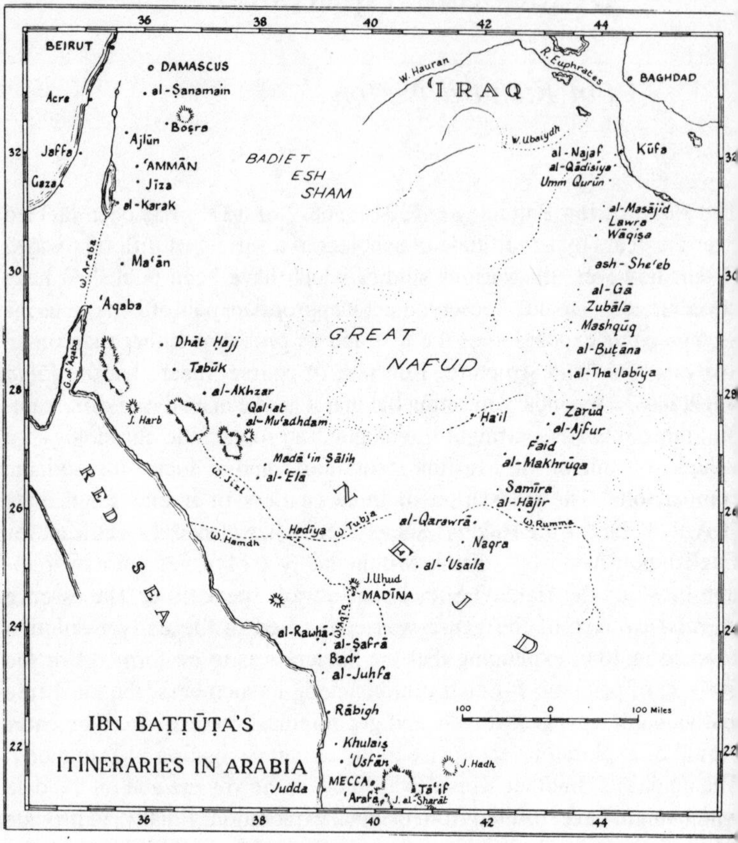

This map is reproduced by kind permission of the Hakluyt Society from H.A.R. Gibb, *The Travels of Ibn Baṭṭūṭa*, (published for the Hakluyt Society, Cambridge, 1958), vol. 1.

or whether there is some kind of identifiable structure upon which the *Riḥla* is built and some paradigm or pattern of widespread applicability by which it is ordered. Such tools of analysis need not, of course, have been present in the mind of the writer as he wrote or, rather, dictated his text. Indeed, it would be extraordinary if Ibn Baṭṭūṭa had thought in any kind of 'structuralist' way at all. What he did do, however, was to give vent to overriding interests and prejudices in the course of his text which we ourselves can now use as part of the meat of our analysis. It is therefore the purpose of this essay to assess what are the 'constants' at work within the frame which has been described. I propose to use, firstly, the three-level method of historiography established by that doyen of the French *Annales* school of history, Fernand Braudel (1902–1985), as a key to unlocking at least some of the structure of the *Riḥla* (*in particular, its Arabian section*) and identifying eventually what I will term the basic 'pilgrim paradigm' of Ibn Baṭṭūṭa.

Braudel's method, in which history is viewed and studied on three levels of (i) enduring geographic and economic structures, (ii) social structures and 'conjunctures',[10] and (iii) events, is best seen in operation in his magisterial three-volume *Civilization Matérielle, Économie et Capitalisme (XVe–XVIIIe Siècle)*.[11] But it also appeared earlier in his famous *La Méditerranée et le Monde Méditerranéen à l'Epoque de Philippe II*.[12] And it is precisely because of the Mediterranean orientation of the latter that I have decided to concentrate on it rather than on the former. In the preface to the first edition of *La Méditerranée* Braudel stressed that his book had three parts: the first studied the history of man 'dans ses rapports avec le milieu qui l'entoure; une histoire lente à couler, à se transformer, faite souvent de retours insistants, de cycles sans cesse'. The second part dealt with 'histoire sociale, celle des groupes et des groupements' and the way in which such forces as economic systems, civilisations and societies interacted in the field of warfare. For war, Braudel emphasised, was the product of more than purely individual responsibility. The last part of *La Méditerranée* was rather more traditional and dealt with the history of events or what had been termed by Paul Lacombe and François Simiand 'l'histoire événementielle'. Braudel summarised his efforts by saying that 'ainsi sommes-nous arrivés à une décomposition de l'histoire en plans étagés. Ou, si l'on veut, à la distinction, dans le temps de l'histoire, d'un temps géographique, d'un temps social, d'un temps individuel'.[13] And he entitled the three parts of his book respectively 'La Part du Milieu', 'Destins Collectifs et Mouvements d'Ensemble' and 'Les Événements, La Politique et les Hommes'.

It is instructive to try and apply the Braudelian categories to the Arabian section of Ibn Baṭṭūṭa's *Riḥla*. And although an *over-rigid* compartmentalisation of data is often unwise, none the less the Braudelian method can be valuable in highlighting aspects both of Ibn Baṭṭūṭa's own mind and the land and age through which he travelled, which might otherwise have been overlooked. Firstly, however, it is necessary to outline briefly the salient features of that first Arabian travelogue. Ibn Baṭṭūṭa made several pilgrimages to Mecca[14] but it is this first visit and first incursion into Arabia that will concern us here.

Ibn Baṭṭūṭa left Damascus with the pilgrim caravan on 1 September 1326. He passed by the great castle of Al-Karak with its legendary crusading associations and entered the desert after passing through Ma'ān which the traveller described as the last of the Syrian towns. He then began to encounter places associated with the Prophet Muḥammad in one way or another: Tabūk to which the Prophet had led an expedition in 631; the well of al-Ḥijr from which the Prophet had refused to drink; and finally, and most notably, the City of Medina with its plethora of associations with the life of the founder of Islam. Relying much on the earlier work of Ibn Jubayr, Ibn Baṭṭūṭa describes in detail the Mosque of Medina where Muḥammad, as well as the two early Caliphs Abū Bakr and 'Umar b. al-Khaṭṭāb, lies buried. He retails, again in some detail, the circumstances of the building of this mosque and the way in which it was gradually enlarged over the centuries.[15]

Ibn Baṭṭūṭa tells us that he stayed four days in Medina and spent each night in the mosque.[16] After leaving the city, he donned the pilgrim garb and entered the state of *iḥrām* near the mosque of Dhū 'l-Ḥulayfa, about five miles away. The last major village through which he passed was Badr, site of the first notable battle between Muḥammad and the Meccans in 624. It is duly noted and eulogised by Ibn Baṭṭūṭa. Finally, with a full heart, the traveller reached Mecca.[17]

Mecca has been the object of his journeying and the importance of this city both for Islam generally, and for Ibn Baṭṭūṭa in particular, ensures that it is treated in page after page of almost fulsome detail. Not only does Ibn Baṭṭūṭa perform the familiar and age-old pilgrim rituals and traditions of *ṭawāf*, running between al-Ṣafā and al-Marwa, and drinking from the well of Zamzam, but he positively revels in every aspect of the city, describing its gates, the Sacred Mosque with the Ka'ba, the city cemetery and even the sanctuaries outside Mecca, and the Meccan mountains and caves significant for early Islamic history.[18] Nor do the inhabitants of Mecca escape his curious attention: he praises the good qualities of the Meccan citizenry and, as is his wont, pays particular attention to the scholars and pious folk who inhabit the city and its environs, recounting several entertaining anecdotes about these people.[19]

Perhaps the kernel of Ibn Baṭṭūṭa's narrative of this, his first visit to Mecca for the pilgrimage, is his description of the *wuqūf* on the plain of 'Arafāt (map: 'Arafa). The event clearly made an extraordinary impression on the young traveller for he notes not only the date of this wuqūf as a Thursday in AH 726 (= 6 November 1326)[20] but records in the same paragraph the names of the commanders of the Egyptian and Syrian caravans at that time and the names of some of the notables who made the pilgrimage that year. The 'Standing' at 'Arafāt is followed by the traditional rush to Muzdalifa, move to Minā, stoning of the pillars and celebration of 'Īd al-Aḍḥā.[21]

Ibn Baṭṭūṭa left Mecca with the Iraqi caravan on 17 November 1326 and travelled back to Medina, where he spent a further six days, before embarking on a quite different route from the inward one, which eventually brought the traveller to Kūfa in Southern Iraq. As he went he once again recorded the historical associations of the places through which he passed: Al-Ajfur, romantically connected with the lovers Jamīl and Buthayna; al-Qādisiyya (map: al-Qādisīya) scene of one of the greatest early Arab victories over the Sassanians in 636 or 637, and Najaf with its Shi'ite heritage.[22]

The above paragraphs give the bare chronological bones of Ibn Baṭṭūṭa's first visit to Arabia for the purpose of making the pilgrimage to Mecca. And the value of the great quantity of material which he provides in his text (despite some obvious plagiarism)[23] has, of course, been much appreciated by scholars from a variety of disciplines, not least that of Islamic art and architecture. But what may have sometimes been neglected in the frequently indiscriminate mining of the *Riḥla* for information by scholars is a real appreciation and ordering of the several different *layers* of information provided by Ibn Baṭṭūṭa. Here the insights of Braudel can be of considerable value.

If we take first the *geographical* level in Braudel's methodology, we find that a vivid awareness of the harshness of the Arabian landscape permeates Ibn Baṭṭūṭa's narrative. This awareness is epitomised best in the constant search for, and references to, water.[24] Ibn Baṭṭūṭa is always delighted by the presence of water whether it be running as at Tabūk,[25] sweet from having been previously brackish as at the Well of Arīs,[26] or simply rain-water collected in tanks.[27] There are numerous references to water and Arabian watering places in his narrative: the principal problem associated with both seems to have been the usual one of continual supply[28] rather than the incidence of malaria.[29] And there are other references to the environment as well: secondary motifs in Ibn Baṭṭūṭa's Arabian section include the terrors of the desert where men can be lost[30] and the fearsome Samoom wind.[31] By contrast with all this, the cities of Medina and Mecca are positive oases of the good life — what Braudel calls 'minuscules points d'appui'[32] — with their mosques and well-stocked markets.[33] The exquisite importance of transport[34] — well-provisioned transport! — becomes excessively clear in such a desert-dominated milieu, and was a prime consideration of Ibn Baṭṭūṭa in Arabia as well as of every other sensible traveller.[35] It is factors such as the above that must have led Braudel to summarise Islam as 'la totalité de ce que le désert implique de réalités humaines, concordantes et discordantes . . .',[36] though he would be wrong if he intended to imply that Islam was *of* the desert, i.e. a desert faith in origin and essence.

In his second layer of analysis, which in *La Méditerranée* is encapsulated under the general rubric 'Destins Collectifs et Mouvements d'Ensemble', Braudel examined the role of interlocking factors such as the economy, trade and transport on the one hand, and social structures such as Empires, societies and civilisations, on the other. He concluded with an analysis of the forms of war.

All these elements are present or implicit, of course, in one form or another in the *Riḥla* of Ibn Baṭṭūṭa. On his first Arabian journey the author noted, for example, the role of the pilgrim caravan as a vehicle of trade.[37] Gibb comments: 'The pilgrim caravans were at all times occasions for trade, especially as they were often exempted from the ordinary transit and custom duties.'[38] Braudel cites the description of an anonymous Englishman who, a few centuries later in 1586, followed an extremely well-endowed caravan to Mecca from an assembly point outside Cairo. It allegedly had about 40,000 mules and camels and 50,000 people including many merchants. As the caravan travelled, it sold some of the rice, tin, grain, silk and coral destined to be exchanged in the markets of Mecca.[39] And, indeed, the caravans in which Ibn Baṭṭūṭa travelled in Arabia, although he gives us no figures, may well have been of a similar magnitude and luxurious nature. The Iraqi caravan in which he left Mecca was clearly a massive one: according to the traveller, the numbers of people were so large that they surged like the waves of the sea, and if anyone left the caravan to relieve himself, he was quite unable to find his place again. The caravan was also endowed, as we have observed, with many water-bearing camels as well as a massive supply of luxuries and food.[40] And Ibn Baṭṭūṭa, like later[41] and earlier travellers, was not unaware of the dangers of a possible attack on the caravan.[42] In a sea-faring context, Braudel described piracy, 'industrie ancienne et généralisée', as a 'forme supplétive de la grande guerre'.[43] On land, raids on the Arabian caravan routes could serve similar or other purposes but were equally ancient and dangerous.[44] Ibn Baṭṭūṭa's caravans were not themselves attacked while he was in Arabia on his first pilgrimage, but his narrative betrays a distinct apprehension about the possibility.

The caravan trade described by the traveller reflected, in some small way, the larger economy of the states through which he travelled. Similarly, the larger empires and civilisations, with their mixtures of societies, which he encountered as he moved on his *Riḥla*, impinged upon him most clearly and obviously in the form of smaller social units or structures. Two important social groupings which he encountered in Arabia were those of the pilgrimage peer group and the *'Ulamā'*.

Ibn Baṭṭūṭa moved or worked, from the inside, with the one as a *ḥājj* and the other as a *'ālim*.[45] His narrative provides abundant evidence of the intricate 'group-ethos' which developed within the caravan with its customs and class structure: for example, it was customary for the Syrian pilgrims on arriving at Tabūk to charge the camp with drawn swords and smite the palm trees with those swords in emulation of the deeds of the Prophet Muḥammad on his expedition to Tabūk in 631.[46] Similarly the pilgrims made a point of drinking a mixture of barley meal and water or butter called *sawīq*, which was mixed with sugar, at the Pass of al-Sawīq. Again the action commemorated a previous one by the Prophet who, finding his companions to be without food in that place, changed sand into sawīq in a miracle which echoed that of the New Testament Cana.[47] The class structure of the pilgrim caravan is reflected in the fact that the Amīrs had their own tanks of water set aside for them at, for example, the spring of Tabūk, unlike the ordinary pilgrims;[48] and it was the Amīrs who assumed the responsibility for filling the water tanks with sawīq and doling it out to the people from them.[49] Wealth and/or high rank and a privileged access to water and associated beverages in the caravan are thus seen to be inexorably linked. Such divisions, to a certain extent, ought to have vanished with the group assumption of iḥrām.[50] But it was only in the rituals of the *Ḥajj* itself, communally celebrated in Mecca and 'Arafāt and its environs, that the pilgrims really merged with their peers and assumed a single corporate identity *par excellence*.

Ibn Baṭṭūṭa's interest in, and encounters with, his fellow-'Ulamā' is a constant *leitmotiv* throughout his *Riḥla*. It is thus no surprise to find the traveller noting by name during the account of his first pilgrimage such individuals as a Mālikī professor,[51] a Zaydī Qāḍī,[52] and the imāms of the four principal *madhāhib* at Mecca.[53] Though Ibn Baṭṭūṭa does not seem to have collected in Medina and Mecca the *ijāzāt* which he claims to have acquired in vast quantities in Damascus just before setting off on his first Arabian journey,[54] it is clear from his accounts of these cities that he enjoyed to the full the company of his academic peers.[55]

Braudel has described events as 'poussière'. For him 'ils traversent l'histoire comme les lueurs brèves; à peine naissent-ils qu'ils retournent déjà à la nuit et souvent à l'oubli'. But every event, 'si bref qu'il soit, porte témoignage . . .'[56] and Ibn Baṭṭūṭa's own first pilgrimage to Mecca and incursion into Arabia is much more than a single Braudelian event, or even a chain of connected events or journeyings, at a particular time. Because of its nature it is a celebration across time and space of a whole series of 'events', or alleged 'events', which took place long before in both the pre-Islamic pilgrimages and those of Muḥammad, and which function as a set of symbols in the present. It is *these* 'events' rather than what Ibn Baṭṭūṭa himself does, and where he goes, which constitute in a major sense the substance of his pilgrimage.

This three-level analysis based on the insights of Fernand Braudel enables us to marshal and present the data in Ibn Baṭṭūṭa's *Riḥla* in a particularly 'compartmentalised' fashion. The question may now be fairly asked: can we identify, through the medium of such a method, certain constants which have a function, relevance, or applicability throughout much of the *Riḥla*, and which may be said to constitute *in toto* a 'pilgrim paradigm' for the traveller? In other words, having achieved its most Islamically perfect form in Arabia because of the pilgrimage and Mecca — (although Mecca may not be the sole focal point of Ibn Baṭṭūṭa's journeyings as it was with Ibn Jubayr)[57] — is there a pattern of intentions which appears to operate in other cities and regions visited in the *Riḥla* as well?

An analysis of the *Riḥla* shows that this is the case. There are a certain number of constants which may be said to transcend, though they may be permeated by, or even a cause of, the traveller's more individual preoccupations or characteristics such as an interest in watering holes or uxoriousness. They transcend simply because of their breadth and the far-reaching nature of their significance for the narrative scope of the entire *Riḥla*; and they may thus be said to constitute a substrate or, better, an underlying 'pilgrim paradigm' for this work. The principal elements of the paradigm are four-fold. Firstly, we may derive from Braudel's generalised primary level of geographic constants the enduring religious geography of an Islamic sacred area, which in Arabia means primarily Mecca and its environs, and in which are celebrated, in a strictly ordered series of rituals, religious 'facts' from the past. Thus there is a linkage between Braudel's first and third levels. Religious geography and the 'facts' such geography has witnessed and absorbed engender a *primal and focal search or journeying to a shrine*, which in the case of Mecca is the Ḥajj to the sacred Ka'ba itself.

Secondly, bearing in mind Braudel's second level of social structures generally, and the grouping of the Islamic 'Ulamā' in particular, we may note Ibn Baṭṭūṭa's *search for knowledge*. The 'Ulamā' as a social and educational group personified and institutionalised knowledge; and travellers like Ibn Baṭṭūṭa implemented the medieval saw which instructed Muslims to seek knowledge even as far as China. This has two facets in the *Riḥla*: Ibn Baṭṭūṭa's desire to associate with, or meet, as many scholars as possible, a feature which is clear in his Arabian narrative, and his almost childlike eagerness to acquire as many of such scholars' ijāzāt as possible, a feature which is, however, lacking in this first Arabian account but prominent elsewhere.[58] Ibn Baṭṭūṭa may be said to have obeyed the saw to the letter in that he actually claims to have visited China and conversed with its academics.[59]

Thirdly, related to and deriving from this second Braudelian level of social structures is our traveller's *search for personal recognition and/or power and massive interest in those who hold power*. The isolation and loneliness felt by the youthful and inexperienced traveller as he sets out[60] are soon replaced by the satisfaction of scholarly converse, recognition in the form of the grant of an ijāza or ṣūfī robe,[61] personal fulfilment in marriage,[62] or the attainment of politico-religious power as in his appointments as Ambassador of Sulṭān Muḥammad ibn Tughluq of Delhi to China,[63] or Qāḍī to the Maldive islands.[64] Ibn Baṭṭūṭa's predilection for recognition by the pious and the powerful appears on his Arabian journey not only in his dropping of the names of jurists and scholars whose converse he clearly enjoyed, but in the way, for example, that he persuades the Commander of the Iraqi caravan himself, Muḥammad al-Ḥawīh, to take him under his wing, even to the extent of having the said Commander pay out of his own pocket the cost of hiring half a double litter as far as Baghdad, for Ibn Baṭṭūṭa.[65] Elsewhere, his interest in the great and the powerful is never far below the surface.[66]

Finally, as a species of Braudelian 'fact' occurring in the present, there is the *search for what might be characterised as the satisfaction of the raḥḥāla impulse*, that inquisitive 'itch' to travel for its own sake, shared to a greater or lesser degree by all real travellers, as opposed to mere tourists, whether they be the ancient, and anonymous, author of the *Periplus of the Erythraean Sea*[67] or the modern Tim Severin.[68] The urge is encapsulated in our medieval traveller's express wish never to travel the same route twice if it be possible.[69]

Ibn Baṭṭūṭa's 'pilgrim paradigm' thus comprises a series of four searches: for the shrine and/or its circumambient religious geography;

for knowledge; for recognition and/or power; and for the satisfaction of a basic wanderlust. To test whether such a paradigm really exists it is useful to look at some of the other cities and regions to which he travels and see if it is applicable there as well. Its various features are not, of course, always totally present and they may, at times, be permeated or changed by the traveller's other interests and prejudices his vivid imagination and, indeed, his capacity for invention. But let us briefly take five cities or regions which are mentioned elsewhere in the *Riḥla* and see whether the pattern which has been posited holds true

In *Najaf*, one of the great Shi'ite centres of culture and learning, Ibn Baṭṭūṭa takes a considerable interest in the alleged tomb of 'Alī[70] and eagerly soaks up information from 'trustworthy individuals' as well as three cripples hailing from Byzantium, Iṣfahān and Khurāsān, about healing miracles occurring every year on a certain 'night of life' (*laylat al-Maḥyā*) at the mausoleum.[71] The power and rank of the *Naqīb al-Ashrāf*, who governs Najaf, exercise the usual fascination over the traveller's mind and Ibn Baṭṭūṭa devotes some space to anecdotal material about a former incumbent of the office, Abū Ghurra.[72] On leaving the city, Ibn Baṭṭūṭa's wanderlust clearly transcends his justified fear of the inhabitants and highwaymen of the area between Najaf and Baṣra.[73]

In *Isfahān* Ibn Baṭṭūṭa chooses to stay in a convent much visited by people seeking *baraka* because it is associated with an ascetic disciple of al-Junayd. The traveller is warmly welcomed and honoured by the Convent Shaykh who ultimately invests him with the robe of the Suhrawardī Ṣūfī order, thereby satisfying in the one action Ibn Baṭṭūṭa's constant yearning for recognition, fascination with *taṣawwuf*, and love of arcane knowledge and lore. The latter is particularly apparent in the way he records in the *Riḥla* after describing the investiture, what he now considers to be his own ṣūfī *silsila* which he has clearly attempted to memorise from the Shaykh himself or his learned associates in the Convent.[74] After Iṣfahān a ten-day journey, with a view to visiting a certain Shaykh in Shīrāz, is contemplated with equanimity or, at least without comment.[75]

Ibn Baṭṭūṭa's one month and six days' sojourn[76] in *Constantinople* is marked by a similar collection of features: he is intrigued by the Christian places of prayer, whether they be the great church of Hagia Sophia or the city's monasteries.[77] He converses at length with the Qāḍī of Constantinople,[78] meets the ruler of the city[79] and also a monk named Jirjīs whom he believes to have been the former ruler.[80] Ibn Baṭṭūṭa's 'raḥḥāla impulse' is clearly indulged to the full in his roaming about the city every day.[81] And the same pattern manifests itself all over again in and around *Delhi*: he provides a vivid description of the great Mosque of Delhi[82] and lauds the power possessed by the much-venerated tomb of the Shaykh Quṭb al-Dīn Bakhtiyār al-Ka'kī of the Chistī order.[83] Ibn Baṭṭūṭa has his ample share of contact with the scholarly and the pious in Delhi,[84] as well as welcome and unwelcome recognition and power. The unstable and bloodthirsty ruler of Delhi, Sulṭān Muḥammad ibn Tughluq, showers him with gifts[85] and ultimately invests him with the Qadiship of Delhi[86] and an ambassadorship to China.[87] In between holding the latter two offices, however, he suffers the indignity of being placed under guard by the Sulṭān, having incurred the latter's displeasure.[88] Finally, his wanderlust surfaces readily in his eagerness to go hunting with the Sulṭān[89] and his (thwarted) attempt to go out on an expedition organised to fight the Sulṭān's enemies as well.[90]

It is, perhaps, in our fifth and final example, Ibn Baṭṭūṭa's sojourn in *Ceylon*, that we come closest to finding articulated the original Meccan paradigm. On Adam's Peak is a shrine or better, place of religious visitation *par excellence*: this is the footprint of Adam[91] and the visit to it has its own peculiar customs and pilgrim rituals.[92] The traveller absorbs (though he does not necessarily believe) the stories of the Yogis,[93] and he finds his lust for proper recognition sated in full measure by the hospitable and kindly reception which he receives from the infidel ruler whom he calls Sulṭān Ayrī Shakarwatī (Arya Chakravarti).[94] The enthusiasm with which Ibn Baṭṭūṭa seeks permission from the latter to undertake the difficult journey to the 'Foot of Adam' is yet a further simple indication of the traveller's innate wanderlust combined with curiosity.[95]

The five examples which we have provided above may not rigidly reflect, or adhere to, what has been termed 'the pilgrim paradigm' in every tiny detail. None the less, that paradigm is sufficiently present in each case: in other words, the illustrations chosen from a number of disparate cities and areas *do* show that there is an underlying, and therefore unifying, set of constants, in the narrative of each visit. The Arabian section of the *Riḥla* does, therefore, present a paradigm of features which are coherent, relevant and applicable to other areas of the text.

Ibn Baṭṭūṭa's work, of course, constitutes a particular development of the *Riḥla* form:[96] it is, so to speak, a canonisation of that form. If we turn back briefly to an earlier, and almost equally famous, *Riḥla*, that of Ibn Jubayr (AD 1145–1217),[97] with which it is logical to make a comparison, we find a much more fluid travelogue: this is the record of a pilgrim journey undertaken for a different purpose, much shorter in terms of both time and distance travelled and not so much a frame story as a simple narrative of a voyage undertaken and experienced.[98] We may conclude with a, perhaps not inappropriate, gardening analogy: if Ibn Jubayr's work resembles the somewhat disordered 'swampy, treeless land about Versailles' in the days before the advent of Louis XIV's master-gardener André Le Nôtre (AD 1613–1700), then Ibn Baṭṭūṭa's paradigmatic frame is akin — without too much exaggeration — to the ordered formalism of that gardener's great achievement at Versailles when he had finished.[99] The 'pilgrim paradigm' which we have proposed is both a 'way of seeing' or examining the age in which Ibn Baṭṭūṭa himself operated as well as a broader representation of some of the primary impulses of that which, for the sake of convenience, we describe loosely as 'Islam' itself.[100]

Notes

1. I am indebted to the writings of my colleague Professor Aziz Al-Azmeh for suggesting to me a 'paradigmatic' approach to the *Riḥla* of Ibn Baṭṭūṭa. See M. Masterman, 'The Nature of a Paradigm' in I. Lakatos and A. Musgrave (eds.), *Criticism and the Growth of Knowledge*, Proceedings of the International Colloquium in the Philosophy of Science, London, 1965, vol. 4 (Cambridge University Press, Cambridge, 1970), pp. 59–90. (I owe this reference to Professor Al-Azmeh.) See especially p. 62, n. 5 and p. 63, n. 11.

2. E.g. by Herman F. Janssens, *Ibn Batouta 'le voyageur de l'Islam' (1304–1369)*, (Office de Publicité, Brussels, 1948).

3. Ivan Hrbek, 'The Chronology of Ibn Baṭṭūṭa's Travels', *Archiv Orientální*, vol. 30 (1962), pp. 409–86.

4. G.-H. Bousquet, 'Ibn Baṭṭūṭa et les Institutions Musulmanes', *Studia Islamica*, vol. 24 (1966), pp. 81–106.

5. J.N. Mattock, 'The Travel Writings of Ibn Jubair and Ibn Baṭūṭa', *Glasgow Oriental Society Transactions*, vol. 21 (1965–66), pp. 35–46.

6. Dorothy Middleton, 'The Hakluyt Society 1846–1923' in *Annual Report and Statement of Accounts for 1984* (Hakluyt Society, London, 1985), p. 14. The relevant Hakluyt volumes are H.A.R. Gibb, *The Travels of Ibn Baṭṭūṭa AD 1325–1354*, trans. from the Arabic text ed. by C. Defrémery and B.R. Sanguinetti, 3 vols. (Cambridge University Press for the Hakluyt Society, Cambridge, 1958–71).

7. Ian Richard Netton, 'Myth, Miracle and Magic in the *Riḥla* of Ibn Baṭṭūṭa', *Journal of Semitic Studies*, vol. 29:1 (1984), pp. 131–40.

8. Ibid., p. 133.

9. For references to Ibn Baṭṭūṭa's editor, Ibn Juzayy, see my 'Myth, Miracle and Magic', p. 132, nn. 4, 6.

10. For a discussion of the word 'conjuncture', see his *La Méditerranée* (1966), vol. 2, pp. 213–20. (Full bibliographical details appear below in n. 12.)

11. (Librairie Armand Colin, Paris, 1979).

12. (Librairie Armand Colin, Paris, 1949; 2nd rev. ed. 1966); trans. of 2nd rev. ed. by Siân Reynolds, *The Mediterranean and the Mediterranean World in the Age of Philip*

II, 2 vols. (Collins, London, 1972).

13. *Méditerranée*, vol. 1, pp. 16–17.
14. E.g. in 1326, 1332, 1349.
15. *Riḥlat Ibn Baṭṭūṭa* hereafter referred to as *Riḥla* (Dār Ṣādir, Beirut, 1964), pp. 110–20.
16. Ibid., p. 126.
17. Ibid., pp. 128–30.
18. Ibid., pp. 130–46.
19. Ibid., pp. 148–68.
20. Gibb, *Travels of Ibn Baṭṭūṭa*, vol. 1, p. 245, n. 225.
21. *Riḥla*, pp. 169–71.
22. Ibid., pp. 172–218.
23. See my 'Myth, Miracle and Magic', p. 132, n. 6.
24. Ibid., p. 132.
25. *Riḥla*, p. 111–12.
26. Ibid., p. 126.
27. Ibid., p. 173.
28. E.g. ibid., p. 174. See also the story recounted on p. 112 in which a caravan's water supplies dried up.
29. See Braudel, *Méditerranée*, vol. 1, pp. 56–9.
30. *Riḥla*, p. 111; see also the reference to the awful wilderness between Tabūk and al-'Ulā, p. 112. For deserts and oases see Braudel, *Méditerranée*, vol. 1, pp. 156–65, 169–70.
31. *Riḥla*, pp. 112–13. See Braudel, *Méditerranée*, vol. 1, p. 223 for the impact of the sirocco and ibid., pp. 229, 231 for that of the mistral.
32. *Méditerranée*, vol. 1, p. 169.
33. *Riḥla*, pp. 132, 164.
34. *Méditerranée*, vol. 1, p. 158.
35. E.g. see the references to provisions and transports, including water-carrying camels for the foot pilgrims, in the Iraqi caravan, *Riḥla*, p. 172.
36. Braudel, *Méditerranée*, vol. 1, p. 171.
37. *Riḥla*, pp. 113, 175.
38. Gibb, *Travels of Ibn Baṭṭūṭa*, vol. 1, p. 159, n. 10.
39. Braudel, *Méditerranée*, vol. 1, pp. 165–6.
40. *Riḥla*, pp. 172–3; see n. 35 above.
41. Braudel, *Méditerranée*, vol. 1, p. 165.
42. *Riḥla*, p. 174.
43. Braudel, *Méditerranée*, vol. 2, pp. 190–1.
44. Compare the Cossack attacks on caravans along the Volga, *Méditerranée*, vol. 1, p. 178.
45. See my 'Myth, Miracle and Magic', pp. 138–9 for an assessment of the kind of 'ālim that Ibn Baṭṭūṭa was.
46. *Riḥla*, p. 112.
47. Ibid., p. 129. See John 2: 1–11.
48. *Riḥla*, p. 112.
49. Ibid., p. 129.
50. Ibid., p. 128.
51. Ibid., p. 110.
52. Ibid., p. 127.
53. Ibid., pp. 150, 151.
54. See my 'Myth, Miracle and Magic', p. 138, esp. n. 40.
55. See, for example, his sharing of the content of a dream with the Imām of the Malikites at Mecca, Abū 'Abdullāh Muḥammad, *Riḥla*, pp. 150–1.
56. *Méditerranée*, vol. 2, p. 223.

57. See my 'Myth, Miracle and Magic', pp. 132–3.
58. For *ijāzāt* acquired in Damascus, see *Riḥla*, pp. 108–10.
59. E.g. *Riḥla*, pp. 633, 637–8.
60. E.g. see ibid., p. 17.
61. E.g. ibid., p. 201.
62. E.g. ibid., pp. 19–20.
63. Ibid., p. 530.
64. Ibid., p. 588.
65. Ibid., p. 172.
66. E.g. see his account of the two Amīrs of Mecca, ibid., p. 148.
67. See the trans. by Wilfred H. Schoff (Oriental Books Reprint Corporation, New Delhi, 1974, [repr. from the Longmans, Green & Co., New York, 1912 edition]), and the more recent trans. by G.W.B. Huntingford (The Hakluyt Society, London, 1980).
68. See his *The Brendan Voyage* (Hutchinson, London, 1978) and *The Sindbad Voyage* (Hutchinson, London, 1982). See also his most recent volume *The Jason Voyage: The Quest for the Golden Fleece* (Hutchinson, London, 1985).
69. *Riḥla*, p. 191.
70. Ibid., pp. 176, 182.
71. Ibid., pp. 176–8.
72. Ibid., pp. 179–82.
73. Ibid., pp. 182–3.
74. Ibid., pp. 200–2. See Ibn Juzayy's somewhat snide commentary on this *silsila*, p. 202.
75. Ibid., p. 202.
76. Ibid., p. 356.
77. Ibid., pp. 351–4.
78. Ibid., p. 355.
79. Ibid., pp. 349–50.
80. Ibid., pp. 349, 354–5.
81. Ibid., p. 350.
82. Ibid., pp. 416–17.
83. Ibid., p. 419.
84. Ibid., pp. 419–20.
85. E.g. ibid., pp. 453, 507.
86. Ibid., p. 512.
87. Ibid., p. 530.
88. Ibid., p. 528.
89. Ibid., p. 517.
90. Ibid., p. 522.
91. Or the footprint of Shiva or Buddha depending on one's religious affiliation! See H.A.R. Gibb, *Ibn Battúta: Travels in Asia and Africa 1325–1354*, The Broadway Travellers (Routledge & Kegan Paul, London, 1929), p. 365, n. 5.
92. *Riḥla*, pp. 598–600.
93. Ibid., pp. 597, 600.
94. Ibid., p. 594.
95. Ibid.
96. See my 'Myth, Miracle and Magic', p. 133.
97. *Riḥla* (Dār Ṣādir, Beirut, 1964).
98. See my article 'Ibn Jubayr: Penitent Pilgrim and Observant Traveller', *UR*, No. 2 (1985), pp. 14–17.
99. See Lucy Norton, *The Sun King and his Loves* (The Folio Society, London, 1982), pp. 39–41.
100. See Masterman, 'The Nature of a Paradigm', pp. 76–77.

4 Some Western Views of the Arab Gulf

Paul Auchterlonie

In 1968 and 1972 Derek Hopwood wrote two bibliographical articles on the Egyptian Revolution[1] and the Arabian Peninsula[2] respectively. Limiting himself to books written by Westerners, he surveyed historical, biographical and political writings, omitting specialised economic and anthropological studies, as well as the wealth of journal literature and most collective works. This essay will work within the same limits, confining itself to serious scholarly works and eschewing both the valuable travel narratives of the nineteenth century and most of the journalistic essays of our own time.

Compared with other parts of the Middle East, there is remarkably little literature in any language on the Gulf as such. There is virtually no evidence to support the geopolitical concept of the Gulf at all in medieval times. The first to see the region as an entity were the British in the nineteenth century, particularly after 1880 when a series of treaties was signed with individual Gulf rulers. Since that date, the Gulf's relations with the West and its role in world affairs have been constant, even dominant, themes in Western writings about the area.

The internal characteristics of the Gulf states, their history and social patterns, have only recently become of interest to Western scholars. The reasons for this are twofold: firstly none of the shaykhdoms has been large enough to support an extensive vernacular literature in history, biography, the Islamic sciences or belles lettres. Only the Sultanate of Oman has had a strong literary tradition but one which only now is becoming accessible to the Western scholar. Faced with a paucity of sources, the latter has turned to richer and easier fields to till. Secondly, the theme of the impact of modernity on traditional societies, which has dominated much of Western academic writing on the Third World this century, is scarcely relevant to Gulf society before the late 1950s.

Moreover, it is worth pointing out that the Arab Gulf has only attracted a sizeable Western population, permanent, temporarily resident or transient, within the past twenty-five years. Since none of the Gulf states was ever a colony or even officially a protectorate, few Europeans had cause to reside there for administrative purposes. Exclusive treaties and small populations precluded the need for large naval or military contingents. Commercial activities attracted few outsiders either, at least until oil began to be extracted in large quantities in the late 1950s. Even the climate and the lack of historical monuments militated against tourism.

It is, therefore, not surprising that the Gulf has inspired few Westerners to put pen to paper. For over 100 years, from Captain Taylor's report of 1818, imperial factors dominate what literature there is. Thenceforth, the geopolitical role of the Gulf has shared the stage with the social, economic and political transformation of the Gulf states. Even today, however, nearly all Western writing on the Gulf is coloured by the region's past and present external relations and security to a degree unmatched by any other Middle Eastern state, and possibly even by the Arab-Israeli conflict itself.

In 1819, the British Government in India sent an expedition against the Qawāsim of Ras al-Khaima, for which the Assistant Political Agent in Baṣra, Captain Robert Taylor, prepared a brief handbook of all the available information on the region. With Britain deeply concerned to maintain maritime supremacy in the Gulf, along with good relations with the local Arab rulers, subsequent political agents augmented and updated these reports. At the same time, a succession of officers from the Survey Service of the Indian Navy charted the coastal waters and explored the shores of the entire region. A selection of their reports was issued as a monograph by the Bombay Government of 1856. Extremely rare, the *Arabian Gulf Intelligence* has fortunately been recently reprinted.[3]

Reading, not surprisingly, like a series of diplomatic despatches, the book is imbued with the authors' obvious desire to maintain British supremacy in the area. Nevertheless, it contains valuable data on trade, religion, customs and inter-tribal relations as well as historical and topographical information. The history of the various tribes extends back to the beginning of the eighteenth century in some cases, and was the basis of all subsequent historical accounts until the second half of the present century.

During the second half of the nineteenth century, British political agents continued to send back regular reports to the Government of British India. Selections from these reports were published in limited quantities in Calcutta, mostly compiled under the direction of J.A. Saldanha and with the title *Précis*.[4] Unannotated, the *Précis* are immensely valuable as raw data on political and maritime affairs in the Gulf. Although they sometimes deal with social and political matters, they do have the disadvantage of always and exclusively representing the imperial point of view; furthermore they have been criticised by J.B. Kelly as being inaccurate and deficient.[5] Nevertheless, the *Précis* contain an enormous, if undigested, amount of information.

Saldanha's *Précis* had been commissioned as essential preparatory work for a gazetteer of Gulf affairs. This appeared between 1908 and 1915, compiled by Colonel J.G. Lorimer, again under the auspices of the Government of British India.[6] The crowning achievement of consular reporting from the Gulf, it is a massive six-volume work divided into historical and geographical parts. Easier to use than the *Arabian Gulf Intelligence* because of its detailed table of contents, the *Gazetteer* expands and completes the information available in its predecessors (except for the United Arab Emirates). With the previous works, it shares a concern for the balance of power between rival shaykhs, for the imposition of exclusive treaties, and for maintaining British predominance, military, naval, commercial and political. The detail of Lorimer's work and the accuracy of his transcription make up for his dependence on other people's reporting, and the appendices on such diverse matters as pearl fisheries, geology, sailing craft, and Christian missions are uniquely valuable. The topographical section can be regarded, as Sir David Roberts has pointed out, as 'the Domesday Book of the Gulf'.[7] Its importance to the British Government can be gauged by the fact that it was not made available to the public until the 1950s and Sir Arnold Wilson does not even quote it in his bibliography to *The Persian Gulf* (see below).

The first Western work on the Gulf wholly by an individual is *Countries and Tribes of the Persian Gulf*, by S.B. Miles.[8] Miles died in 1914, the same year as Lorimer, and like him he was a servant of the Government of British India, occupying the post of Political Agent in Muscat from 1872 to 1886. Here, however, the similarity ends, for, whereas the *Gazetteer* was a government-sponsored undertaking designed to promote imperial ends, Miles's book is a scholarly history of the Gulf, and of Oman in particular. Miles was a man of curiosity, determination and scholarship who was clearly sympathetic to Islam and the Arabs of the Gulf. He was conversant with the major Arabic sources (references to which were, unfortunately, not supplied by the author, who died before the book went to press) and this is reflected in the considerable detail given to the history of the area before 1800. Miles also travelled extensively in both Oman and the rest of the Gulf and his book is an invaluable record of flora, fauna, topography and tribal affiliations. A landmark in the literature on the Gulf, *Countries and Tribes of the Persian Gulf* is the first Western work to accept the Arabs on their own terms.

The imperial era closes with Sir Arnold Wilson's history of the

Gulf.[9] It is a comprehensive work beginning with prehistory and ending with the advent of the twentieth century. While the early part of the work is based on Arabic and Persian texts (mainly in translation), the later history of the Gulf is almost exclusively that of its relations with the European powers. Wilson does not share Miles's enthusiasm for the Gulf as a region *per se*, but merely sees it as an area where Britain (or England, as he puts it) can pursue her *mission civilisatrice*. Listing Britain's achievements in the Gulf, he declaims: 'We have maintained order and thereby promoted trade; we have raised the standard of living and thereby encouraged the spread of education; we have fostered the growth of individual freedom and of aspiration to succeed in life — this is what we understand as civilisation.'[10]

Wilson's history is separated chronologically from the next work by a thirty-year gap and, spiritually, by the ending of the imperial mentality. No longer was it necessary to collect, collate and summarise historical and geographical data for the purposes of rule and government. This was now the era of the political scientist, the academic historian, and the incoming oilfield worker. Diplomatic paternalism still existed, but it was tempered with the realisation that the era of empire was drawing to a close and that the Gulf states were on the verge of social transformation. Maureen Tweedy's *Bahrain and the Persian Gulf*[11] is a slight illustrated handbook designed for the new British resident. Full of social information on how to visit the wife of a shaykh and the amenities offered by the Gymkhana Club in Bahrain, it paints a charming if unsophisticated picture of a traditional society uncertain of its future. There is little depth or perception in this book, but a good deal of sympathy with the indigenous culture. It is a book entirely of its period.

The Golden Bubble[12] is a rather more important work than Tweedy's. Apart from anything else, it is the first genuine travel book on the Gulf, a point the author makes vigorously in the first chapter, when he describes how H.M. Passport Office was extremely reluctant to grant him a visa for Bahrain and Kuwait, on the grounds that no one ever went there to write a book. Roderic Owen lived in the Arab quarter of Muharraq, whence he travelled up and down the Gulf, meeting shaykhs, political agents, Arabs, Persians and oilmen. Impressed by Sir Charles Belgrave's immense knowledge of Bahraini society and by the courtesy and friendliness of the Gulf rulers, he was clearly less taken by the rigid regard for protocol of some of the political agents. His conversations with all walks of life led him to make interesting observations on Egypt's role in Gulf politics, on the medical treatment of women, and on the attitude of the educated Bahrainis to the High Executive

Committee, among other matters. Never trivial, often perceptive, Owen's book is a colourful portrait of the first stirrings of a society in change.

Jean Jacques Berreby's *Le Golfe Persique*[13] is the first major French work to deal with the Arab Gulf (he himself had produced a much briefer book two years earlier). The author sees the Gulf states as test-tubes in which the conflict between traditional life-styles and imported Western fashions are to be studied. He does not, however, probe beneath the surface and is content in most of the book to restate the geopolitical role of the Gulf in European terms.

The final book from the 1950s is Sir Rupert Hay's *The Persian Gulf States*.[14] Designed to introduce the Gulf to the Western visitor, the book is at its most informative on the role of the British residency and the relationship between the Gulf rulers and their subjects. Sir Rupert, who was for eight years Political Resident in the Persian Gulf, is, in general, understanding of the social customs of the Arabs, refusing to condemn the institution of slavery, making no criticism of Islamic practices, and reserving his indignation solely for the custom of providing all members of a shaykh's family with pensions. Hay's views, nevertheless, are coloured by Britain's pre-eminence in the region and he regards with alarm the possibility of democracy or independence in the Gulf states. The work of an honest and a modest man, but not a disinterested one.

John Marlowe's *The Persian Gulf in the Twentieth Century*[15] is a move away from the handbook formula; like Wilson's study, it surveys the history of the Gulf from the viewpoint of world politics. Economic and diplomatic considerations dominate to such an extent that there are more entries in the index for Russia/USSR than for any single Gulf state. Much space is taken up by oil revenues and defence pacts (e.g. CENTO), and there is remarkably little on internal developments in the Gulf. What information there is, is accurate but bland; it has neither the charm of Tweedy, nor the perception of Owen, nor the informed opinion of Hay. This book, like several others by Marlowe, is really an investigation — not an unduly hostile one — into Britain's imperial role in a particular corner of the Middle East.

The first major work on the Gulf by a Western academic is J.B. Kelly's *Britain and the Persian Gulf*, published in 1968.[16] This had been preceded in 1964 by *Eastern Arabian Frontiers*,[17] a study of rival territorial claims to the oasis of Buraymī, which, while not dealing with the Gulf in general (it was restricted to Oman, Saudi Arabia and the Trucial States), shows Kelly's scholarship and his ability to clarify complex issues of international diplomacy. It also demonstrates his unequivocally pro-British stance. Kelly's second book is a meticulous and very detailed account of British involvement in the Gulf between 1795 and the signing of the first exclusive treaty (with Bahrain) in 1880. Kelly bases himself mainly on British archival documents and provides an enormous amount of factual detail. While rarely interposing his own comments on events, there is no doubt of his complete belief in the justice of Britain's role in the Gulf and in the need to maintain the security of British India and the safety of British maritime commerce.

Kelly's third book, however, does not disguise his feelings at all, in particular his disgust at the British Government's withdrawal of troops from the Gulf in 1971 and his distaste for the states which subsequently obtained independence. *Arabia, the Gulf and the West*[18] is a collection of nine essays, three of which deal exclusively with the Gulf. While Kelly makes a certain number of valid points regarding vacillating British politicians, excessive expenditure, and under-privileged immigrants, his language is intemperate and his claims often unsubstantiated by references to sources. His preface indicates his line of attack by defining the Gulf as 'turbulent, backward, intrinsically unstable'. Never at a loss to impute disreputable motives to Gulf rulers, his overstated language devalues his scholarship and his message.

At first sight, B.C. Busch's book, the first by an American scholar, might seem to be a continuation of Kelly's massive study of the period 1795–1880, for it is entitled *Britain and the Persian Gulf, 1894–1914*.[19] Despite a considerable use of British archives, however, Busch's emphasis on the area is different from Kelly's; instead of seeing it as merely an unruly area for Britain to pacify and administer, Busch focuses on the Gulf as an area of international rivalry. Quoting Bismarck's remark that the Gulf was one of three 'wasps' nests' in international affairs (outside the Balkans), he goes on to discuss French, Ottoman, German and Russian challenges to British supremacy. Apart from the opening chapter, the Gulf Arabs play the role of backdrop to the imperial players. A valuable piece of scholarship, but a one-sided one.

Quite the opposite from diplomatic history is the *Area Handbook for the Peripheral States of the Arabian Peninsula*.[20] Prepared by Stanford Research Institute for the Foreign Area Studies Program of the American University, its foreword claims that it is 'designed to be useful to military and other personnel who need a compilation of basic facts'. Dealing with the two Yemens, as well as the Gulf states, it is not uncritical in its views. It points out the problems of limited franchise, curtailed trade unions, and expatriate workers, but does not analyse them in depth. Slightly dull, as all compendia tend to be, it compresses a multitude of facts into a small compass. As these facts are under-analysed, the *Handbook* itself has dated rapidly.

R.M. Burrell's brief monograph *The Persian Gulf*[21] is significant in a number of ways; it appears to be the first book by a political scientist on the Gulf, it is the first book to discuss Gulf security, and it is the first book to make predictions as to the future course of events there. The work surveys the economic and political situation in the Gulf states themselves rather than just their relations with outside powers, concentrating on areas likely to bring instability to the region. Social change and expatriate labour are both omitted, however, in favour of freedom of navigation, oil production, military capacity and external threats.

John Duke Anthony's book on *The Arab States of the Lower Gulf*[22] (Bahrain, Qatar and the Emirates) is the first to examine the area on the basis of class and to study the shaykhdoms as independent states. Working in terms of elites, bourgeoisie, and political dynamics, the author examines the structure of government, the conflict between different ethnic elements, and foreign affairs. Although constantly stressing the transition from virtual protectorate to independent state, Anthony does not really analyse major changes in the social fabric, like the impact of urbanisation on a basically bedouin people, or the development of the economy. A work of some perception, but not one that always gives the impression of a close acquaintance with day-to-day life in the Gulf.

The second book in French on the Gulf is *Les Émirats Mirages* by Gabriel Dardaud and Simonne and Jean Lacouture.[23] It is divided into two parts, the first of which, *Hier*, is a historical survey of the Gulf, summarising existing interpretations. The second, *Aujourd'hui*, based on two journeys to the Gulf by the Lacoutures uses interviews and first-hand observation to examine a variety of issues: industrialisation in the United Arab Emirates, business sponsorship in Kuwait, women's education in Bahrain, the war in Dhofar. Hostile to Western influence in the Gulf, the Lacoutures nevertheless do not hesitate to judge Gulf Arabs by Western standards. The first work overtly critical of the path taken by the rulers of the Gulf in modernising their territories, *Les Émirats Mirages* is a significant piece of serious journalism. Contradictory, inflexible, perceptive, it raises a host of important questions.

David Long's *The Persian Gulf*[24] devotes much space to economic and political organisation, to foreign policy formulation, and to the role of language, religion and tribe on national unity (though these three factors are still under-represented). A useful handbook full of facts and figures, it sometimes gives the impression that the author may not have visited the region himself. There are none of the personal reflections, anecdotes or asides which distinguished the works of the 1950s. A political scientist's textbook rather than an attempt to understand the Gulf Arab and, through him, the Gulf.

At first sight nothing but a picture book, the text of Simon Jargy's *Émirats Arabes du Golfe*[25] is not as bland as it might appear. It discusses the problems of the urbanised bedouin, the high level of imported labour, and paternalistic rule. The level of analysis, however, never rises above the superficial and the work remains no more than a well-illustrated introductory handbook.

Molly Izzard's *The Gulf: Arabia's Western Approaches*[26] is an unsatisfactory amalgam of history, reminiscence, anecdote and social comment. It is difficult to see to what end the book was written, since it satisfies none of the categories outlined above. Some of the information, notably that on British firms trading in the area in the nineteenth century is interesting, but most is easily accessible in more detail and accuracy elsewhere. A confusing and confused book.

It is difficult to decide whether *Security in the Gulf*[27] is a monograph or not; originally prepared as four separate volumes, these were collected into a single book and reissued as volume seven of the Adelphi Library, retaining the pagination of the originals. The four volumes are entitled: *Domestic Political Factors*, a collection of four short papers; *Sources of Inter-State Conflict* (R. Litwak); *Modernization, Political Development and Stability* (A. Plascov); *The Role of Outside Powers* (S. Chubin). Although uneven in its treatment of the various stages (Oman receives scant mention throughout), this is a perceptive, critical, well-informed quartet of studies. More than any other book, it highlights the difficulties the Gulf states face in modernising their societies: the reaction of conservative Muslims, the decline of agriculture and ultra-rapid urbanisation, political opposition, and rampant consumerism. The other main theme of inter-state and supra-state conflict is dealt with very fully. A valuable contribution to Gulf studies.

The final work in this section is John Bulloch's *The Gulf: a Portrait of Kuwait, Qatar, Bahrain and the UAE.*[28] It has the advantages of most works of serious journalism — amusing anecdotes, personal observations and unsubstantiated assertions — allied with the disadvantages — few facts and figures, lack of organisation, concentration on the obvious. Fortunately, the advantages outweigh the disadvantages since Bulloch has a sound grasp of Arab society, Islamic religion and Middle Eastern history. As a light-hearted personal corollary to the meatier academic works, it has its place.

While the Western literature on the Gulf as a whole may be described as meagre, certainly in comparison with countries like Egypt or Iraq, that on individual Gulf states is even more exiguous. Only Oman and Kuwait have had enough written on them to allow valid comparisons between authors to be drawn.

Kuwait, as the first of the Gulf shaykhdoms to achieve independence, has attracted considerable attention from serious Western writers, at least relative to Bahrain, Qatar and the UAE. The doyen of Kuwaiti scholarship is H.R.P. Dickson, a political officer in Iraq and the Gulf for 20 years, thereafter chief local representative of the Kuwait Oil Company in Kuwait. Derek Hopwood discussed *The Arab of the Desert*,[29] an unparalleled description of tribal life in and around the shakydom, in his second article. Dickson followed this 20 years later (Dickson's first book was completed in typescript in 1936, although published after the war) with *Kuwait and her Neighbours*, a detailed history of the state mainly between 1915 and 1945.[30] History is perhaps rather a grand term for a series of personal reminiscences, some of which touch on diplomatic matters of import, others being mere anecdotes. The work is interspersed with zoological data contributed by Dickson's wife. *Kuwait and her Neighbours* does not stand comparison with Philby's work as a personal view of history, but it does give an authentic picture of all classes of Kuwaiti society between the wars.

Dickson was survived by his wife Violet and his married daughter Zahra Freeth, both of whom produced books on Kuwait. Perhaps the best known is *Kuwait: Prospect and Reality* written by Mrs Freeth in collaboration with H.V.F. Winstone.[31] Historical in tone for the most part, the information it contains is almost exclusively taken from travel narratives, earlier historical accounts, and Colonel Dickson's own writing. Only in the section on oil is there evidence of original research and the use of archival material. The work concludes with a survey of independent Kuwait which, while not sycophantic, is uncritical, particularly regarding political institutions. Not sufficiently analytical to be political science, nor sufficiently original to be historical research, the book has the air of a superior travel guide, giving facts about Kuwait but little idea of how Kuwaitis live or see themselves.

Kochwasser's *Kuwait*[32] gives much more detail than Winstone and Freeth on modern Kuwait but still manages to present a mass of economic data uncritically. There is almost no analysis of the real impact of development on a traditional people, merely the feeling that a great deal of money is being spent. Seemingly writing to explain Kuwait to travel-hungry Germans, Kochwasser does discuss important subjects like religion and the pearl-fishing industry, but lacks the scholarship to put them into historical context. Nevertheless Kuwait does come across as an Arab state with an Arab heritage, whereas Freeth and Winstone sometimes make it appear just a small pebble on the shores of Britain's imperial ocean.

Finally, Jacqueline Ismael, a Canadian social scientist, provides the first analysis of any Gulf state in terms of dependency theory.[33] Once the opening chapters, replete with Weberian terminology, have been passed, the book settles down to examining the pearling industry in the early twentieth century, political structures both pre- and post-independence, and the effect of oil wealth on Kuwaiti society. Despite the theoretical framework, Ismael does not offer any radical new insights; she does, however, manipulate her data critically and offers a considerable amount of valuable information on subjects such as immigrant labour and the rise of education.

Oman, due to its size as much as its tradition of local historiography, has attracted more attention than any other Gulf state. The first work of modern scholarship is Robert Landen's *Oman since 1856*.[34] Using newly developed historical techniques, Landen explores Omani history in the second half of the nineteenth century, giving due weight to social, economic and religious factors. In his study he reaches some interesting conclusions: firstly, he recognises the tension between coast and interior, between a moderate and a conservative view of the world; secondly, he shows that British suzerainty imposed different norms of conduct on the Gulf's traditional political *mores* and caused the Gulf's political geography to become fossilised; thirdly, he shows that Oman's maritime economy declined sharply from 1856 onwards due to external economic competition and internal political disruption; fourthly, he detects a change in British imperial philosophy between 1860 and 1890, by which latter date it had acquired a much more jingoistic and racialist tenor, with inevitable repercussions on the Gulf. Full of insights, Landen's acute analyses and his acquaintance with new developments in historical method give his book a depth met with all too infrequently in Gulf studies.

Certainly, Landen's scholarship is a refreshing contrast to Wendell Phillips's *Oman: a History*,[35] which is almost entirely an unanalytical political narrative based in the main on a few Arab chronicles. Describing recent Omani history, Phillips becomes an apologist for the Āl Bū Sa'īd dynasty, taking their part in both the Buraymī dispute and the Dhofar rebellion. Useful as a collection of facts, the book does little with them.

Phillips's other book, *Unknown Oman*,[36] is a record of his travels through Oman and some of the Emirates. A hotch-potch of medical, social, historical and legal observations, these are fortunately of enough interest to excuse their lack of organisation. Phillips was clearly impressed by and knowledgeable about bedouin society, and *Unknown Oman*, despite its confusions, does give an authentic picture of traditional life beset by change.

Ian Skeet's *Muscat and Oman*[37] is derivative as history but valuable as a survey of the country before the deposition of Sa'īd b. Taymūr. Skeet is well informed, interested in all aspects of Omani life, and endowed with a retentive memory and quick intelligence, even to understanding the complexities of multi-currency transactions in the Maṭraḥ bazaar. His evaluation of Sulṭān Sa'īd is as a man of great caution, unwilling to spend money and distrustful of education and outside influences. Skeet has some sympathy with the Sulṭān's position, but clearly foresaw his eventual deposition; although the book was published in 1974, it was written in 1968. The author clearly found a certain attraction in the infinite variety and inconsistency of Omani life and communicates it to his readers in what is an affectionate and colourful portrait of a changing society.

While Skeet was in Oman only during Sulṭān Sa'īd's reign, John Townsend was Development Adviser to both Sulṭān Sa'īd and his successor Sulṭān Qābūs from 1971 to 1975. *Oman, the Making of a Modern State*[38] is the record of his achievements and his failures as he sought to bring progress and modernity to one of the world's most underdeveloped states. Townsend details the economic and social progress of Oman but never fails to set it in its political context. He sees Sulṭān Qābūs as an effective head of state, expert in military matters, but untrained in financial ones, which led to the failure of several development projects. The role of expatriates, outside powers, and Zanzibari Arabs is given considerable weight, but there is little consideration of the effects of religious or tribal conflicts within Oman.

John Peterson in *Oman in the Twentieth Century*[39] emphasises four themes: the nature of the ruling family; administration, both political and financial; the government's relations with the tribes of the interior; and the role of external powers. This is the only book to examine systematically and in detail the complex question of tribal policies in the hinterland, and Peterson's views of the various internal challenges to the Āl Bū Sa'īd dynasty are judicious and well informed. Deliberately it would seem, he does not dwell on personalities and the reader learns of Sulṭān Sa'īd's deposition almost with surprise; nor is the development question tackled in any depth. Nevertheless, this remains the most knowledgeable survey of Omani politics up to the *coup d'état*, and with Skeet and Townsend forms an essential trilogy for understanding Oman.

Oman: the Reborn Land[40] by F.A. Clements is a straightforward account of life in Oman after 1970. Clements, a professional librarian and not an Arabist, does not entirely disapprove of Sulṭān Sa'īd's policy of cautious development, but cites the Sulṭān's complete disregard of public relations as one of the chief reasons for his downfall. On the other hand, Clements gives unqualified (and uncritical) approval to the social, economic and, above all, educational developments sponsored by Sulṭān Qābūs, and is convinced of their popular appeal. Unfortunately, he provides little evidence for his conviction, which is not one shared by all writers on Oman.

Liesl Graz in *The Omanis*[41] sees them as a proud, confident people, whose fortune is that there is enough wealth to introduce some facets of development, yet not enough to permit the state to indulge in extravagant luxuries. Consequently, projects have been selective and modernisation has been tempered with caution. Graz investigates some of the problems occasioned by increased national wealth, such as the insufficiency of native-born Omani teachers, the much increased demand for medical care, and the influx of South Asian labour. She emphasises the crucial role of the Sulṭān and his system of absolute monarchy, albeit seasoned by the counsels of ministers and relatives. In her final chapter, she discusses Oman's role in the world, not as the West but as the Omanis see it.

In Graz's final chapter the wheel has come full circle. While no book written before 1950 could even contemplate the Gulf other than as a cog within Britain's imperial machine, recent literature has concentrated on the Gulf states as entities in their own right. Discussions of naval supremacy and commercial rivalry have now given way to debates on immigrant labour, urbanisation and the diffusion of state power. Government-sponsored reports have yielded to Weberian tracts like Ismael's and unsophisticated travelogues like Skeet's. Yet two themes predominate: what is the Gulf's position in the world, and how are the Gulf states coping with the pressures of modernisation? While the oil continues to flow, there is little likelihood that tomorrow's books will treat different themes from those of today — or even yesterday.

Notes

1. D. Hopwood, 'Some Western Views of the Egyptian Revolution' in P.J. Vatikiotis (ed.), *Egypt since the Revolution* (Allen & Unwin, London, 1968), pp. 181–95.

2. D. Hopwood, 'Some Western Studies of Saudi Arabia, Yemen and Aden' in

D. Hopwood (ed.), *The Arabian Peninsula: Society and Politics*, (Allen & Unwin, London, 1972), pp. 13–27.

3. *Arabian Gulf Intelligence*, (Oleander, Cambridge, 1983). Reprint of *Selections from the Records of the Bombay Government*, new series, no. XXIV: *Historical and Other Information Connected with the Province of Oman, Muskat, Bahrein and Other Places in the Persian Gulf*, compiled and edited by R.H. Thomas, (Bombay Education Society Press, Bombay, 1856).

4. Seventeen *Précis* were compiled by J.B. Saldanha between 1904 and 1906, and a further *Selections from State Papers, Bombay, regarding the East India Company's Connection with the Persian Gulf, with a Summary of Events, 1600–1800*, was compiled in 1908. All eighteen items have been reprinted as *The Persian Gulf Précis 1903–1908*, (Archive Editions, Gerrards Cross, 1986).

5. J.B. Kelly, *Britain and the Persian Gulf, 1795–1880*, (Clarendon Press, Oxford, 1968), p. 860.

6. J.G. Lorimer, *Gazetteer of the Persian Gulf, 'Omān and Central Arabia* (6 vols, Superintendent Government Printing, India, Calcutta, 1908–1915). (Twice reprinted.)

7. D. Roberts, 'The Consequences of the Exclusive Treaties: a British View' in B.R. Pridham (ed.), *The Arab Gulf and the West*, (Croom Helm, London, 1985), p. 13.

8. S.B. Miles, *The Countries and Tribes of the Persian Gulf*, (2 vols, Harrison, London, 1919; reprinted in one vol., Cass, London, 1966).

9. A.T. Wilson, *The Persian Gulf: an Historical Sketch from the Earliest Times to the Beginning of the Twentieth Century*, (Clarendon Press, Oxford, 1928).

10. Wilson, *Persian Gulf*, p. 272.

11. M. Tweedy, *Bahrain and the Persian Gulf*, (East Anglian Magazine, Ipswich, 1952).

12. R. Owen, *The Golden Bubble: Arabian Gulf Documentary*, (Collins, London, 1957).

13. J.J. Berreby, *Le Golfe Persique*, (Payot, Paris, 1959).

14. R. Hay, *The Persian Gulf States*, (The Middle East Institute, Washington, DC, 1959).

15. J. Marlowe, *The Persian Gulf in the Twentieth Century*, (Cresset Press, London, 1962).

16. J.B. Kelly, *Britain and the Persian Gulf, 1795–1880*, (Clarendon Press, Oxford, 1968).

17. J.B. Kelly, *Eastern Arabian Frontiers*, (Faber, London, 1964).

18. Idem., *Arabia, the Gulf and the West*, (Weidenfeld & Nicolson, London, 1980).

19. B.C. Busch, *Britain and the Persian Gulf, 1894–1914*, (University of California Press, Berkeley, 1967).

20. *Area Handbook for the Peripheral States of the Arabian Peninsula*, (United States Government Printing Office, Washington, DC, 1971).

21. R.M. Burrell, *The Persian Gulf*, (Library Press, New York, 1972).

22. J.D. Anthony, *Arab States of the Lower Gulf: People, Politics, Petroleum*, (The Middle East Institute, Washington, DC, 1975).

23. G. Dardaud, S. Lacouture, J. Lacouture, *Les Émirats Mirages: Voyage chez les Petrocrates*, (Éditions du Seuil, Paris, 1975).

24. D.E. Long, *The Persian Gulf: an Introduction to its Peoples, Politics and Economics*, (Westview Press, Boulder, 1976; rev. ed. 1978).

25. S. Jargy, *Émirats Arabes du Golfe*, (Hachette Réalités, Lausanne, 1976).

26. M. Izzard, *The Gulf: Arabia's Western Approaches*, (John Murray, London, 1979).

27. S. Chubin, R. Litwak, A. Plascov, *Security in the Gulf*, (Gower, Aldershot, 1982).

28. J. Bulloch, *The Gulf: a Portrait of Kuwait, Qatar, Bahrain and the UAE*, (Century Publishing, London, 1984).

29. H.R.P. Dickson, *The Arab of the Desert: a Glimpse into Badawin Life in Kuwait and Saudi Arabia*, (Allen & Unwin, London, 1949).

30. Idem., *Kuwait and her Neighbours*, (Allen & Unwin, London, 1956).

31. Z. Freeth and H.V.F. Winstone, *Kuwait: Prospect and Reality*, (Allen & Unwin,

London, 1972).

32. F.H. Kochwasser, *Kuwait: Geschichte, Wesen und Funktion eines modernen arabischen Staaten*, (Erdmann, Tübingen, 1969; rev. ed., 1975).

33. J.S. Ismael, *Kuwait: Social Change in Historical Perspective*, (Syracuse University Press, New York, 1982).

34. R.G. Landen, *Oman Since 1856: Disruptive Modernization in a Traditional Arab Society*, (Princeton University Press, Princeton, 1967).

35. W. Phillips, *Oman: a History*, (Longman, London, 1967).

36. Idem., *Unknown Oman*, (Longman, London, 1966).

37. I. Skeet, *Muscat and Oman: the End of an Era*, (Faber, London, 1974).

38. J. Townsend, *Oman: the Making of a Modern State*, (Croom Helm, London, 1977).

39. J.E. Peterson, *Oman in the Twentieth Century: Political Foundations of an Emerging State*, (Croom Helm, London, 1978).

40. F.A. Clements, *Oman: the Reborn Land*, (Longman, London, 1980).

41. L. Graz, *The Omanis: Sentinels of the Gulf*, (Longman, London, 1982).

5 Hispano-Arabic Historiography: The Legacy of J.A. Conde

Richard Hitchcock

This present venture into Hispano-Arabic historiography is the product of two decades of frustration and a growing feeling of exasperation. The frustration arises out of a conviction that English-language students of the Muslim period of the history of the Iberian Peninsula may be being nurtured, if not wholly then substantially, on unreliable, inaccurate and misleading accounts. The prototypical textbooks in English, in so far as I am aware of them, are those of Watt, Chejne, Livermore, Lomax, Glick, Hillgarth, O'Callaghan, MacKay and Collins, not to mention Michael Brett and Jan Read.[1] Montgomery Watt's book, the one most frequently quoted and recommended, is avowedly a synthesis based on secondary sources; that is to say that Watt, although an Arabist, did not, in this instance, choose to re-evaluate the primary sources for the history of the period. He expresses an admiration for the *Histoire de l'Espagne Musulmane* of Évariste Lévi-Provençal, whose three volumes, in his words, 'take the story to 1031 and completely supersede the earlier works'. Watt recognises that 'for the period after 1031 there is no such historiographical tradition and no single work covering the period in any detail'. He goes on: 'This is a serious gap in modern historical studies and is reflected in the sections on this period [from 1031 to 1492] in large composite works and in the smaller popular books on Islamic Spain.'[2] Watt himself makes no claim for filling this gap. He follows one of the alternatives open to historians, and that is, he asks questions. Indeed, the final page of his Introduction consists almost solely of a string of pertinent questions relating to Islamic Spain. These questions are taken up again in the final section of the book entitled: 'The Intrinsic Greatness of Islamic Spain.' Not surprisingly, no definitive solution is offered to such questions as 'Was it [Islamic Spain] mainly a passive recipient or did it make any distinctive contribution to Islamic culture as well?'[3] In a characteristically judicious manner, Montgomery Watt poses such questions for others to ponder over.

It is not that Watt's book is inadequate. It does have the merit of being eminently readable and thought-provoking in its presentation, but there is a nagging feeling that it is all *déjà vu*, and that it is one side of a familiar coin minted long ago, certainly in the nineteenth century, maybe even earlier. Watt, it appears, expected such criticism and perceptively pre-empted it in the following comment:[4]

> since the standard view of the earlier history of Islamic Spain is thus mainly the work of two closely associated men [he is referring to Reinhard Dozy and Évariste Lévi-Provençal], it may be that when some scholar with a different perspective familiarises himself with all the material the general line of interpretation will be modified.

Such an attempt has not to my knowledge been made in the English language, if one excepts Anwar Chejne's *Muslim Spain. Its History and Culture*, barely a quarter of which is concerned with history proper. To quote Chejne himself:[5]

> This book is not intended to be a definitive work on the subject, but rather a general study of the history, culture, and intellectual life of Muslim Spain. It is an attempt to give a panoramic view of the wide field of Hispano-Arabic culture; to indicate its nature, scope, and importance; and to show its dependence on and relation to the mainstream of Islamic culture.

It is not difficult to pick holes in such an approach, nor indeed in the work itself, but its encyclopedic nature and its extensive notes and bibliography, despite inexactitudes, confer on it a distinctive value as a source of reference.

Thomas Glick may be categorised as 'a scholar with a different perspective' with his *Islamic and Christian Spain in the Early Middle Ages. Comparative Perspectives on Social and Cultural Formation*.[6] This book is extensively innovative in its comparative approach, with numerous insights into the social, economic and cultural structure of the Peninsula, but it is difficult to get a sense of the passing of historical time. Although there is some adhesion to chronological limits, the centuries are seemingly merged and crucial issues such as the nature of Islam and the nature of Christianity in the Peninsula seem at times to be blurred. This may be a mistaken reaction, because Glick, in his Introduction, quite clearly acknowledges the significance of the two cultures, Islamic and Christian. 'Only by identifying with both cultures', he argues, 'and with one no more than the other, can the historian entertain any reasonable hopes of filtering out some of the more flagrant biases that have so persistently plagued this area of investigation.'[7] This statement has the ring of sincerity and sounds plausible, but it is in itself, one may point out, a biased statement with its use of emotive phrases such as 'flagrant biases' and 'persistently plagued'. This criticism does not invalidate the approach, but rather serves to demonstrate one of the fundamental problems facing the historian. According to Glick: 'Certain national schools of historiography — the Spanish is the case in point — seem less able than others to disentangle present myths from past ones', but this need not necessarily be either a national or, more specifically, a Spanish failing.[8] The point is that it is all very well 'striving to be objective', but such an approach is only, I believe, of relative value. If the historian is to be an interpreter, then does he not leave behind some of his objectiveness in the process? W.M. Watt carefully avoided such pitfalls by posing questions without addressing himself to their resolution. Glick's concerns are of a much more complex nature, and the resulting book is correspondingly weightier in its analyses and more far-reaching in its implications. One wonders, nevertheless, about the fundamental approach. The questions that inform it emerge, it seems to me, as a consequence of a view of history, and not as a direct result of reading and pondering the primary sources. This is not to say that such sources have not been consulted, but it is to imply that the resultant history is hindered by the self-confessed desire for maintaining an objective approach.

The primary sources, be they Arabic, Latin, or Romance texts, hold the key to the history of the 700 years of independent Muslim domination of the Iberian Peninsula or part of it. Cannot these texts be allowed to speak for themselves? This, of course, is not an original question and, indeed, three different answers can be readily identified. One has only to consider the manifold interpretations of the history of the Muslim presence in the Peninsula to reach the non-controversial conclusion that the most popular answer to this question is no. It is blatantly apparent, however, that in discussions of such interpretations, the texts themselves have faded into the shadows. What forms the subject of debates is, more often than not, albeit less obtrusively in some instances than in others, a philosophy of history, whether knowingly or unwittingly elaborated. As a recent example, I refer to Robert Burns's reactions to criticisms of his interpretation of 'Muslim-Christian interaction or Mudejar evolution' — his words. Dolefully remarking that 'Rejecting both sides means being perceived by each camp as adhering to the other', and 'Conceding merit to an aspect of either becomes proof of complicity', Burns observes that, in his case, this procedure becomes 'disconcertingly grotesque'.[9] In the Preface to *Muslims, Christians, and Jews in the Crusader Kingdom of Valencia. Societies in Symbiosis*, Burns comments on Pierre Guichard's belief that he, Burns, follows 'the Nationalist school of "continuity" between the Islamic and Christian Spains, and of "optimism" consequently, in refusing to see the damage done by the colonialist crusaders to the essential structure of Islamic society'.[10] 'Such positions are anathema to me', he writes, and he is concerned to demonstrate his refutation. Underlying the strength of this reaction to Guichard is Burns's belief in the aptness of the terms 'crusade' and 'colonialism' which he uses to describe thirteenth-century Valencia. No one would deny him this right, but phrases such as 'Too narrowly political or ideological a study . . . can obscure the social reality' are revealing and, one might say, self-incriminating.[11] For 'study' here read 'interpretation', and the phenomenon is precisely as I have been describing it.

The second answer to the question whether the texts can be allowed to speak for themselves is yes, but with modifications. That is to say, the texts need not necessarily be interpreted, but they need to be ordered and categorised because they are so divergent. The material needs to be carefully classified and placed in order. This is, I believe, by and large the approach of Lévi-Provençal. The later part of Glick's work, the section on technology for example, and the studies of Juan Vernet may also come into this category. The third answer to the question, and the most obvious one, is yes. The texts can be allowed to speak for themselves, and this I believe by and large was the reasoned decision of the first historian of Muslim Spain, José Antonio Conde. In the Prologue to a work conceived at the very beginning of the nineteenth century, Conde made the following significant claim for his work: 'The student of History, then, may read this book as one written by an Arabic author, since it is in effect a faithful translation of, and extracts from, large numbers of those authors.'[12]

It is no coincidence that these preliminary observations have led so soon to Conde. I have been convinced for many years that the fount of Hispano-Arabic historiography is not to be encountered in the meritorious efforts of Lévi-Provençal nor in those of his francophile Dutch predecessor Dozy. It had its origins in the careful scholarship of an Arabist who, contrary to the dismissive taunts to which both he and his works had been subjected for over a century, knew precisely what he was about. He was aware, not only of the problems to be encountered in such a bold enterprise, but also of the need for a serious philosophy of history. Conde writes:[13]

> The knowledge of the Arabic language only, if unaccompanied by critical judgment and acquaintance with historical literature, does not suffice to enable an author to make choice of useful and judicious extracts from those works amidst which the notices required are scattered and discriminated without order or arrangement.

is acknowledged intention was to give a faithful version of Arabic ritings: 'to repeat what they relate has been my constant care, and I ropose to do so, in almost every case, in their own words faithfully anslated, and no others'.[14] He was anxious that, in his endeavours, he ould be seen to be '*fiel y exacto*'. This concern was recognised as raiseworthy by the English translator Mrs Jonathan Foster, who ommented[15]

> on the admirable manner in which the learned and conscientious author completed his work . . . He frequently allows the Arabian writers to speak for themselves, and with so felicitous an effect, that the reader may almost hear the voices of the speakers, conducting him to the land of the patriarchs.

In the second half of the eighteenth century, Arabic studies were rought within the reach of European scholarly enquiry. Cañes, a Franscan who had lived in Damascus, published a grammar and an extenve Spanish/Latin/Arabic dictionary, although mainly for the purpose f proselytising.[16] Michael Casiri [al-Ghazīrī], a Syrian Maronite, was nployed at the Royal Library in Madrid. He concluded his life's work f cataloguing the Arabic manuscripts of the Escorial in 1770, a project hich took him approximately 20 years.[17] The entries contain ımmaries and comments on the contents, and indicate Casiri's familiarity ith many of the manuscripts which he catalogued. Casiri's work rovided a basis for future studies on Spanish Islam and, indeed, James Ionroe has pointed out that Gibbon, in the section devoted to Spanish ılam, drew extensively on information made available by Casiri in his *ecline and Fall of the Roman Empire*.[18]

Conde was born in 1765 and studied Arabic and history from an early ge. He may be said to have continued the scholarship of the Spanish rabists of a generation earlier, but the impetus for his work was clearly rovided by the Arabic manuscripts in the Library of the Escorial, over hich he had charge. His first work on an Arabic topic seems to have een a partial translation of Al-Idrīsī's *Geography*, published in 1799, y which time he was the archivist-librarian of the Royal Library.[19] The part relating to al-Andalus is translated and is accompanied by th customary critical apparatus. The Arab text and Spanish translatio occupy 130 facing pages. There are over 100 further pages of note elucidating particularly the Arabic forms of Spanish place-names. Thes notes enable the reader to judge Conde's familiarity with the Arabi language and, also, incidentally, with the Greek and Hebrew language as well as with Arabic and Spanish history and geography. Nobody seem to have taken this book into account, although it may perhaps hav acquired a certain readership, since its republication, in an excelle facsimile, by Atlas in 1980. This is a useful, eminently manageabl edition of a primary text, which is evidence of Conde's philological expe tise, and also serves as an expression of his high esteem of the Arabi language, which he praises in fulsome terms as an excellent languag being spoken 'with the same elegance on the banks of the Guadalquiv and Tagus, as in the Yemen and on the shores of the Dijla'.[20]

Conde's prowess as a numismatist was recognised when, in 198 his address to the Royal Academy of History in 1804 was republishe with a flattering Prologue, in the course of which his paper is describe as 'probably the first modern work in Spanish on this subject'.[21] Cond aware that he was a pioneer in this field, provides a scholarly accou of Arabic coinage minted in the East, before discussing at length, an chronologically, the successive mintings by Muslim rulers in al-Andalu The coins are illustrated, described, identified and placed in the historical context. The Arabic texts of the inscriptions together with translation in Castilian are also supplied.[22]

Everything then seems to have been set fair for the preparation an publication of a *magnum opus* on the Muslims in Spain. Contemporar events, however, intervened. Conde was a close friend of the famou Spanish playwright Leandro Fernández de Moratín, whose first cousi he was to marry much later. From 1797 to 1808 Conde was an integr part of Moratín's life, as is testified by the latter's journal.[23] Morati visited Conde almost every night for eight years. The two we *afrancesados* and when Godoy fell in 1808 they were obliged to leav Madrid, to return a year later with the French. By 1811 it appears fro private correspondence that Conde had his manuscript largely complet but was looking for further material on the kingdom of Granada. When King Joseph Bonaparte left Madrid in 1813 Conde went with hi and stayed in Paris for a year, taking advantage of the occasion to g to know the French orientalist Silvestre de Sacy. Conde returned to Spai in 1814, principally to check details of that part of the history alread written, and also to consult a copy of a manuscript of al-Maqqarī's *Na al-Ṭīb*. Conde recounts how in 1807 he petitioned Charles IV to order a copy of the manuscript of this work to be made. This manuscript was in the Biblioteca Real, in Paris, and Charles agreed to finance the project. De Sacy and Langlès supervised the copy which was completed by 1818. It was sent to Madrid, but to Conde's chagrin he was not able to consult it, nor did he know of its whereabouts when writing the Prologue to his *Historia*.[25] When Maqqarī's work was eventually published, in partial translation, by Pascual de Gayangos in 1843, it was soon apparent how sensational a discovery it was, and how vital and fundamental a source, and how beneficial it would have been to Conde's work. Conde was virtually under house arrest, unable to leave his house in Madrid, and only permitted to move freely in that city from 1816 onwards. He was reincorporated into the Academies of Language and History, where his seat had been declared vacant in 1814, but his prime concern was to see his work through the press.

Conde had apparently seen the first volume in proof just before he died on 12 June 1820. The three volumes of the work were published in 1820 and 1821, although it is generally acknowledged that Conde himself was only wholly responsible for the first volume. The comparative lack of notes, even in this first volume, was seemingly Conde's decision, and has attracted much criticism, but this is not an indictment of Conde's scholarship. He was quite capable of supplying appropriate apparatus as is indicated by his edition of Idrīsī. In a notice appended to the second volume, the editor points out in tones of scarcely veiled despair that this second volume was published despite the fact that Conde had hardly left it in a publishable state.[26] In the preliminary notice attached to the third volume which comprises mainly the Granadan period, the editor reverts to the same theme. Conde, it is claimed here, left a draft of a small glossary of Arabic words found throughout the work. Although the glossary was incomplete the editors decided to attach it to the work. There were no indices.

I have dwelt at length on the preparation and publication of this work because of the impact it was expected to make, and which it did in effect make at the time. There had been enormous advance interest in Conde's history with notices in the *Memorias de la Real Academia de la Historia*, published the previous year. The list of subscribers, drawn from all walks of society and numbering at least 250, is provided in the third volume. A German translation appeared almost immediately, and a French one in 1825, although Mrs Foster's English translation did not appear for a further 30 years. For a quarter of a century the work held sway as a general source book for the history of the Muslims in Europe, and as such it was extensively imitated and plagiarised. Its lack of index and of notes, a deficiency made good, however, in the English version, is certainly a drawback when it comes to consultation, but it is nevertheless precisely what it says, a *History of the Dominion of the Arabs in Spain* to give it the title into which it was translated in English.

Subsequent analyses of Conde's work, and a comparison of the contents with the Arabic sources he provides in the Prologue to volume one, have made it possible to identify these sources in large measure.[27] As he had claimed, he did translate substantial sections of these sources, including the poems which are such a characteristic feature, and which do confer, on the first volume at least, a notably Arabic flavour. Conde, albeit posthumously, had succeeded in filling a void. From henceforward, there would be an eminently readable history of the Muslim state of al-Andalus.

There were a few dissenting voices for 30 years, but these were as nothing when compared to the dose of vitriol which the Dutchman Dozy administered to Conde's *opus* in 1849.[28] One can say quite confidently that Dozy's vicious attack on Conde led ultimately to the latter's fall from grace as an accredited historian of Muslim Spain. In the second part of the century Conde's work was to be supplanted by one written by Dozy himself. The introduction to Dozy's *Recherches* takes the form of a letter to the two French scholars, Reinaud and Defrémery. In extraordinarily strong language Dozy impugns Conde's proficiency as an Arabist, even going so far as to say that Conde only knew the Arabic characters and little of the Arabic language: 'Conde a travaillé sur des documents arabes sans connaître beaucoup plus de cette langue que les caractères avec lesquels elle s'écrit.' Furthermore, 'Suppléant par une imagination extrêmement fertile au manque des connaissances les plus élémentaires, il a, avec une impudence sans pareille, forgé des dates par centaines, inventé des faits par milliers, en affichant toujours la prétention de traduire fidèlement des textes arabes.'[29] For Dozy, it was not only that Conde was inadequately prepared professionally for his task. He charged Conde with forging documents, concealing information and making false claims, skilfully covering up the traces of his deceit. Moreover, those who have used Conde as a source should forget all they have learnt: 'car on devra bien considérer désormais le livre de Conde comme non avenu'. He concludes devastatingly, and I translate: 'it would be easier to clean the stables of Augeas than to correct all the faults and refute all the lies which are rife in Conde's book'.[30] These libellous statements were in fact dropped from later editions of Dozy's *Recherches*, not, as one critic has suggested, because he repented of them, but rather ecause the damage had been done. The readership of the day were onvinced by Dozy, whose view that Conde was an ignorant falsifier f data persisted throughout the second half of the nineteenth century.

The most scholarly attempt to reassess Conde's contribution to the istory of Muslim Spain was made by Barrau-Dihigo in 1906. Barrau-ihigo undertook the daunting task of trying to determine whether Conde 'as true to his word, that his history was compiled on the basis of selected rabic accounts. He compared texts with sources and found nothing einous. Conde did use Latin sources, of which the most conspicuous 'as the *Historia Arabum*, but the obvious point can be made that Rodrigo sed Arabic material himself, so in effect Conde was merely borrowing rabic material at second hand. In Barrau-Dihigo's words: 'L'imposture e Conde est ici plus apparente que réelle.'[31] Conde used Arabic ources directly, as he claimed he did, but not all the ones that are now onsidered to be the *sine qua non* for any history of Muslim Spain, for xample Ibn Idhārī, Ibn al-Athīr, Ibn Khaldūn and Al-Maqqarī, although e may have come across 'la substance de leurs oeuvres' in manuscripts the Escorial library. He did have recourse to the sources listed in the ntroduction to his *Historia*. There is no question of Conde being oroughly vindicated, but Barrau-Dihigo does validate his good faith. 'onde was a precursor, a pioneer, who succeeded in his declared aim f giving the impression that one is reading an Arabic author when eading his book. There is nothing deliberately spurious in his work. Ioreover, as Barrau-Dihigo points out, 'Conde est dans une certaine esure responsable des beaux travaux de Dozy, lequel ne lui a point ayé la dette de la reconnaissance qu'il avait involontairement contractée nvers lui.'[32]

More recently, in a fascinating and detailed account, Manuela Ianzanares de Cirre resurrects the whole controversy, making use of e partial biography of Conde published by Roca in 1904. Manzanares e Cirre identifies and isolates Dozy's criticisms, with the interesting esult that most of them appear to be rather trivial. She also addresses tention to four places in Dozy's book where he has a grudging kind ord for Conde. She seems to have been the first Arabist to have checked ozy's accusations, and she reaches the following conclusion: 'Cuando asunto es realmente notable, salvo pequeñas y humanas excepciones, ozy tiene que confesar que Conde no se equivoca de una manera tan bsoluta como él quiere hacer ver.'[33] Dozy was, it is now generally ecognised, too severe in his judgement of Conde, but the intensely ersonal tone of his slanderous accusations leads one to suppose that ctors other than academic ones motivated them, although these have never been established. One has tended to accept the explanation of Francis Griffin Stokes in his Introduction to his own translation of Dozy's *Spanish Islam*, namely:[34]

> it did not enter into the head of the prosperous scholar of Leyden to make allowances for the difficulties under which the Spanish historian laboured. Historical inaccuracy was in Dozy's eyes a crime — and the slipshod historian, a criminal.

I believe Dozy's demolition of Conde inflicted incalculable damage on the image that Muslim Spain presented to the world at large. What purported to be an accurate and scholarly history was irremediably discredited. However, the legacy of Dozy's criticisms is interesting. The mantle of authority in matters Hispano-Arabic passed from Conde to Dozy. Dozy's work was the one which held sway until the 1930s, when Lévi-Provençal brought it up to date. Of course, in the next decade the mantle was to pass from Dozy to Lévi-Provençal himself, where, to a greater or lesser extent, it still remains. The curious and revealing fact, however, is that there is, I believe, a genetic affinity between the works of Conde, Dozy and Lévi-Provençal. This is the decisive point at issue Dozy replaced Conde with a liberal helping of the same brew, and much later on, Lévi-Provençal expanded and rewrote Dozy.

It will be recalled that Conde chose to allow the texts to speak for themselves. Dozy's procedure should therefore be scrutinised. He start from the premise, demonstrably false, that he is traversing ground 'hitherto untrodden', 'existing treatises on the subject' being 'wholly valueless', because 'they are all based on the labours of Conde — or the labours that is to say, of a writer who had but scant materials at hi disposal, who was unable, from the inadequacy of his linguisti attainments, to understand the documents to which he had access, and who lacked the historic sense'.[35] Dozy expresses his own *modu operandi* as follows:[36]

> Since it has not been my intention to compile an arid and severel scientific treatise, . . . I have refrained from overloading my page with excess of detail, . . . I have not hesitated, upon occasion, to en liven the drama of political history with interludes of personal adven ture; for, in my opinion, it is too often forgotten that without the relie afforded by picturesque details and the side-lights thrown by them upon contemporary manners, all history is apt to be colourless and

> insipid, . . . [and finally] . . . I am convinced that an undue display of erudition would not tend to add vivacity or lucidity to its pages; I have therefore refrained from the lavish use of notes, references, and quotations.

Dozy's *Spanish Islam*, although professing to pioneer the subject, is cast in the same mould as Conde's work. Both are elegantly written, eminently readable, unashamedly anecdotal, replete with familiar details and data, and encased within the same chronological framework. One such detail concerns the library of al-Ḥakam II, the son of 'Abd al-Raḥmān III. Al-Ḥakam was renowned as a scholar, and is reputed to have had an extensive library. In Dozy's words:[37]

> The catalogue of the Khalif's library occupied forty-four volumes, of which each comprised twenty sheets — or fifty according to some chroniclers — though they contained only the titles of the works. Some writers assert that the number of volumes amounted to four hundred thousand.

These absurdities, given the ring of veracity by reference to 'chroniclers', were thought worthy of inclusion by Dozy, without critical appraisal or explanation. Conde provides fuller background material:

> In Bagdad Alhaken had also an agent for . . . the purchase of valuable books, Muhammad Ben Tarhan namely. He also kept accomplished copyists in various cities, to the end that he might obtain manuscripts of their best writings.

Then, after referring to the arrangement of the books into various subjects, Conde comments:[38]

> Aben Hayan, speaking of the books he [Alhakem] collected, tells us that the catalogues . . . extended to forty-four volumes, each containing fifty sheets: these being filled with the names of the books and the authors alone. According to Telid El Feti, the general index . . ., was not completed until some time after his death, and in the reign of Hixem his son.

The somewhat more adventurous claims which Dozy thought worthy of inclusion are omitted by Conde, whose account has, by the by, the greater ring of conviction. In this century, Lévi-Provençal talks of 'un catalogue méthodique' which according to Ibn Ḥazm had no less than 44 'registres' each of 50 leaves.[39] He mentions the figure of 400,00 volumes and gives as his sources, Ibn al-Abbār, Maqqarī, and Ib Khaldūn.

Had Lévi-Provençal borne Conde in mind, this ludicrous figure migh not have been perpetuated. As it is, historians have been fascinated b it, and it is sad but significant that Collins, giving his source as Maqqarī should have repeated the same detail, without comment, in his recen book: 'His library is recorded as containing four hundred thousan volumes, with a catalogue of forty-four volumes.'[40] Now Maqqarī, i the appropriate section, translated by Gayangos, is more specific an consequently more revealing. The details of the literary treasures in al Ḥakam's immense collection of books proceed from Ibn Khaldūn, an Ibn al-Abbār, who transcribes Ibn Ḥazm as follows:[41]

> I was told by Talīd the eunuch who was keeper of the library an repository of sciences in the palace of the Beni Merwān, that th catalogue only of the books consisted of forty-four volumes, eac volume having twenty sheets of paper, which contained nothing els but the titles and descriptions of the books.

But it is an unnamed historian who is responsible for mentioning th much-repeated total of books assembled:

> Al-hakem . . . amassed such a collection of books that it is imposs ible to estimate even approximately either their value or their number some writers stating that they amounted to four hundred thousan volumes, and that when they were removed [from the palace] si months were expended in the operation.

Gayangos in his annotation of these passages, remarks that 'this state ment is likewise found in Casiri (II, p. 37) and Conde (I. 459) wh borrowed it from the same sources. It is no doubt exaggerated, unles the forty-four volumes, of which the unfinished catalogue is said to hav consisted, contained also a biography of the authors'.[42] In so far as reconstruction is possible of the process of transmission, the Arabi source is first Maqqarī, then Ibn al-Abbār, then Ibn Ḥazm who got th information at second hand, then an unnamed historian who puts a figur on the number of books. None of the European partisans of this legen have seen fit to record Gayangos's prudent note of caution.

This example of what might be most charitably described as a uncritical procedure on the part of historians since 1843, draws the kin

·f problems that I have been describing into sharp focus. Those who .ave read accounts of the Umayyad period in al-Andalus have come to ssociate Al-Ḥakam II's reign with one of vigorous cultural activity, and .ave been led to recognise his patronage of learning as indicative of ·rodigious erudition. Such impressions may or may not correspond to he reality of the situation, but an approach, more alert to the complex-ies of Arabic historiography, would, I am certain, lead to the dismantling f countless myths.

These reflections on Hispano-Arabic historiography prompt me to azard several conclusions which may be considered presumptuous. The :nglish-language reader is confronted with a view of al-Andalus that vas constituted in the first half of the nineteenth century, primarily by :onde, then continued by Dozy, and later expanded and revitalised by .évi-Provençal. There has been some superficial tinkering, rectification ·f errors, and partial reassessments in the light of newly discovered infor-nation. Where new theories have been formulated, these have often been s a consequence of various ideologies being superimposed upon secon-ary sources. My concluding remark bears on the frustration that is felt .ow when reading present-day accounts which quite evidently form part f Conde's legacy. It seems to me to be essential for there to be some wareness or acknowledgement of the historiographical tradition of the ·ast 200 years, and far more important to do this, in fact, than to pay ip-service to transient ideological trends.

lotes

1. W. Montgomery Watt, *A History of Islamic Spain*, (Edinburgh University Press, .dinburgh, 1965); Anwar G. Chejne, *Muslim Spain. Its History and Culture*, (University f Minnesota Press, Minneapolis, 1974); H.V. Livermore, *The Origins of Spain and 'ortugal*, (Allen & Unwin, London, 1971); Derek W. Lomax, *The Reconquest of Spain*, Longman, London, 1978); Thomas F. Glick, *Islamic and Christian Spain in the Early liddle Ages*, (Princeton University Press, Princeton, 1979); J.N. Hillgarth, *The Spanish 'ingdoms 1250–1516*, (2 vols, Clarendon Press, Oxford, 1976–78); Joseph F. O'Callaghan, *History of Medieval Spain*, (Cornell University Press, Ithaca, New York, 1975); Angus 1acKay, *Spain in the Middle Ages. From Frontier to Empire, 1000–1500*, (Macmillan, .ondon, 1977); Roger Collins, *Early Medieval Spain. Unity in Diversity, 400–1000*, Macmillan, London, 1983); Michael Brett, *The Moors, Islam in the West*, (Orbis, London, 980); Jan Read, *The Moors in Spain and Portugal*, (Faber, London, 1974). The latter vo works, despite being less well known, have commendable qualities.
2. Watt, *Islamic Spain*, p. 186.
3. Ibid., p. 2.
4. Ibid., p. 186.
5. Chejne, *Muslim Spain*, p. V.
6. *Glick, Islamic and Christian Spain*. Glick was not the first to deal with medieval

Spain as one entity. In Spanish, Luis G. de Valdeavellano's *Historia de España*, Prime Parte, (2 vols., Revista de Occidente, Madrid, 1952), was a monumental achievemen

7. Glick, *Islamic and Christian Spain*, p. 4.
8. Ibid., p. 3.
9. Robert I. Burns, SJ, *Muslims, Christians, and Jews in the Crusader Kingdom Valencia. Societies in symbiosis*, (Cambridge University Press, Cambridge, 1984), p. 1
10. Ibid., p. XVIII.
11. Ibid., p. 171.
12. José Antonio Conde, *Historia de la dominación de los árabes en España, saca de varios manuscritos y memorias arábigas*, (3 vols., García, Madrid, 1820–21), vo 1, p. XVII. The English is taken from the translation by Mrs Jonathan Foster, *Histo of the Dominion of the Arabs in Spain*. Translated from the Spanish of Dr J.A. Cond (3 vols., H.G. Bohn, London, 1854–55), vol. I, p. 18.
13. Condé, translated by Mrs Foster, *Arabs in Spain*, vol. 1, p. 17.
14. Ibid., p. 18.
15. Ibid., p. VI.
16. Miguel Cañes, *Diccionario español-latino-arábigo*, (3 vols., Sancha, Madrid, 1787 See also Elías Terés, 'El diccionario español-latino-arábigo del P. Cañes', *Al-Andalu* vol. XXI (1956), pp. 255–76. His *Gramática arábigo-española vulgar y literal* was publishe by Pérez de Soto in Madrid in 1775.
17. Miguel Casiri, *Bibliotheca Arabico-Hispanae Escurialensis*, (2 vols., Antonio Pér de Soto, Madrid, 1760–70).
18. James T. Monroe, *Islam and the Arabs in Spanish Scholarship*, (E.J. Brill, Leide 1970), p. 34.
19. Josef Antonio Conde, *Descripción de España de Xerif Aledris, conocido por Nubiense*, con traducción y notas, (La Imprenta Real, Madrid, 1799), facsimile editio (Ediciones Atlas, Madrid, 1980).
20. Ibid., p. III. My translation.
21. Josef Antonio Conde, *Memoria sobre la moneda arábiga, y en especial la acuña en España por los príncipes musulmanes*, leída . . . el 21 de julio de 1804, facsimile editic with a prologue by J.J. Rodríguez Llorente, (Editora Mayrit, Madrid, 1982). My translatio
22. In the light of later criticisms of Conde's work as a historian, it has been considere appropriate to affirm the worth of his scholarship as an Arabist.
23. Leandro Fernández de Moratín, *Diario (Mayo 1780–Marzo 1808)*, edición anota por René y Mireille Andioc, (Castalia, Madrid, 1967).
24. The life and works of Conde are studied by Manuela Manzanares de Cirre, *Arabist españoles del siglo XX*, (Instituto Hispano-Arabe de Cultura, Madrid, 1972), pp. 49–7 making use of several earlier accounts, including that of Pedro Roca, 'Vida y escrit de D. José Antonio Conde', *Revista de Archivos, Bibliotecas y Museos*, vol. VIII– (1903–4).
25. Conde, *Historia*, p. XXIV.
26. Conde, *Historia*, vol. II, p. 457: 'Sin división de capítulos, sin la correspondenc de los años, y sin otras perfecciones que ordinariamente dejan los autores para la pren ¿quién supliría la falta de Conde, de Conde empapado en la materia de su obra, y de cuy conocimientos debían esperar no solamente exactitud, sino luces nuevas en todos los punt que toca'?
27. L. Barrau-Dihigo, 'Contribution à la critique de Conde', in *Homenaje a don Fra cisco Codera*, (Mariano Escar, Zaragoza, 1904), pp. 551–69.
28. R.P.A. Dozy, *Recherches sur l'Histoire Politique et Littéraire de l'Espagne penda le Moyen Âge*, (E.J. Brill, Leiden, 1849), Tome I.
29. Ibid., p. VII.
30. Ibid., p. X.

31. Barrau-Dihigo, 'Contribution', p. 559.
32. Ibid., pp. 568–69.
33. Manzanares de Cirre, *Arabistas españoles*, p. 70.
34. Francis Griffin Stokes, *Spanish Islam: A History of the Moslems in Spain by Reinhart Dozy*, (Chatto & Windus, London, 1913), p. XXII.
35. Ibid., p. XXXV. Dozy wrote these words in 1861, some 12 years after the publication of his *Recherches*.
36. Ibid., pp. XXXV–XXXVI. Dozy does, however, append to each chapter the Arabic sources from which the material within it was garnered.
37. Ibid., p. 454.
38. Conde, translated by Mrs Foster, *Arabs in Spain*, vol. I, pp. 460–61.
39. E. Lévi-Provençal, *Histoire de l'Espagne Musulmane*, vol. III, *Le Siècle du Califat de Cordoue*, (Maisonneuve, Paris, 1953), p. 498.
40. Collins, *Early Medieval Spain*, p. 173.
41. Aḥmad Ibn Muḥammad Al-Maqqarī, *The History of the Mohammedan Dynasties in Spain*, translated by Pascual de Gayangos, (2 vols., Oriental Translation Fund, London, 1840–43), vol. II, p. 169.
42. Ibid., vol. II, p. 473.

PART TWO

THE POLITICAL, SOCIAL AND CULTURAL EVOLUTION OF THE GULF

6 Wahhabite Polity

Aziz al-Azmeh

An Iraqi opponent of the Wahhabite movement[1] in the early part of the present century could not comprehend why the Wahhabites were bent on inverting the correct order of things, as he understood it, in terms of which the Ḥijāz and Najd were connected. Whereas the Najdī Wahhabites had considered the Ḥijāz to be territory to be conquered, subjugated, and corrected, being technically *dār al-ḥarb*, it was in fact Najd (or rather the southern parts of it) which, in the early years of Islam, was the abode of the anti-prophet Musaylima, and was thus accursed territory that could in no way figure as *dār al-hijra*, as the Wahhabites claimed.[2] The repudiation of the irenical character of the mutually recognised and validated schools of Sunnī law was one of the charges most often levelled against the Wahhabites. Stress was laid on their radical intolerance of all but their own adepts to the extent of ascribing unbelief (*takfīr*) to all others, a feature that was often compared to the original position of the universally proscribed Kharijites,[3] and such stress was the substance of the very earliest critical pronouncements against the Wahhabites.[4] Muḥammad b. 'Abd al-Wahhāb himself devoted a lengthy epistle to refuting, among other charges, the charge that he was seeking to transcend the four schools of Sunnī law,[5] and this charge seems to have been quite persistent, having been repeated in a threatening letter sent by the then Pasha of Damascus to Su'ūd b. 'Abd al-'Azīz in 1808, in which the Ottoman official stated that the Wahhabites were ignorant bedouins without instruction in the fundamentals of the four schools.[6] There was indeed much confusion pertaining to the articles of Wahhabite belief, not to speak of events inside Najd; Muḥammad b. 'Abd al-Wahhāb was accused of sorcery,[7] and the fable according to which he fled 'Uyayna as a result of having murdered its ruler Ibn Mu'ammar in the mosque became a fact to a contemporary British consular report.[8] The incomprehension and misinformation in which Wahhabism was and is still engulfed is due to more than the fact that their works were little known outside Arabia (with the exception of India) until well into this century,[9] and certainly to more than the undoubted intellectual poverty and aridity of such works or to the relative isolation of Najd. The anti-Wahhabite polemic[10] was due principally to a primary and original trait of the Wahhabite movement and its concomitant ideology: that of making an absolute demarcation between an expanding polity and all its surroundings.

The social and political dimension of Wahhabite ideology is the setting of strict limits of exclusivity to a particular *'aṣabiyya* (tribal power group), thus rendering all that is external to this expanding 'aṣabiyya social, political, and geographical territory whose plunder and subjugation are legitimate, indeed, incumbent upon members of this exclusive group.[11] *Kufr* (unbelief) is an attribute of others and, in the accentuated Wahhabite form, of otherness *tout court*. It is an attribute which makes conquest and subjugation incumbent, under the banner of *jihād*, both as the political act of an expanding polity and as a legal-religious obligation. This exterior of kufr comprises not only idolatrous religions, nor is it confined to non-Islamic monotheism, but describes non-Wahhabite co-religionists as well. Ibn 'Abd al-Wahhāb himself emphasised this, justifying it on the analogy of Muḥammad himself having fought believers in the one God.[12] The hallowed principle of Sunnī Islam, according to which all those who profess the *shahāda* are Muslims, is ejected in favour of the assertion often made by Wahhabite divines that even sheer reserve towards the necessity of pronouncing non-Wahhabites (generically dubbed *mushrikūn*) to be *kuffār* (unbelievers) and of fighting them in itself constitutes kufr.[13] Sulaymān b. 'Abdillāh b. Muḥammad b. 'Abd al-Wahhāb, a prominent grandson of the movement's founder, banned not only alliance with the kuffār, but also their employment, consultation, trust, visiting, advice, friendship, emulation, trust, and cordiality and affability towards them.[14] Needless to say, it was not always that the full rigour of these principles was brought to bear; this was dependent on the political and social conditions of the time. The third Saudi *Imām*, Su'ud b. 'Abd al-'Azīz b. Muḥammad, was particularly noted for his severity,[15] while the population of Qaṣīm in the north of Najd and their local divines were known for their relative leniency and considered neither the Ottomans nor other Muslims generally to be kuffār.

In the first instance, the concrete manifestation of otherness that is to be suppressed was the particular Najdī forms of *shirk*. This comprised such matters as the idol Dhā 'l-Khilṣa, destroyed very early in the history of Wahhabism,[16] against which apparently infertile women rubbed their buttocks in the hope of fertility.[17] Najdī shirk also involved the sanctification of the dead and supplication and sacrifice at their shrines, such as that of Zaynab bint al-Khaṭṭāb at Jubayla, where people sought success in business, or the cult of the male palm tree, at Bulaydat al-Fiḍḍa and elsewhere, to which spinsters flocked praying for matrimony, and much else.[18] The felling of sacred trees and the destruction of shrines (not the obliteration of graves or their desecration) were some of the very first acts of Ibn 'Abd al-Wahhāb, who was particularly vehement in his condemnation of devotional acts directed towards any objects of sanctity other than God; these included supplication to the *jinn*, the celebration of feasts connected with the birth of persons of sacred attributes (including that of the Prophet himself), the use of talismans and of sorcery, and similar actions imputing potency to mere creatures.[19] Some of the first acts of the Wahhabite forces of Su'ūd b. 'Abd al-Azīz upon the invasions of Mecca in 1803 and Medina in 1805 were the destruction of sacred domes designating shrines.[20] Over a century later, the Saudi Government destroyed the dome of a shrine in Jidda supposedly containing the remains of Eve, and banned popular devotions at the site.[21] To these local iniquities were added others derived from conditions farther afield. One prominent Wahhabite divine in 1808 included amongst iniquitous practices in Syria the drinking of alcohol, the smoking of tobacco, the playing of cards and listening to popular storytellers.[22] Finally, Shi'ite Muslims throughout the history of Wahhabism and until the establishment of Saudi Arabia have been a favoured target of unremitting Wahhābī ferocity, ideological as well as military; the Ismā'īlī Shi'ites of the Banū Yām in 'Asīr were eventually converted.

There can be little doubt that the Wahhabite assault on popular practices and on other manifestations of devotional and doctrinal difference was not only one directed against dogmatic and devotional aberrations, but was also the counterpart of the fact that these were not only aberrant, but also and decidedly local. This acted to fragment religious authority in this world as well as in others, and militated against the emergence of a political authority which, busily devouring and incorporating social and geographical territory into a unifying vortex, was sustained by the Saudi-Wahhabite alliance.[23] Prior to the emergence of the Wahhabite state of the Su'ūd family, scholarly activity in Najd was scanty, although it was on the increase along with the growth in population in general, and urbanised habitation in particular, during the seventeenth century.[24] Much of this learning was cultivated in the context of connections with Damascus and (to a smaller degree) other centres where Hanbalism was in currency; indeed, the *adhān* in Burayda in the early part of this century was described by one observer as having been delivered in the tones of Syria.[25] Ibn 'Abd al-Wahhāb himself belonged to a prominent scholarly family, and his twenty or so marriages,[26] some to members of the princely families of Mu'ammar and Su'ūd, indicate social alliances concomitant with the politico-religious alliance in which his career and those of his descendants find their bearings.[27]

The role of Wahhābī divines is inseparable from the role of Wahhabite doctrine and its emphasis on the application of Islamic law; aspects of this will be analysed further below. The most direct aspect of the social alliance between divines and Saudi princes is the direct political role of the former. Though it may be true that the original compact between Muḥammad b. ʻAbd al-Wahhāb and Muḥammad b. Suʻūd at Dirʻiyya, the first Saudi capital, was one in which the divine was 'the senior partner',[28] this is only so in the sense that it was he who was in charge of the legal system. Yet the pre-eminence of the Āl al-Shaykh, the descendants of Ibn ʻAbd al-Wahhāb, in the legal and religious institutions of successive Saudi states is a factor connected both with their position in family alliances and their capacity formally to charter transfers of power.[29] Acting upon the hallowed principle repeated by Ibn ʻAbd al-Wahhāb, that power is legitimate however it may have been seized, and that obedience to whoever wields this power is incumbent upon all his subjects — so much so that the prerogatives of the Imamate belong to the holder of power irrespective of his own status[30] — the senior ranks of the Wahhabite devotional and legal institutions have acted as legitimisers of the successive transitions of power within the House of Suʻūd, both peaceful and seditious. It appears that, in all cases, such legitimation, *bayʻa*, was always undertaken at the behest or command of the effective ruler.[31] In the period of turmoil and internecine Saudi struggle in the 1860s and 1870s which saw eight changes of supreme Saudi authority in Riyadh between the death of Fayṣal b. Turkī in 1865 and 1877, the position of the Wahhabite hierarchy embodied in Āl al-Shaykh was one of attempts to reconcile, followed by the recognition of the victorious party.[32]

The Āl al-Shaykh have therefore been rather like the house clerics of the Saudi clan, to whom their loyalty never wavered even in the worst days of Egyptian occupation in the early nineteenth century or during the ascendancy of the Āl Rashīd of Ḥā'il. For leadership in the desert polity which the Saudi states were, was the prerogative of a particular clan within a possible wider federation, and this polity was based on the absolute pre-eminence of a particular family combined with the political peripheralisation of others. As always, desert polity is based on the patrimonial ascendancy of a particular clan — here the Suʻūds — which holds in tow an alliance of other clans which are by definition tributary and excluded from power. And whereas the leading clan — the only one, strictly speaking, which can arrogate to itself a political role — does not base its emergence to leadership on the extraction of public surplus but derives its wealth from private property and trade, its role as political leader, and the geographical expansion of this role, is based on systematic utilisation of public surplus, a fact which is made possible by the tributarisation of subject populations.[33] A similar situation, that of the Rashīdī state at Ḥā'il, has been described in an excellent account as a trade state at the core, and a tribute state at the periphery,[34] and one could well say the same about the successive Saudi states. Built upon the settled population of al-'Āriḍ (the early Islamic Yamāma), it came to command and extract surplus from the trade of Qaṣīm, whose rival towns of Burayda and 'Unayza sat astride the important Baṣra-Medina route and held one of the key routes to Kuwait; others to Kuwait and Bahrain passed in more southerly territory. These territories were early incorporated into the Saudi state, although they seem to have been prepared readily to turn against it in times of crisis, as during the Egyptian intervention.[35] From the Gulf Najdī trade reached as far as India, and 'Unayza traders had a stake in a pearling trade whose main buying organisation was, in the early part of this century, represented by a M. Rosenthal of Paris, known locally as Ḥabīb.[36] Besides trade in necessities, the export of horses was sometimes significant and sometimes in decline.[37] Also in the territorial core of Wahhabite polity was an erratic, but sometimes flourishing, agriculture.[38]

The bedouin tribes, however, were connected with this system only in so far as trade routes passed through their territory, *dīra*, and from this passage they extracted protection fees and offered guidance services. The 'Ajmān, for instance, controlled routes between Najd and both Kuwait and Ḥasā. Similarly, other tribes of the surrounding territories, such as 'Utayba, Āl Murra, Muṭayr, 'Aniza (to which the House of Su'ūd 'belong'), Shammar, and others, controlled routes leading to other territories, the Ḥijāz, Syria, and elsewhere. But for these tribes to come to be considered as anything other than idolators, they had to be incorporated into the political system whose core was (and still is) the Saudi clan. This entailed these tribes becoming tributaries to the centre of power in southern Najd, and this, in its turn, entailed not only their subjection to taxation (in kind such as camels), but also their exclusion from the political sphere. The centralisation in the extraction of surplus and the elimination of the role of these nomadic tribes in the extraction of surplus for their own benefit, as they did from protection fees (*khuwwa*) paid by agriculturalists and by traders passing through tribal territories, implied more than the technical reorganisation of such extraction in general by relegating this task to a central authority which then redistributed to every group its proper due. It also implied political eradication, that is, the abrogation of tribal right for the benefit of a political right exclusively exercised by the centre. This new political right erected over the debris of tribal right is itself derived from an eminently tribal concept, that of protection, *ḥimāya*, exercised by the central authority,[39] in exactly the same way as the nomadic tribes had hitherto offered protection and thus politically neutralised settled and trading groups in return for taxation. The relation of power expressed in its exercise, and thus the exercise of politics, by certain groups, and the exclusion of others from it, is the means by which tribal society is stratified. This self-same process is repeated, in reverse, in the subjugation of nomadic tribes to the centre.[40]

Martial nomadism is thus emasculated by its reduction to the same vulnerability and susceptibility to fiscal subjugation, with its concomitant political obliteration, that had been the lot of the weaker agricultural settlements. In the religious terms of Wahhabite divines and of the principles of government they imparted to the House of Su'ūd, this reduction of nomads, agriculturalists, and townspeople equally into subjects of the Saudi polity, this compact of protection and allegiance, was expressed in terms of the canonical alms tax, the *zakāt*.[41] Religious ordinances advocated by reformists are never disembodied, and their practical translation in the Wahhabite instance is a compact of protection between unequal parties modelled on tribal relations. The one is unthinkable without the other. It appears that the Saudi clan, by means of the military forces it could muster from the 'Āriḍī population and its own domestic militia (*fidāwiyya, zghurtiyya*), and by skilful manipulation of desert and international diplomacy, not to speak of the use of vast wealth accruing from agriculture, trade, and various forms of tribute, was capable of turning itself into the only unit in the territory of faith which plays the role hitherto performed by martial nomadic tribes; the erstwhile masters of the desert are thus transformed into tribal tributaries connected to the House of Su'ūd by ties of obligation brought about by unequal power. That is why the founder of Saudi Arabia invoked ties of kinship with tribal groups way out of his areas of control to express his bid for expansion.[42]

With the zakāt the criterion of inclusion within the exclusive group is indicated; the group comprises the parties to a compact of unequal power, sharing a common exterior which exists for the purpose of expansion. The incursions of Wahhabite forces into Iraq, Syria, the Ḥijāz, the Yemen, and Oman in the early nineteenth and early twentieth centuries are instances of this. War being one vital manner in which tribal groups cohere, it is clearly impossible effectively to detribalise tribes and to atomise tribesmen by means of subjection to zakāt and simultaneously to have them as tribal units with a tributary status; the only effective solution to this was agricultural settlement and the physical obliteration of tribal military force, both of which 'Abd al-'Azīz was to attempt in the first third of this century, succeeding in the second.[43]

Zakāt is only one manifestation, albeit one of great importance, of the tendency of Wahhabism to homogenise that society subject to the control of the House of Su'ūd. *Shar'*, of which zakāt is an instance, is certainly the method whereby society is homogenised, rid of its irregularity, and deconstituted so that it becomes more amenable to central direction. *Lex talionis* was one thing that the shar' imposed by Wahhabism on both nomads and townspeople abolished; it prescribed the substitution of money for blood, but this worked imperfectly,[44] indicating an as yet unconsummated project. The prohibition of usury, widely used amongst the bedouin,[45] is a similar issue. Customary marriage not involving a proper Muslim contract, and the customary division of inheritance whereby women were deprived of canonical shares, were common practice, particularly amongst bedouins,[46] who in some cases favoured the marriage of women who were already married but whose husbands were in captivity.[47] It was not until Saudi power was consolidated by means of zakāt-collecting local agents that the shar' and precepts derived from it were applied by the legal authorities answerable to the Wahhabite divines.[48] Just as local devotions detracted from the authority of the centre, so did local customs for which there was the possibility of a central provision that could be enforced by the corps of Wahhabite *'ulamā'*. In all cases, Wahhabism in its devotional as well as its legal aspects seems an element for the homogenisation of society.

But this homogenisation had limits that we have already touched upon, namely, the fact that domination of the tributary type exercised by tribal polity based on the absolute monopoly of power by one particular clan requires the maintenance of tribal particularism and of the social system of stratification prevalent in the desert. Homogenisation is a political, not necessarily a social, process. It is thus not surprising that, despite the vehemence of Wahhabite proselytism, the Ṣulubba were untouched by it, although they did not dwell *in partibus infidelium* but nevertheless revered the stars and held beliefs akin to heathens.[49] But this finds its explanation in their caste-like social inferiority and occupational stratification. Conversely, status and political necessity were allowed to override the requirements of the shar' in cases of personal status touching princely or royal personalities. The frequent marriages of members of the Su'ūd clan, in some instances for no more than one or two nights, are sometimes reminiscent of Shi'ite *mut'a* marriage, proscribed by all legal schools of Sunnī Islam.[50] Particularity could not be eliminated as totally as Wahhabite doctrine might require, and it is undoubtedly true that the ethos of Wahhabism, with its embeddedness in tribal society, militated against the very homogenisation it prescribed and required for its total practical consummation. This is why the administration of legal as opposed to customary justice, especially the attempts to eliminate the right of asylum and blood revenge, was at best very imperfect and had to await the modern Saudi state for its serious implementation.[51] It is according to this contextual condition, or reality-principle, of Wahhabite fundamentalism that Wahhabite polity, with the definitive establishment of the state in the first quarter of the twentieth century, becomes strictly Saudi polity. Saudi polity tributarises other clan groups, no longer nomadic, and ties them as clans stratified according to a particular pecking order to the redistribution of Saudi wealth; for plunder is substituted subsidy and the privileges of citizenship, such as the legal sponsorship of foreign businesses (*kafāla*), akin in many ways to the exaction of protection money (*khuwwa*). Thus tribalism becomes ascendant, not merely a *modus vivendi* or a traditional structure of society. For its part, Wahhabism abstains willy-nilly from ordering society, and becomes a state ideology in the most common acceptation of 'ideology'. Wahhabism remains pervasive not only in the educational system, the media, and public discourse in general, but also in international proselytising and other activities, not to speak of its spectacular performances in the shape of the public punishment of errants and criminals, much reminiscent of the Roman circus. Indeed, the Saudi-Wahhabite alliance reminds one of one Roman principle of statecraft, *panis et circenses*.

Yet Wahhabism preserves its integrity entire. For despite complications of unwieldy reality, Wahhabism sought the abstraction of society according to a utopian model whose current name is 'fundamentalism', denoting the attempt to fashion society according to a fundamental model already accomplished. Like all fundamentalism, Wahhabite doctrine[52] is cast in the mode of revivification. It purports to detail the exemplary behaviour of the Prophet and his contemporaries, and to utilise this register of exemplaries as a charter for reform. The fundamentals of rectitude are contained in this register, and the history that intervenes between the occurrence of exemplary acts and today is an accident that no more than sullies and corrupts its origin, and which therefore can be eliminated, as history is the mere passage of time, not the work of social, political and cultural transformations. It is not perchance or an act of incomprehensible blindness to the facts of history that causes the fundamental doctrinal texts of the Wahhabite movement — Ibn 'Abd al-Wahhāb's *Kitāb al-Tawḥīd* and its main commentaries and glosses[53] — to contain little concrete reference to contemporary reality, but to be rather like commentaries on this reality in a different medium, that of detailing exemplary acts and sayings culled from historical and scriptural knowledge. The two are set in parallel registers and are expressed in terms of today's fundamentally right bearings, making the iniquities of today less historical realities than supervening mistakes which can be eliminated by reference to exemplary precedent.

History is therefore reversible; alternatively, that history which interjects itself between the fundamental examples of the past and today is liable to elimination. Wahhabite doctrine not being historical scholarship, this position finds its bearings in the social and political being of this doctrine. For the import of fundamentalism is to require its (willing or unwilling) adherents to become subject to its requirements, that is, to lay Wahhabite territory open to the authority of Wahhabism, and therefore subject to the Saudi polity. By requiring subjection in principle to the authority whose voice is Wahhabism, this doctrine simultaneously renders these subjects open to the dictation of cultural and societal relations whose ground and condition are this authority. In short, Wahhabite fundamentalism puts forward a model whose task is to subject local societies with their customs, authorities, devotions, and other particularities to a general process of acculturation[54] which prepares them for membership in the commonwealth whose lynchpin and exclusive *raison d'être* is the absolute dominance of the House of Su'ūd.

Such is the import of the abstraction from contemporary reality which marks all fundamentalism: an absence is engendered, which is filled by interpretations provided by those with the means of enforcing an interpretation. It leaves the way open for the social and political contexts of fundamentalist doctrine to weave themselves into the terms of fundamentalist discourse, and by so doing to translate the terms of this discourse into contemporary facts and realities. The abstract reference of Wahhabite ideology has its counterpart also in the infinite possibilities for endowing it with meaning by those capable of enforcing a particular interpretation. The major one in this context is the abstract exterior, open for correction and demanding of struggle: instead of local and other infidels, the spectre of Communism is posited by the Saudi state, autonomously and in tandem with its almost utter dependence on the United States, as the primary evil and manifestation of kufr and shirk. Fact and fantasy become tokens of one another. Wahhabism thus seeks to flatten the contours of societies under its authority and to prepare them for the receipt of new form by those powers who wield the ultimate authority and the ultimate sanction of force — the House of Su'ūd. Thus the definition of the interior in terms dictated by political authorities is the counterpart of the iniquitous exterior defined by the divines of Wahhabite doctrine.

The definition of this interior is based on the fundamentalist mode of perceiving this interior, in the sense that presentation of the present in terms of scriptural and historical examples eliminates its reality and transforms it into a *tabula rasa* on which the authoritarian writ can be inscribed. This is the import of the execration of *taqlīd* from the days of Ibn 'Abd al-Wahhāb,[55] in line with a long Hanbalite tradition. And since law perhaps best reflects the transformations of reality, it is there that the encounter between Wahhabite doctrine and the political and social reality for which it is the charter is best regarded; the legal system of the Saudi state is based on the twin pillars of devotional severity, whose ultimate authority is the Qur'ān and the *sunna* as mediated by the authority of Wahhabism and its professionals (imāms, *muṭawwi'* corps), and of legal liberalism, one of whose most important categories is that of public welfare or the common weal, *maṣlaḥa*.[56] The liberalism of the Saudi legal system is not only manifested in the wide use of discretionary legislation based on the notion of maṣlaḥa, in line with Hanbalite tradition, but in a strong tendency towards doctrinal eclecticism, and the wide use of non-Hanbalite law,[57] particularly after 1961.[58] All in all, economic legislation in Saudi Arabia has been consonant with conditions prevalent there. 'Islamic banking', for instance, is consonant with conditions of speculative capitalism such as exist in Arabia today, and is in many ways reminiscent of European banking practices in the early nineteenth century.

Maṣlaḥa and devotional puritanism therefore become the twin pillars of the construction of the Wahhabite interior,[59] and both have the sanction of Wahhabism and its professionals. The King's prerogative as imām in the conduct of politics according to the shar' becomes referred to as *ijtihād*.[60] Thus when a *fatwā* pronounced the insurance of commercial goods to be illegal, King 'Abd al-'Azīz reversed the ruling on the grounds of public interest.[61] And when the Wahhabite divines wanted to abolish the commercial codes of the Ḥijāz which had been modelled on the Ottoman *Mejelle*, 'Abd al-'Azīz desisted and, when this code was overhauled in 1931, it was simply purged of reference to interest and was still modelled on the Ottoman code of 1850.[62] The king's position was clear from the outset. He declared publicly that he would abide by the judgements of Ibn 'Abd al-Wahhāb and others only if they were demonstrable with reference to the scriptures;[63] direct reference to scriptures with the elimination of intervening authorities implies *ipso facto* a call for reinterpretation. Such is the real import of the rejection of taqlīd and the injunction to ijtihād.

The Saudi-Wahhabite alliance therefore subjected populations to legal abstraction, cleared the way for legislation in line with the discretionary requirements of what is habitually termed 'development', and inflicted upon this population a constant social invigilation and control undertaken by the corps of *muṭawwi'ūn* who assure adherence to standard devotions and precepts of public puritanism. This last function assures the control over social relations that obtain in the tribal society which Saudi polity has always considered to be its natural domain, relations that entail the strict exclusion of women, the observance of very conservative attitudes, and other means of severe social control, in addition to rituals of inwardness, such as public punishments. Such puritanism has often been the counterpart of economic liberalism, and Saudi Arabia is no exception. Yet the constraints on tribalism as well as on the consummation of a strict and integral Wahhabite order, both the results of practical Wahhabism, have resulted in two major episodes that have disturbed the Saudi-Wahhabite order.

The first was the series of events which led to the final military elimination of the Ikhwān during the late 1920s. These were irregular forces levied from settlements of bedouin populations known as the *hujar*, modelled on the *hijra* of Muḥammad and designed as places of exemplary life and repositories of military manpower at the disposal of the Saudi state, and established from about 1908 onwards at various strategic locations in Najd on tribal territories belonging to the clans.[64] They were therefore tribal-military settlements, extensively subsidised by 'Abd al-'Azīz,[65] and marked by the observance of strict codes of fundamentalist morality, including a vestimentary code.[66]

'Abd al-'Azīz did not construct a civic militia in the hujar — he had his townsmen for this purpose — but constructed tribal abodes with definable boundaries. We have seen that the Wahhabite-Saudi alliance deprives social collectivities of a political constitution, but preserves them as social units. This applies especially to nomadic tribal groups, which sustained their social being by raids into infidel territory, not only for booty, but for the maintenance of desert social stratification, as has already been suggested. When the borders of present-day Saudi Arabia were solidifying as a result of agreements and treaties, mainly with Great Britain, the checks put on bedouin raiding activity led to a situation expressed by one of the leaders of the Ikhwān revolt, Fayṣal al-Duwaysh, chief of the Muṭayr and of the Arṭawiyya hijra, as one in which 'we are neither Moslems fighting the unbelievers nor are we Arabs and Bedouins raiding each other and living on what we get from each other'.[67] The Ikhwān had indeed 'worked themselves out of a job',[68] and a conflagration was inevitable and was predicted by a discerning ethnologist.[69]

The exterior was no longer to be territory open to conquest and subjection, as it should be with Wahhabite doctrine, and the revolt of the Ikhwān might have turned into a general rebellion had it not been for the fact that an analogue of external plunder was found: oil, the wealth accruing from which is redistributed after a patrimonial manner according to the pecking order required by, and conducive to, the maintenance of tribal structures and status. The distinctions brought about by wealth and privilege, the correlatives of the tribal structure, define a novel exterior, that of expatriates employed in Saudi Arabia, over and above the local exterior, women.

So much for the disturbing social consequences of Wahhabite polity. As for the ideological consequences of this polity, i.e. of the Wahhabite-Saudi alliance, these have taken a form unchanged since 1927 when the Ikhwān, in full rebellion, charged 'Abd al-'Azīz with violating the relationship of interior and exterior by sending his son Su'ūd to Egypt (occupied by a Christian power and inhabited by infidel Muslims), using wireless telegraphy and other works of the devil, not compelling the Shi'ites of Ḥasā to adopt the Wahhabite creed, and so forth.[70] Indeed, the Ikhwān had been suspicious of 'Abd al-'Azīz's dealings with infidels from a much earlier date; in 1918 they were not enthusiastic about the campaign against the Wahhabite Ḥā'il, on the assumption that they were playing a British political game.[71] Very much the same sort of objection to the political power of the Saudi state was voiced by the participants in the seizure of the Great Mosque with the Ka'ba at Mecca in November 1979 — the second episode to disturb the Saudi-Wahhabite order. One chief iniquity and manifestation of kufr is the constant contact and co-operation with Christians; and the state which pretends to *tawḥīd*, the technical name of Wahhabism, in fact performed the unification, tawḥīd, between Muslims, Christians and polytheists, confirmed Shi'ites in their heresies, and, while it combated fetishism, instituted the fetish of money.[72] The facts of today, in perfectly fundamentalist manner, are assimilated to scripturalist models and are made to translate them, and the prime motif of the group which precipitated the events of 1979 was the assimilation of contemporary events to eschatological events,[73] which justified their messianic revolt.

The Wahhabite divines who condemned the 1979 rebels to death[74] are truer representatives of Wahhabism than the dead puritans. The grand Muftī of Saudi Arabia, Shaykh 'Abd al-'Azīz b. Bāz, a signatory to the death sentence,[75] did not seem to disagree with the theses of the rebels who had read some of their treatises to him, but simply declined to specify the object of criticism as the present Saudi state.[76] The secret of fundamentalism resides in the absence of specification, in the very tokenism of the letter, in the parallelism but never in the identity of the scriptural and the real registers. The latter can therefore be the meaning of the former through the imputation of such meaning by the agency that has the power and authority to posit, consolidate, and enforce meaning. The impossibility of utopia derives from the impossibility of conflating the two registers and contexts of reference, the scriptural and the real. Juhaymān al-'Utaybī and his followers conflated the two registers and identified them. They consequently read the eschatological script as an immanent chiliasm, precipitating their mundane perdition. Without the distinction between the registers which allows the powers that be to penetrate the script and infuse it with their power, fundamentalism becomes redundant, an idle chiliasm without a chance in this world.

Notes

1. I use this term in preference to *Muwaḥḥidūn* used by the Wahhabites because it is common and because the latter is confusing, being used by the Druze and, indeed, by all Muslims, to designate themselves.

2. M.Sh. Alūsī, *Tārīkh Najd*, ed. M.B. Atharī, (Al-Maṭba'a al-Salafiyya, Cairo, AH 1343/AD 1924), p. 50.

3. Ibid., p. 50 ff.

4. For instance, Al-Jabartī, *Min Akhbār al-Ḥijāz wa Najd fī Tārīkh al-Jabartī*, ed. M.A. Ghālib, (Dār al-Yamāma, n.p., 1975), p. 97.

5. Ḥ. Khalaf al-Shaykh Khaz'al, *Ḥayāt al-Shaykh Muḥammad b. 'Abd al-Wahhāb*, (Maṭābi' Dār al-Kutub, Beirut, 1968), p. 119 ff.

6. Fleischer (tr.), 'Briefwechsel zwischen den Anführender Wahhabiten und dem Paša von Damascus', *Zeitschrift der Deutschen Morgenländischen Gesellschaft*, vol. xi (1857), p. 441.

7. Ibn Bishr, *'Unwān al-Majd fī Tārīkh Najd*, (2 vols., Maṭābi' al-Qaṣīm, Riyadh, AH 1385, 1388/AD 1965, 1968), vol. 1, p. 18.

8. M.A. Khan, 'A Diplomat's Report on Wahhabism in Arabia', *Islamic Studies*, vol. 7 (1968), p. 40.

9. M. Kurd 'Alī, *Al-Qadīm wa 'l-Ḥadīth*, (al-Maṭba'a al-Raḥmāniyya, Cairo, 1925), p. 157.

10. See M.R. Riḍā, *Al-Wahhābiyya wa 'l-Ḥijāz*, (Maṭba'at al-Manār, Cairo, AH 1344/AD 1925), for a critical exposition, and see in general Z.I. Karout, 'Anti-wahhabitische Polemik im XIX. Jahrhundert', unpublished Doctoral Dissertation, University of Bonn, 1978.

11. The best account of the social and political bearings of Wahhabite ideology and of the overall history of the movement is that of W. Sharāra, *Al-Ahl wa 'l-Ghanīma: Muqawwimāt al-Siyāsa fī'l-Mamlaka al-'Arabiyya al-Su'ūdiyya*, (Dār al-Ṭalī'a, Beirut, 1981).

12. *Majmū'at al-Tawḥīd*, (Ri'āsat Idārāt al-Buḥūth al-'Ilmiyya wa'l-Iftā' wa 'l-Da'wa wa 'l-Irshād, Saudi Arabia, n.d.), p. 52 and *passim*.

13. Ibid., p. 284 and *passim*.

14. Ibid., pp. 121–2 and cf. pp. 251 ff., 288–9, 292.

15. Alūsī, *Tārīkh Najd*, p. 94.

16. H. Wahba, *Arabian Days*, (Arthur Barker, London, 1964), pp. 99 and 112.

17. Ibn Bishr, *'Unwān al-Majd*, vol. 1, p. 6.

18. Wahba, *Arabian Days*, p. 87.

19. For instance, Ibn 'Abd al-Wahhāb in *Majmū'at al-Tawḥīd*, pp. 9–10, 58, 66 and *passim*.

20. Jabartī, *Akhbār al-Ḥijāz*, pp. 92, 104.

21. Ḥ. Wahba, *Jazīrat al-'Arab fī 'l-Qarn al-'Ishrīn* (Lajnat al-Ta'līf wa 'l-Tarjama wa 'l-Nashr, Cairo, 1967), p. 31. For practices of talismans and magical healing in today's Ḥijāz, see M. Katakura, *Bedouin Village. A Study of a Saudi Arabian People in Transition*, (University of Tokyo Press, Tokyo, 1977), pp. 68–9.

22. Fleischer, 'Briefwechsel', p. 438.

23. Sharāra, *Al-Ahl wa 'l-Ghanīma*, p. 91.

24. U.M. Al-Juhany, 'The History of Najd prior to the Wahhabis. A Study of the Social, Political and Religious Conditions in Najd during Three Centuries', unpublished PhD Thesis, University of Washington, 1983, p. 250 ff. On population, see p. 165 ff. It must be stressed that Juhany's conclusions are based on sketchy source material and that they should be treated with some caution as indicating general trends rather than anything else.

25. H. St.John B. Philby, *Arabia of the Wahhabis* (Frank Cass, London, 1977, repr. from Constable, London, 1928 ed.), p. 195.

26. Khalaf al-Shaykh Khaz'al, *Ḥayāt al-Shaykh Muḥammad b. 'Abd al-Wahhāb*, p. 341.

27. Ibn 'Abd al-Wahhāb's sworn and active enemy was his own brother: ibid., p. 205 ff.

28. M.J. Crawford, 'Wahhābī *'ulamā'* and the Law, 1745–1932', unpublished M.Phil. thesis, University of Oxford, 1980, p. 38.

29. Ibid., pp. 42 ff., 52.

30. Khalaf al-Shaykh Khaz'al, *Ḥayāt al-Shaykh Muḥammad b. 'Abd al-Wahhāb*, p. 140.

31. For instance, Ibn Bishr, *'Unwān al-Majd*, vol. 1, pp. 96, 101, 203; vol. 2, p. 60.

32. See the discussion of this by M.J. Crawford, 'Civil War, Foreign Intervention and the Question of Political Legitimacy: A Nineteenth-Century Sa'ūdī Qāḍī's Dilemma', *International Journal of Middle East Studies*, vol. 14 (1982), p. 227 ff.

33. For the stratification of Najdī society, see Juhany, 'History of Najd', p. 173 ff.

34. H. Rosenthal, 'The Social Composition of the Military in the Process of State Formation in the Arabian Desert', *Journal of the Royal Anthropological Institute*, vol. 95 (1965), p. 184 ff, and *passim*.

35. Ibn Bishr, *'Unwān al-Majd*, vol. 1, p. 240.

36. Philby, *Arabia of the Wahhabis*, p. 285.

37. For instance, R.B. Winder, *Saudi Arabia in the Nineteenth Century*, (Macmillan, London, 1965), p. 214; J.G. Lorimer, *Gazetteer of the Persian Gulf, 'Omān and Central Arabia* (6 vols., Superintendent Government Printing, India, Calcutta, 1908–1915), vol. I, Pt. 2, p. 2335 f; Philby, *Arabia of the Wahhabis*, p. 216.

38. For a full description of the earlier period, see Juhany, 'History of Najd', p. 182 ff.

39. Cf. Sharāra, *Al-Ahl wa 'l-Ghanīma*, p. 67.

40. On the Saudi taxation system, see for instance, Winder, *Saudi Arabia*, p. 211 ff.

41. Cf. C.M. Helms, *The Cohesion of Saudi Arabia* (Croom Helm, London, 1981),

p. 152 ff.

42. Kh. Ziriklī, *Shibh Jazīrat al-'Arab fī 'Ahd al-Malik 'Abd al-'Azīz*, (N.p., Beirut, 1970), p. 290, and A. Rihani, *Maker of Modern Arabia*, (Houghton Miffin, Boston and New York, 1928), pp. 60–61.

43. See the detailed account of J.S. Habib, *Ibn Saud's Warriors of Islam. The Ikhwan of Najd and their Role in the Creation of the Sa'udi Kingdom, 1910–1930*, (E.J. Brill, Leiden, 1978).

44. For instance, Winder, *Saudi Arabia*, pp. 158–9.

45. J.L. Burckhardt, *Notes on the Bedouins and the Wahábys*, (Henry Colburn & Richard Bentley, London, 1831), vol. 2, p. 150.

46. Ibid., vol. 1, pp. 107, 131; J. Chelhod, *Le Droit dans la Société Bédouine*, (Marcel Rivière, Paris, 1971), pp. 70–71, 134; J. Henninger, 'Das Eigentumsrecht bei den heutigen Beduinen Arabiens', *Zeitschrift für vergleichende Rechtswissenschaft*, vol. 61 (1959), p. 29.

47. Ziriklī, *Shibh Jazīrat al 'Arab*, p. 464.

48. For instance, Burckhardt, *Bedouins and the Wahábys*, vol. 1, pp. 99, 101, 120; vol. 2, pp. 136–9.

49. For a description, see Lewis Pelly, *Journal of a Journey from Persia to India through Herat and Candahar. By Lieut. Colonel Lewis Pelly . . . also Report of a Journey to the Wahabee Capital of Riyadh in Central Arabia*, (Printed for Government at the Education Society's Press, Byculla, Bombay, 1866), p. 189 ff.

50. One could also cite as evidence of animist manifestations (or survivals) the *wasm* with which 'Abd al-'Azīz branded his camels, described by Philby, *Arabia of the Wahhabis*, p. 53 and sketched in H.R.P. Dickson, *The Arab of the Desert* (Allen & Unwin, London, 1949), p. 420.

51. Cf. for instance Winder, *Saudi Arabia*, p. 208.

52. A thorough sketch can be found in H. Laoust, *Essai sur les Doctrines Morales et Politiques de Takī-d-Dīn Aḥmad b. Taimīya*, (Institut Français d'Archéologie Orientale, Cairo, 1939), bk. 3, ch. 2.

53. Sulaymān b. 'Abdillāh b. Muḥammad b. 'Abd al-Wahhāb's *Taysīr al-'Azīz al-Ḥamīd fī Sharḥ Kitāb al-Tawḥīd*, (Al-Maktab al-Islāmī, Damascus, n.d. [1962]), is a detailed linguistic and historical commentary; *Fatḥ al-Majīd* by 'Abd al-Raḥmān b. Ḥasan Āl al-Shaykh, (Maktabat al-Riyāḍ al-Ḥadītha, Riyadh, n.d.), is in many ways a summary of its predecessor, while the same author's *Qurrat 'Uyūn al-Muwaḥḥidīn fī Taḥqīq Da'wat al-Anbiyā' al-Mursalīn*, (Maktabat al-Riyāḍ al-Ḥadītha, Riyadh, n.d.), is a collection of glosses on the original.

54. Cf. Sharāra, *Al-Ahl wa 'l-Ghanīma*, p. 101.

55. Text in *Majmū'at al-Tawḥīd*, p. 60.

56. See, for instance, Crawford, 'Wahhābī *'ulamā'* ', pp. 68, 110.

57. For instance, ibid., pp. 70–71.

58. A.W.I. Abu Sulaiman, *The Role of Ibn Qudāma in Ḥanbalī Jurisprudence*, unpublished PhD. thesis, University of London, 1970, p. 248.

59. Cf. O. Carré, 'Idéologie et Pouvoir en Arabie Saoudite et dans son Entourage', in P. Bonnenfant (ed.), *La Péninsule Arabique d'Aujourdhui* (Editions CNRS, Paris, 1982), vol. 1, pp. 242–3 and *passim*.

60. Crawford, 'Wahhābī *'ulamā'* ', p. 111.

61. Wahba, *Arabian Days*, p. 94.

62. Crawford, 'Wahhābī *'ulamā'* ', p. 97; Wahba, *Jazīrat al-'Arab*, p. 319 ff.

63. A. Riḥānī, *Tārīkh Najd al-Ḥadīth*, vol. 5 of Riḥānī, *Al-A'māl al-'Arabiyya al-Kāmila*, (Al-Mu'assasa al-'Arabiyya li 'l-Dirāsāt wa 'l-Nashr, Beirut, 1980), p. 374.

64. A. Musil, *North Neğd. A Topographical Itinerary*, Oriental Explorations and Studies, no. 4, (American Geographical Society of New York, New York, 1928), p. 283.

65. Habib, *Ibn Saud's Warriors*, p. 143.

66. Ibid., p. 33 ff.

67. Ibid., p. 136.
68. Ibid., p. 119.
69. Musil, *Northern Nejd*, p. 303.
70. Habib, *Ibn Saud's Warriors*, pp. 122, 135. On the curious controversy over telegraphy, see Wahba, *Arabian Days*, pp. 57–58.
71. Philby, *Arabia of the Wahhabis*, p. 102.
72. Juhaymān b. Muḥammad b. Sayf al-'Utaybī, *Da'wat al-Ikhwān: Kayfa Bada'a wa ilā ayn Tasīr* (n.p., n.d.), pp. 32–3; idem., *Al-Imāra wa 'l-Bay'a wa 'l-Ṭā'a wa Kashf Talbīs al-Ḥukkām 'alā Ṭalabat al-'Ilm wa 'l-'Awāmm* (n.p., n.d.), p. 28.
73. 'Utaybī, *Al-Fitan wa Akhbār al-Mahdī wa 'l-Dajjāl wa Nuzūl 'Īsā b. Maryam wa Ashrāṭ al-Sā'a* (n.p., n.d.), *passim*; idem., *Al-Imāra*, pp. 20–21.
74. The text of this *fatwā* and other documentation is contained in 'A. Maṭi'nī, *Jarīmat al-'Aṣr. Qiṣṣat Iḥtilāl al-Masjid al-Ḥarām* (n.p., Cairo, 1980), pp. 43–44.
75. Ibid., p. 45.
76. 'Utaybī, *Da'wat al-Ikhwān*, p. 8.

7 Saudi Arabia: Political and Social Evolution

Keith McLachlan

Saudi Arabia — The Immature State

The Kingdom of Saudi Arabia cannot be classified as a modern state except in the sense that it exists at the time of writing as a national entity. Measured by most objective criteria, including the maturity of its economic, social or political structures, the country is more characterised by traditional attributes than those features normally associated with the modern or 'developed' world. This view is not a criticism, implied or otherwise. But it is as well to appreciate that the designation of Saudi Arabia as a structurally complex and advanced country is likely to be misleading.[1]

This essay will hope to show that economic and material evolutions of significant parts of Saudi Arabia have been extremely rapid. But social development has been at best patchy, while elaboration of the political system has been so slow as to be imperceptible. It is an interesting irony in Saudi Arabia and a number of other oil-rich states that the arrival of substantial oil incomes has militated against achievement of economic maturity since the petroleum sector has brought lopsided growth, diminishing the roles played by productive agriculture, trade and industry. So far in Saudi Arabia, oil wealth has also served to fossilise the political system since oil income has been concentrated in the hands of the ruling family and used as an instrument for securing its continued monopoly of political power. It might be argued that the history of Saudi Arabia is the history of a few families and, since the turn of this century, the saga of the House of Su'ūd.[2] Without the strong hand of 'Abd al-'Azīz ibn Su'ūd (1880–1953), the lands of the bulk of the Arabian Peninsula might never have been united under one flag. The political acumen of Ibn Su'ūd's successors and not least Fayṣal (1906–1975) helped the country to survive both internal problems and threats to domestic stability from abroad. The Kingdom is of very recent origin, however, and national cohesion is not a matter that can be taken for granted. Regional, tribal and family sentiments remain strong. National territorial integrity will always be in question for as long as unsettled boundary disputes, that affect most of the southern and eastern frontiers, persist.[3]

Examination of Saudi Arabia must be undertaken within inter-Arab, Islamic and international frameworks since the state has a high degree of external dependency. Saudi Arabia created an important role for itself within the Arab world, especially during the rule of Fayṣal as prime minister and king (1958–1975, with short intervals out of office), when it acted as a mediator on the one hand and a mobiliser of moderate Arab opinion on the other.[4] During the 1970s, as its oil wealth grew, so the state became a paymaster to the Arab countries and an attempted purchaser of influence, albeit with objectives little different from those espoused during the earlier period.

The Kingdom's role as custodian of the most holy shrines and a centre of pilgrimage for the entire Islamic world has given it a clear status, though pilgrimage took place for centuries before the emergence of the country in its contemporary form. Expansion of Saudi Arabian participation in the international institutions concerned with Islam has been considerable, though as much stimulated by the country's ability to fund them as by acceptance of its leadership on other grounds. Even in the arena of Islamic organisations and the guardianship of the holy places, there has been challenge to the state and the monarchy. Confrontation has come most recently from Iran, where the Islamic Republic, established during 1979, has appeared to ignore the Islamic Conference and its committees on the matter of the ending of the war against Iraq, treating its emissaries with disdain. The very nature of the Shi'ite establishment in Iran since the revolution, and the religious alignment against orthodox interpretations of Islam as practised in Saudi Arabia or other Arab states, has challenged traditional religious authorities. The close linkage in Saudi Arabia between the ruling house and the Wahhābī teachings of the Ḥanbalī School of Islamic jurisprudence makes Iranian criticism an attack on both the principal pillars of the state. Dedication to an aggressive republicanism in Iran has added to the apparent challenge to the legitimacy of the monarchy in Saudi Arabia arising in the Islamic domain.[5]

If Saudi Arabia has been able to develop only a small and disputed role as a leader within the Islamic world or may be regarded as comparatively insignificant as a player in inter-Arab politics, it cannot be denied that it has a special position *vis à vis* the strategy of the United States in the Middle East.[6] The Saudi Arabian relationship with the USA arises from a complex and changing history that is unique for the Americans within the Middle East region.[7] The linkage through the

perations by ARAMCO since 1933 has given the US oil industry and
ie US diplomatic service extremely close contacts with the Government
f Saudi Arabia and most organs of state over an extended period. The
resence of US companies and advisers has left an indelible impression
n Saudi Arabia and has ensured that the first point of reference for Saudi
rabian leaders in foreign affairs on all matters other than those
xclusively concerned with religion is the USA. The reverse of the coin
that the United States has increasingly seen Saudi Arabia as a prin-
ipal plank for ensuring political stability in the Arabian Peninsula and
rab Gulf area, as a source of moderation within OPEC and OAPEC,
nd as an ally against Russian penetration of the Middle East as a whole.
is important, too, in any consideration of Saudi Arabian legitimacy
s a sovereign state to take account of the apparent underwriting of the
itegrity of the country by the USA, especially since 1980.[8]

he Territorial Evolution of Saudi Arabia

rabia before 1914 was nominally under the control of the Turks. In
eality, the appointment of Ḥusayn ibn ʻAlī ibn Muḥammad ibn ʻAwn
s Sharīf of Mecca in 1908 had left the new Turkish administration much
eakened in Arabia and increasingly faced by pan-Arabist sentiments
iat were antipathetic to Turkish nationalism. A tentative alliance of
onvenience in the Peninsula between several of the principal Arab
aders and the British during the 1914–18 war enabled the Arabs to
eclare their independence from the Turks. Five separate political units
ere recognised, including Saudi Arabia, Ḥijāz, ʻAsīr, Ḥā'il and Yemen.

For Saudi Arabia, the events surrounding the Arab revolt, despite
ie small part that it played, enabled it to consolidate what had been no
iore than an often precarious zone of influence around Riyadh in the
losing decades of the nineteenth century into an independent Emirate
f Najd by 1918. This was a major achievement for the House of Suʻūd
nd was only made possible by a prolonged struggle with ʻAbd al-ʻAzīz
on Rashīd, whose family had formerly controlled the main settlements
i the Najd as allies of the Turks.

In continuing military operations during the period 1920–22, Ibn Suʻūd
ursued the successors of Ibn Rashīd, capturing Ḥā'il in 1921. In the
ollowing year the oases of Taymā', Khaybar and Jawf, lying on the
rontier with the Ḥijāz, were captured. This opened the way, after
etbacks in Transjordan, to the invasion of the Ḥijāz in 1923–25. Mean-
hile, the ʻAsīr and the Empty Quarter were occupied, the former in

1920, when Sayyid Muḥammad al-Idrīsī accepted Saudi authority, and the latter in 1925. A revolt in the 'Asīr in 1925 was put down and war broke out with the Yemen in 1934, which finally saw the region consolidated under the control of Ibn Su'ūd.

The territorial expansion of Saudi Arabia was accomplished with remarkable rapidity, credit for which rests largely with Ibn Su'ūd. He was aided by the close alliance of his House with the Wahhābī movement.[9] He had an element of spiritual as well as family legitimacy in his assertion of leadership against the Sharīf of Mecca. The Ikhwān, the dedicated Wahhābī warriors of the Peninsula, were an important component of Ibn Su'ūd's military forces. Their intervention during the invasions of Ḥā'il and Ḥijāz was critical in enabling him to win the day. The reputation of the Ikhwān both as fighters and merciless conquerors[10] was instrumental in demoralising enemies of the Wahhābī expansion under Ibn Su'ūd. Ibn Su'ūd also had the tacit support of the British in so far as he was the only realistic means through which political stability could be achieved in the Peninsula, especially in view of the political ineptitude of the Sharīf of Mecca, his only serious rival. In areas such as Transjordan, Kuwait and Iraq, where the British had treaty relations with client states that bordered Saudi Arabia, incursions by the Ikhwān were dealt with firmly and Ibn Su'ūd, though making whatever political capital from the activities of the Ikhwān that was feasible on each occasion, was never slow to repudiate them when it suited him.

Total consolidation of the Peninsula was beyond Ibn Su'ūd, even had he wished it. The British were ensconced in Aden and the Aden Protectorate as the colonial power. Elsewhere in Kuwait, Iraq and Transjordan British influence, often expressed in a military presence, made expansion difficult. In the Gulf coast region, treaty relations between the British and local rulers in Abu Dhabi, Dubai, Ras al-Khaima, Ajman, Fujairah, Sharjah and Umm al-Qaiwain had the same effect. In respect of Yemen it appeared that Ibn Su'ūd had few ambitions. Even following the hostilities of the Saudi-Yemeni war of 1934 only minor local adjustments were made to borders, despite the fall of much of northern Yemen to Saudi troops. In the east, Oman, like Yemen a Muslim state, was not apparently envisaged as an area where the young Saudi state should have territorial ambitions, although disputes concerning the boundary between the two states have persisted through to the present day.

Internal acknowledgement of the House of Su'ūd culminated in 193[illegible] after the suppression of the Ikhwān challenge to his authority, when Ibn Su'ūd was crowned King of Saudi Arabia, replacing his former designation as King of Ḥijāz and Najd. The most important of external recognitions came from Great Britain through the Treaty of Jidda of 1927. During the 1930s treaties were arranged with Transjordan in 1933, and with Bahrain, Iraq and Egypt in 1936, by which time Saudi Arabia was an entirely accepted national state. The new country had exemplary credentials. It had been formed by an Arab dynasty and made up of exclusively Arab and Islamic fabrics, unlike many other Arab states, which were essentially created by colonial interests.

Yet Saudi Arabia was not accorded a warm welcome by the Arab nationalist movement of the period. Sentiment of the time, which has persisted, albeit in modified form, through to the contemporary era in forms such as Ba'th socialism, was republican, socialist and, if not secular, at least modernist rather than fundamentalist in religious outlook. The dynastic roots of the House of Su'ūd and its association with tribal groupings were at odds with the prevailing dedication to written constitutions, models for which had been constructed in Turkey and Iran, and modern (or by definition 'democratic') political structures. At the same time, the attachment of Ibn Su'ūd to the Wahhābī movement alienated many of the Islamic communities which were averse to the basic and in some cases questionable tenets of the Wahhābīs. Arab nationalists were critical of the lack of intellectual depth of the Saudi leadership and the want of an Arab political ideology behind the Saudi conquest or acquisitions through tribal/kinship alliances. None the less, the elaboration of structures of government at national and provincial levels by Ibn Su'ūd and his successors, together with reinforcement of the House of Su'ūd by inter-tribal marriage, often on a grand scale, brought considerable continuity and national integration,[11] which contrasts with the experiences of many other Arab countries, where regimes have been unstable and institutions constantly changing despite their dedication to political ideologies.

The Trappings of Maturity: Economic Change

The economic base level on which economic and indeed social changes have taken place in the present century was extremely varied. The greater area of the country — for the most part virtually waterless desert — offered limited opportunities for grazing by nomadic pastoralists. Occasional oases on the Red Sea coast and the hills inland, such as Jidda and the better watered lands of the 'Asīr, were rare relief from an otherwise unyielding landscape. The central zone of the Peninsula, in addition to the unpromising deserts of Nafūd, Dahnā' and Rub' al-Khālī, was occupied by a number of well-developed oasis settlements, including Jawf, Ḥā'il, Burayda, 'Unayza, Shaqrā and Riyadh. Together with their settlements, they represented 'a not uncultured and not uncomfortable urban life'.[12] The Ḥasā region of the eastern Peninsula also sustained a number of oases, notably Al-Hufūf, 'Ujayr and Qaṭīf.

The economy was organised in a regional and local system on an agricultural base that was split between settled oasis farmers on the one hand and nomadic herdsmen on the other. Inter-regional trade was limited to small-scale exchanges and inhibited by poor lines of communication, lack of security for travelling traders and the poverty of much of the population. Only the annual *ḥajj* brought in outside wealth on a significant scale, depending on the numbers of pilgrims, political conditions in the Islamic world and health conditions in the countries of origin of the pilgrims.

Proclamation of Ibn Su'ūd as King of Saudi Arabia in 1932 was followed in November 1933 by the assignment of a petroleum concession to California Arabian Standard Oil Company (later renamed the Arabian American Oil Company, generally known as ARAMCO). Exploration activity was slow and, other than initial payments made for securing the concession by CASOC, the income effects of the oil venture were restricted and felt only in the most modest of ways, beginning with expenditure by the US company on exploration and development and the first exports of oil to the Bahrain refinery in September 1938. Development of the Saudi Arabian oilfields was slowed down by the outbreak of the Second World War and, despite construction of improved facilities in 1944, the country did not become a serious exporter of oil until the 1950s (Table 7.1).

Oil revenues very soon replaced the ḥajj and other economic activity as the principal income of the state. Comparatively gradual increases in oil income in the early years sheltered the traditional economy since the new wealth was absorbed in the towns and by government agencies. Under Ibn Su'ūd revenues from oil were spent wisely. Other than consumption by the royal family and expenditures abroad by them, monies were channelled into the construction of railway, road, port, airline[13] and other systems that assisted political or economic integration of the state. With considerable and mainly well-directed guidance from ARAMCO, attempts were made to underpin agriculture and to establish some industrial plants.

Above all, however, Saudi Arabian oil revenues until the 1970s were used to preserve the position of the House of Su'ūd by subsidising tribal notables and purchasing political support/quiescence in rural areas.

able 7.1: Saudi Arabia — Oil Production (000 b/d)

939	11	1962	1,525
940	14	1963	1,630
941	12	1964	1,730
942	12	1965	2,025
943	13	1966	2,395
944	21	1967	2,600
945	58	1968	2,830
946	164	1969	2,995
947	246	1970	3,550
948	391	1971	4,500
949	477	1972	5,730
950	547	1973	7,345
951	760	1974	8,350
952	820	1975	6,970
953	840	1976	8,525
954	950	1977	9,235
955	970	1978	8,315
956	975	1979	9,555
957	985	1980	9,990
958	1,005	1981	9,985
959	1,000	1982	6,695
960	1,245	1983	5,330
961	1,390	1984	4,589
		1985	2,600[a]

ote: a. Estimates for first six months.
ources: *BP Statistical Review of the World Oil Industry* (various years) and .H. Longrigg, *Oil in the Middle East*, (Oxford University Press, London, 954).

mployment of Saudi Arabians in the army, the national guard and other gencies was an important vehicle for underpinning and sheltering the ountry from radical change. Traditional occupations in agriculture and erding were preserved in this way so that Saudi Arabia was still reporting no less than 70 per cent of its indigenous labour force in agriculture n 1960 and some 60 per cent in 1980.[14]

The balance between oil revenues and domestic development, mainained until 1973 by the existence of a viable oasis agriculture, subsidised astoralism, some state-sponsored industrialisation and the activities urrounding the annual ḥajj, was sharply broken in the aftermath of the il price 'shock' of October 1973. There was a marked increase in oil evenues flowing to the Saudi Arabian exchequer (Table 7.2), which reated an acute discontinuity in economic and, by implication, social ffairs.

Conventional national accounting suggests that between 1973/4 and 979/80 the non-oil sector as a whole had actually increased its contribuion to national output from about 27 per cent to 38 per cent. During

Table 7.2: Saudi Arabia — Oil Revenues ($mn)

1940	1.5	1976	30,754.9
1950	56.7	1977	36,538.4
1960	333.7	1978	32,233.8
1965	664.1	1979	57,522.0
1966	789.9	1980	102,212.0
1967	903.6	1981	113,200.0
1968	926.4	1982	76,000.0
1969	949.2	1983	47,600.0
1970	1,214.0	1984	57,900.0[a]
1971	1,884.8	1985	38,700.0[a]
1972	2,744.6		
1973	4,340.0		
1974	22,573.5		
1975	25,675.8		

Note: a. Estimates.
Sources: *OPEC Annual Statistical Bulletin* (various years) and Yusif A. Sayigh, *The Economies of the Arab World*, (Croom Helm, London, 1978), p. 144.

the same period, productive activities such as agriculture, manufacturing industry and construction were also calculated to have enhanced their position from 11 per cent to 16 per cent of output.[15] Such an analysis might be considered profoundly misleading.[16] It is more realistic to look at the Saudi Arabian economic structure in the light of the full effects of the oil industry on it and to compute the changing roles of the oil and non-oil sectors, respectively, on this basis. In such an analysis it can be seen that the Saudi Arabian economy, far from maturing by way of diversification away from hydrocarbons and growth of real output in other productive sectors, has become even more oil-dependent since 1973 than it was previously. In 1980, approximately 70 per cent of the Gross Domestic Product of the country was generated by oil against 50 per cent in 1970, according to the calculations of Stauffer and Lennox.[17]

The Government of Saudi Arabia has made strenuous efforts to diminish its dependence on oil. Few major oil-exporting states have undertaken so expensive and thorough a programme of industrialisation as Saudi Arabia,[18] except possibly for Iran in the late 1960s and early 1970s. But as both Stevens[19] and Barker[20] have pointed out, industrialisation is surrounded with problems of raising the value to Saudi Arabia of its hydrocarbon exports and creating linkages between the new sector and the rest of the local economy. There is an ultimate irony, too, that industrialisation of the kind pursued by Saudi Arabia was principally hydrocarbon-based and therefore heightened rather than reduced the state's dependence on the oil sector.

In so far as the country seems destined to remain reliant on oil, with all the connotations that has, it is inevitable that the economy will stay heavily skewed towards the primary sector. A secondary measure of Saudi Arabia's lack of economic diversity and immaturity is its labour force. The Saudi section of the labour force is small, amounting to 1.56 million in 1984/5.[21] The work force as a whole (including non-Saudi Arabians) is also overwhelmingly concentrated in agriculture (24 per cent), community and social services (20 per cent), public administration (13 per cent) and other sectors reliant for funding on the oil-based economy. Only 4.2 per cent of all workers are in manufacturing industry and most of them are foreign workers. The effects of easy access by most Saudi Arabian nationals to comfortable employment of a sinecure kind have been augmented since 1973 by an increasing proportion of Saudi Arabians who do not participate in paid economic activity at all. Even the most favourable of economic commentators has pointed out that the trend in the 1980s was towards a lower male Saudi Arabian participation rate in the work force,[22] while female participation is virtually negligible at slightly over 100,000 persons. At the most conservative estimate[23] foreigners comprised some 43 per cent of the total labour force in 1984/5. These characteristics, together with considerations of low skills and moderate health standards among Saudis, underline the reliance by the country on oil revenues and the poverty of real domestic labour resources. In such circumstances the 'maturity' of the economy and of the state as a whole must be questioned.

Modernisation and the Saudi Arabian Social Structure

The great strength of the social structure of the country lies in its tribal system. But, as in many other states of the region,[24] tribes are looked upon as a mixed blessing by rulers bent on consolidating the role of the central government and modernising the national economy.[25] The cohesion of tribal organisations has been eroded gradually since the turn of the century by a number of important pressures. The Ikhwān warrior forces that were formed to extend the frontiers of Wahhabism were non-tribal. They operated altogether outside the established system and were in many ways destructive of the weaker tribal groups with which they came into opposition during the early decades of the twentieth century.[26] In effect, while the Wahhābī movement underpinned the family and tribal position of the Saudis, it tended to diminish the importance of other tribal units within the Peninsula.

In the period since the consolidation of the Saudi Arabian state by Ibn Su'ūd two influences have worked towards diminishing tribal institutions. First, there is evidence that the central authorities have deliberately attempted to enhance their own positions at the direct expense of the tribes and that official policies for rural development have been designed to accelerate detribalisation. Second, and perhaps far more effective than the specific policies for the dismantling of tribal organisations, has been the increasingly fierce adverse impact of oil-sponsored development activities on the economic base of the tribes.

Motivations for the Saudi Arabian Government to undertake policies for diminishing the power of the tribes are disputed. Wagstaff[27] suggests the view that the tribes of Saudi Arabia were challenged because the nomadic way of life was not compatible with the demands of Islam. Another argument is that the tribes were an obstacle to the management of the regions by the central government and that agricultural policies were used to destroy pastoralism as a means, ultimately, of eliminating the tribal system.[28] Certainly, the political motivation in Saudi Arabia for reducing the authority of the tribes was powerful. Ibn Su'ūd was well aware of the route to power that he himself had taken, an important component of which was manipulating tribal alliances, buying influence among tribal leaders, and creating marriage links with other clan chiefs. Survival of the House of Su'ūd depended on the twin policies of retaining the loyalty of the principal tribal notables while simultaneously removing their institutional power bases. Creation of Ikhwān *hujar* or settlements of Wahhābī warriors, of which some 200 were set up between 1912 and 1932, was a step in this process,[29] later made more universal through government-financed bedouin settlement schemes throughout the Kingdom. By the 1960s the position of the House of Su'ūd was so strong that even a weak monarch (King Su'ūd) gave no opening for serious tribal dissent against its rule.

In addition to the conflict between the Su'ūd dynasty and the continued existence of autonomous tribal groups, there was an inexorable need for the Saudi state to impose its control on tribes and tribal confederations that overlapped national frontiers. Embarrassing border skirmishes with the British in Iraq and the Government of Transjordan in the early 1920s put into question the integrity of the state and its ability to abide by international agreements. Cross-border raiding and even alliances by tribes that disregarded the frontiers of modern states were too damaging for the new Saudi Arabian Government to contemplate. In 1925 the authorities annulled all tribal rights to raiding and movements across ational frontiers. The bedouin have taken many years to come to terms vith the concept of fixed-line national boundaries. As late as the mid-980s Saudi Arabian herders felt able to move between the desert pastures n Saudi Arabia and Kuwait, apparently still able to disregard factors f nationality and the apparatus of the modern state.[30] It is indicative f the change in Saudi Arabia during the course of the twentieth century nat the comings and goings of the bedouin noted by observers in Kuwait ave become incongruous and anachronistic in the fifty years following ne first unification of the tribes of the Peninsula within the Saudi state.

The direct effects of agricultural development on the tribal system vere remarkable. Legislation in 1925 noted above, and in many ways nerely a confirmation of the Ottoman Land Codes of the mid-nineteenth entury, began the process of moving ownership of land and water esources from the domain of the tribal community to the individual. n practice, men no longer needed to remain within a system in which and was owned jointly by the tribal members and allocated on criteria f communal requirements. Private rights in land and water were nevitably at the expense of the tribe. This was underscored by new laws assed in 1953 (Rangeland Decree) and 1968 (Public Land Distribution)rdinance) which opened up rangelands for general as opposed to tribal se and liberated the individual in respect of commercial transactions n land and water holdings, respectively.[31]

A further strand of agricultural policy that undermined tribal strength vas the sedentarisation programme. Aided by ARAMCO, the state has ought to set up new agricultural settlement schemes using irrigation. uch projects were intended to be settled by the bedouin but, despite fficial optimism, those bedouin who took up places on the agricultural states retained both their herds and their mobility. Yet land allotment vas successful in weakening tribal authority, since each settler increased is and his family's economic independence from the tribe even if astoralism as such was not abandoned.

Conscious efforts by the government to reduce the influence of tribal uthority were complemented by unplanned pressures of economic hange that affected all parts of Saudi Arabian society, whether urban r rural, sedentary or pastoral. Among the most damaging factors was mployment with the government. Development and other activity timulated by oil wealth created considerable demand for labour. Rural reas provided a portion of the supply and by 1977 it was reported that pproximately one-third of bedouin families had at least one of their umber working for the government.[32] Taken together with the many pportunities for work with foreign companies and the indigenous private sector, government employment drew tribal peoples to temporary o permanent residence outside their traditional areas and severed thei economic dependence on the functioning of the tribe. This form of chang was particularly powerful during the 1970s and early 1980s under th influence of growing state expenditures through the development plans

The Saudi Arabian social structure was forced into change from on essentially tribally-based in pastoralism within traditional territories t one located in urban areas and detribalised, notably since the beginnin of the era of high oil revenues. But the alteration in Saudi attitudes wa less radical than might be supposed. If the tribe has lost importance the extended family has not. Kinship links are maintained in what is carry-over of tribal *mores*, where intermarriage is controlled to sustai family integrity and reputation. Patronage and clientship are articulate through the extended family or tribal linkages. The geographical patter of the former family-tribal system has been difficult to destroy. It i estimated that approximately a third of all Saudi Arabians live withi their tribal territories and that up to one-quarter of the bedouin are sti engaged in agricultural pursuits for part if not all of the year.

It is argued with some merit that Saudi Arabian society is increas ingly tribal, in so far as the indigenous population has to struggle wit the establishment of a new identity in the face of incursions by foreigner that make up the backbone of the private sector work force. In this situa tion, it becomes less important which tribe a Saudi Arabian is from tha that he is of provable tribal connection within the Kingdom.[33] Kuwait which had to face problems of social identity earlier than Saudi Arabia set a similar pattern of attitudes and dress to differentiate Kuwaitis fron non-Kuwaitis. In Kuwait, however, social and intertribal difference between Kuwaitis themselves did not die out and there is reason to believ that the Saudi Arabians will follow the same course.

The loss of the rural nomadic areas of the state has been the gain o the urban areas. Estimates suggest that some 70 per cent of the Saud Arabian population was resident in urban areas in 1981.[34] The enor mous social stresses that have arisen from rapid urbanisation in citie that were less than ideally planned are well documented.[35] Th difficulties of bedouin settlement in towns are equally argued extensivel in the literature.

Cognisance of the great strides forward that have been made in th social field in Saudi Arabia can be made, especially in the field of materia provision.[36] Construction of schools, hospitals, clinics and an immens range of facilities was undertaken at great speed during the 1970s an early 1980s. Progress in making gains in standards of health and educatio amongst the Saudi Arabians was less dramatic. Life expectancy averaged some 55 years for the population as a whole in the early 1980s. Only the People's Democratic Republic of Yemen, the Yemen Arab Republic and Sudan were worse placed in the Arab world. Adult literacy rates in Saudi Arabia remained abysmally low at 25 per cent, albeit much improved on 20 years earlier. In real terms, the country made rapid improvements in areas of human welfare but stayed relatively in the lowest international rank. Oil income singularly failed to buy those improvements in human conditions that are not susceptible to instant cures. The dichotomy between material wealth and physical facilities *vis à vis* the low educational and health status of a large proportion of the Saudi Arabian people was a constant source of social friction both among the Saudi Arabians themselves and between Saudis and better-educated foreigners whom they employed.

In all, the country has undergone tremendous change in its social character, especially when measured by numbers of hospitals and schools, by the degree of urbanisation and by the level of peace and security enjoyed by its detribalised subjects. Yet changes are more apparent than real and were made on so low a base as to leave the nation in a state of social flux but far from achieving maturity in either demographic[37] or structural contexts.[38]

Conclusions

Saudi Arabia is a very recent creation as a sovereign state. It has been shown in this discussion that Saudi Arabia emerged from a politically fissiparous region with poor potential for unification. That it achieved nationhood at all must be regarded as a considerable achievement, mainly to the credit of Ibn Su'ūd and his close supporters. Centralisation of the state continued with few interruptions and may be deemed to be the causative factor behind much of what is done in the name of security, defence or economic development. The present organisation of provincial areas, which has witnessed the gradual elimination of tribal influence in the factional sense,[39] together with appointment of regional governors not representative of local tribal interests, has taken much of the power from tribal leaders other than those of the House of Su'ūd. Indeed, both in the provinces and at the centre of power, the large Su'ūd family has systematically kept all lines of authority closely within its grasp. Political evolution towards a recognisable form of 'constitutional monarchy' has been negligible, though continuing liaison with major families, religious leaders and technocrats by the ruling group has given a unique indigenous means of achieving a limited political consensus.

International recognition of Saudi Arabia is universal. Despite boundary disputes with its neighbours, lack of a fulfilling role in inter-Arab politics and the threat of political instability arising from the Gulf War, the Kingdom has retained its territorial integrity. The special role as keeper of the Islamic holy places, growing internal defence capability and close underwriting from the USA appear to have given the country an element of immunity from the more dangerous pressures acting against its interests.

Trends in social and economic development have not led to the Kingdom taking on mature structures. On the contrary, clear evidence has been given that oil wealth has created growing dependence on oil exports, external supplies of goods and use of foreign labour. At the same time, social change, though rapid in its external forms, has not yet lifted health and educational standards to international norms. Saudi Arabian society has become much divided by the impact of high levels of spending on development activity, and there are no obvious solutions emerging from within the country itself to the problems of social alienation. With society in such uncertain flux and population numbers rapidly increasing, the country cannot be thought of as having established mature (albeit constantly developing) demographic or social forms.

It might be concluded, therefore, that evolution of the country from traditional to modern society is far from being completed. Much of the cause for Saudi Arabia's low status in this respect can be found in the inherently minimal levels of material welfare at the time the unitary state was declared. The very nature of Saudi Arabia as an oil producer has led its economy to be profoundly skewed as a result of the speed of induced growth and the structural dependence on a single export commodity. Long-term improvements might be made to solve the problems of the quality of human resources, given patience and skill. Cures for the economic and political imbalances brought on by the dominance of oil within the state might be less easily prescribed.

Notes

1. Peter Mansfield in his book *The Arabs*, Revised edn., (Penguin Books, London, 1978), p. 400, partly with ironic intent no doubt, characterises Saudi Arabia as a 'Financial Superpower'. Any analogies with Switzerland, the United Kingdom or the USA in this context must, however, be treated as polite hyperbole.

2. J.G.P.M. Benoist-Méchin, *Ibn-Séoud; ou la Naissance d'un Royaume*, (Livre de

oche, Paris, 1955).

3. William C. Brice, *South-West Asia*, (London University Press, London, 1966), p. 392–6.

4. Willard A. Beling, *King Faisal and the Modernisation of Saudi Arabia*, (London, 'room Helm, 1980), pp. 184–98.

5. Iranian antagonism was articulated, among other means, by politicisation of Iranian ilgrim groups visiting Saudi Arabia during the *ḥajj*. Iranians were encouraged by their overnment to use the ḥajj to proselytise among other visiting nationalities and to voice pecific revolutionary demands that conflicted with the Saudi Arabian political position. he conflict was manifested in radio exchanges between the two sides (see *Survey of World roadcasts*, 30 July 1985, ME/8016/A77).

6. Anthony H. Cordesman, *The Gulf and the Search for Strategic Stability*, Westview/Mansell, Boulder/London, 1984), p. 57.

7. Helen Lackner, *A House Built on Sand: A Political Economy of Saudi Arabia*, Ithaca Press, London, 1978), pp. 131–4.

8. John Bulloch, *The Gulf* (Century Publishing, London, 1984), pp. 67–8.

9. Michael M.J. Fischer, 'Competing Ideologies and Social Structure in the Persian ulf' in A.J. Cottrell (ed.), *The Persian Gulf States*, (Johns Hopkins University Press, altimore, 1980), pp. 517–18.

10. During the conquests of the Ḥijāz, for example, the Ikhwān were reputed to have laughtered more than 300 persons after the surrender of Ṭā'if in 1923.

11. A.D. Drysdale and G. Blake, *The Middle East and North Africa: A Political eography*, (Oxford University Press, New York, 1986), Chapter 7.

12. Stephen H. Longrigg and James Jankowski, *The Middle East: A Social Geography*, evised edn., (Duckworth, London, 1970), pp. 154–5.

13. Wolfgang Schuster, *Wirtschaftsgeographie Saudi Arabien mit besonderer erucksichtigung der staatlichen Wirtschatslenkung* (VWGO, Vienna, 1979), pp. 184–98.

14. Of total civilian employment, including all foreign labour, agriculture took 40 per ent in 1974/5 and was expected to drop to 24 per cent in the year 1984/5 according to IERIP, *Saudi Arabia*, (University of Pennsylvania/Croom Helm, London, 1985), p. 178.

15. Ministry of Planning, *The Third Development Plan*, (Saudi Arabia, AH 1400/AD 979), p. 28.

16. T. Stauffer and F.H. Lennox, *Accounting for "Wasting Assets"*, (OPEC, Vienna, 984), pp. 37–42.

17. Ibid., p. 37.

18. Ragaei El Mallakh, *Saudi Arabia: Rush to Development*, (Croom Helm, London, 982), pp. 105–10.

19. Paul Stevens, 'Saudi Arabia's Oil Policy in the 1970s' in Tim Niblock (ed.), *State, ociety and Economy in Saudi Arabia*, (Croom Helm, London, 1982), pp. 214–34.

20. Paul Barker, *Saudi Arabia: The Development Dilemma*, (EIU, London, 1982), p. 63.

21. MERIP, *Saudi Arabia*, p. 179.

22. John R. Presley, *A Guide to the Saudi Arabian Economy*, (Macmillan, London, 984), p. 46.

23. Ministry of Planning, *The Third Development Plan*, (Saudi Arabia, AH 1400/AD 979).

24. R. Tapper (ed.), *The Conflict of Tribe and State in Iran and Afghanistan*, (Croom Ielm/St Martin's, London/New York, 1983), pp. 26–31.

25. B.D. Clarke, 'Tribes of the Persian Gulf' in A.J. Cottrell (ed.), *The Persian Gulf tates*, (Johns Hopkins University Press, Baltimore, 1980), p. 494.

26. British Admiralty, *Western Arabia and the Red Sea*, Geographical Handbook Series, Admiralty, Naval Intelligence Division, London, 1946), p. 396.

27. J.M. Wagstaff, *The Evolution of Middle Eastern Landscapes*, (Croom Helm, ondon, 1985), p. 258.

28. Barker, *The Development Dilemma*, p. 51.

29. Christine Moss Helms, *The Cohesion of Saudi Arabia*, (Croom Helm, London 1981), pp. 135–42.

30. A.A.S. Al-Moosa, 'The Bedawin Shanty Settlements in Kuwait', unpublished Ph Thesis, University of London, 1976, Chapter 1.

31. See Hassan Hamza Hajrah, *Public Land Distribution in Saudi Arabia*, (Longman London, 1982) for a discussion of the benign effects of land allotment policies.

32. P. Cole, 'Pastoral Nomads in a Rapidly Changing Economy: The Case of Saud Arabia' in Tim Niblock (ed.), *Social and Economic Development in the Arab Gulf*, (Croon Helm, London, 1980), p. 111.

33. Ibid., p. 118.

34. IBRD, *World Development Report*, (Oxford University Press, London, 1984), p 191.

35. N.C. Grill, *Urbanisation in the Arabian Peninsula*, University of Durham, Occa sional Papers Series No. 25 (University of Durham, Durham, 1984), pp. 62–80.

36. Presley, *A Guide to the Saudi Arabian Economy*, p. 115.

37. R. McGregor, 'Saudi Arabia: Population and the Making of a Modern State' i J.I. Clarke and W.B. Fisher (eds), *Populations of the Middle East and North Africa*, (Univer sity of London Press, London, 1972), pp. 235–9.

38. For an educated view of social realities in the Arab states of the Gulf see Gle Balfour-Paul, 'The Impact of Development on Gulf Society' in M.S. El Azhary (ed.) *The Impact of Oil Revenues on Arab Gulf Development*, (Croom Helm, London, 1984) pp. 185–96.

39. Nassir A. Saleh, 'Provincial and District Delimitation in the Kingdom of Saud Arabia' in J.I. Clarke and H. Bowen-Jones (eds), *Change and Development in the Middl East*, (Methuen, London, 1981), p. 316.

8 Hashemite Iraq and Pahlavī Iran

Anthony Parsons

I have not written this chapter as a scholarly analysis of the rise and fall of the Hashemite dynasty in Iraq and the Pahlavī dynasty in Iran. A great deal has already been written about the former and the collapse of the latter is still too close in time to lend itself to academic treatment. I served in both countries as a diplomat — in Iraq in the 1950s and in Iran in the 1970s — and have since reflected on those features of both regimes which contributed first to their apparent stability and continuity and finally to their downfall. My observations and conclusions are therefore very much those of an individual, one who was enabled to study both countries from the relatively limited standpoint of a government official.

By way of introduction, it is ironical that Iran and Iraq, which have so much in common, should find themselves engaged in a long and costly war. Both countries have disparate populations comprising large ethnic and sectarian minorities. Both countries had a long tradition of absolutist, monarchical rule stretching back in the case of Iraq to the 'Abbāsid Caliphate; in the case of Iran, if the Pahlavī version is accepted, for 2,500 years. Both countries were heavily exposed to European domination in the first half of the twentieth century. Iran was the first Middle Eastern state in which oil was discovered in commercial quantities, Iraq the second. The holiest shrines of the Shi'ite sect are in Iraq, with many more in Iran in cities such as Mashhad, Qumm and Shīrāz. The security and freedom of passage through the Arab Gulf is a vital interest both of Baghdad and Tehran.

And yet the historical rivalry between the two states, which, in modern times, dates back to the sixteenth century period of Ottoman expansionism and the reaction to this phenomenon of the Safavid Shāh, has persisted to the present day, culminating, after the fall of the respective monarchies, in an armed conflict far bloodier and more damaging to both sides than any of the wars and battles of their joint past.

Hashemite Iraq

There are now 160 states which are members of the United Nations. Of these 90 are in Africa and Asia. The majority of these states, especially in Africa and Western Asia, were originally artificial creations of outside powers, their frontiers owing more to inter-play between Western imperialists than to intrinsic evolution based on ethnic, cultural or political homogeneity. Against this background, it is remarkable that so few of these newly independent entities have fragmented in the post-independence period and that the overwhelming majority increasingly demonstrate the characteristics of established nations. Modern Iraq is a case in point. To some extent the state conformed to the pattern of an ancient geographical expression of the same name, but its boundaries were based on an assembly of three former Ottoman provinces — Mosul, Baghdad and Baṣra — reflecting Anglo-French agreement on the distribution of respective spheres of Middle Eastern interests following the collapse of the Ottoman Empire in 1918. Ethnically and from the sectarian viewpoint Iraq could hardly have contained more disparate elements, with Kurds, Turks and Turcomans in the north, not to mention other, non-Muslim, minorities, Sunnī Arabs in the centre and Shi'ite Arabs in the south.

In the first 30 years of its existence, a number of internal and external factors helped to maintain Iraq's unity and integrity. In the 1920s Republican Turkey recognised an international award on the northern frontier between the two states, thus removing a potential threat to the province of Mosul, including the oil-bearing area. In the south-west, Britain helped to ward off Wahhābī raiders from the Arabian Peninsula. To the west, Syrian foreign policy was under the control of the French mandatory power and relations between Iraq and Transjordan were tranquil owing to the fact that the respective rulers were full brothers. To the east, Iran, following the collapse of the Qājār dynasty and the accession to power of Riżā Shāh Pahlavī, was too weak and too preoccupied with national rehabilitation to offer a threat.

Internally the safeguards were more precarious and the country owed much to the prestige and diplomatic skill of King Fayṣal I. Although lacking direct connections with any of the geographical or tribal components of modern Iraq, and in spite of his more or less accidental accession to the throne — the original plan having been that Fayṣal should be King in Damascus and 'Abdullāh (of Transjordan) King in Baghdad — Fayṣal demonstrated considerable statesmanship in negotiating full independence from the British and in reconciling the disparate elements in his own country. He was helped by the reputation he brought with him as the main military and political leader of the Arab Revolt and also by the resolution and political adroitness of the group of ex-Ottoman officers who constituted the nucleus of governmental leadership. Even so, the new state had a difficult passage and King Fayṣal's premature death in 1933, only a year after Iraq had been unanimously admitted to membership of the League of Nations, was a blow to stability.

In the 1920s a national army had been created with British assistance, which undoubtedly played an important part, and was to do so again, in maintaining the unity of the state. However, with King Fayṣal's dominant and restraining presence removed, it was not long before the army developed the habit of intervention in domestic politics. In his book *Independent Iraq* (Oxford University Press, 1951), Majid Khadduri identifies no less than seven military *coups d'état* between 1936 (General Bakr Ṣidqī) and 1941 (Rashīd 'Ālī and General Amīn Zakī). Contemporary commentators tend to overlook the fact that this politicisation of the Iraqi officer corps long ante-dated the period after the Second World War during which, especially in the years between 1947 and 1970, this phenomenon became such a commonplace throughout the Arab world.

By the time I joined the staff of the British Embassy in Baghdad at the turn of the year 1951/52, Iraq's fortunes appeared to be in the ascendant. For ten years, with the exception of the riots which had wrecked a new draft treaty (the Portsmouth Treaty) tentatively concluded with Britain in 1948, the country had experienced internal tranquillity. The Regent, Prince 'Abdulilāh (King Fayṣal II was still at school at Harrow) and the coterie of politicians led by Nūrī Pasha Sa'īd, who had shared power since the creation of the state, seemed to have the domestic situation under control. And the economy was beginning to take off. Iraq was the first Arab state in which oil had been discovered — in 1927 — and, by the 1950s, particularly with the temporary loss to the international market of Iranian crude following Dr Muḥammad Muṣaddiq's nationalisation of the Anglo-Iranian Oil Company in 1951, Iraqi production was rising to a level sufficient to generate enough revenue to finance a major programme of economic and social development. The Army, which had acquitted itself far from discreditably in the Arab-Israeli wars of 1948–49, seemed to have lost its taste for politics. In the region, Iraq was emerging as a leading Arab power. Jordan and Lebanon were too small to compete; Syria was racked by post-independence military *coups*; Egypt in the last days of the monarchy had yet to realise its pan-Arab potential; Saudi Arabia and the Mutawakkilite Kingdom of the Yemen were introverted and withdrawn; the remainder of the Arab world was still under European rule or protection. To the superficial observer, Iraq was on the way to becoming a stable, modernised, influential regional power, certainly far in advance of neighbouring Iran.

And yet a serious malaise infected the country. The constitution, a curious amalgam of Ottoman theory and British practice, had failed to secure the loyalty of the people. Elections were regularly held but they were widely regarded with contempt and anger as a fraud, a convenient means of rewarding loyalty and strengthening support for the unchanging political coterie. The parliament was an elaborate sham and was seen as such. Cabinet changes were frequent but they did not introduce new blood. The same old faces appeared in different guises. 'If you have a small pack of cards, you must shuffle it frequently', as Nūrī Pasha used to say. The Iraqi people, traditionally submissive to strong leadership, respected the old Pasha even if they did not love him: for the Regent there was widespread dislike. Etiolated, epicene and pleasure-loving, Prince 'Abdulilāh was the antithesis of a popular leader, nor did he possess the diplomatic skills of his uncle, King Fayṣal I. Iraq's foreign policy alignment had many opponents, especially amongst the younger and newly educated generation. The British connection, once a political asset, was becoming a liability. Britain was perceived by the Iraqi youth not only as a fading 'imperialistic' power which was maintaining their country in a state of tutelage humiliating to an independent state, but also as the betrayer of the Palestine cause and the sponsor of Zionism in the Middle East. The existence of an Anglo-Iraqi Treaty, the presence of British Royal Air Force bases, the ubiquitousness of the British presence and influence, the evidence of the almost symbiotic relationship between Britain and their own rulers, were all sources of growing dissent.

Nor was the government succeeding in outdistancing political discontent through the positive benefits of economic progress. The Development Board was investing the oil revenues in infrastructural projects, mainly related to communications, flood control and irrigation. The fruits of these programmes would be harvested in the long term: meanwhile, there were few eye-catching schemes such as low-cost housing and educational expansion (in 1954 there was no university in the old capital of the 'Abbāsid Empire) which would have attracted popular support. The sceptical citizens of Baghdad were disposed to conclude that the oil revenues were disappearing into the pockets of the pashas.

None of this would have been crucial if the people had possessed the means to bring about change, or at least to influence their rulers, by peaceful means. But, with the political system discredited, the only levers of change available were riot (as happened shortly after I arrived in 1952 when the Baghdad mob took over the city for a few days until the Army restored order) or military *coup*.

The Revolution in Egypt in 1952, which brought Jamāl 'Abd al-Nāṣir (Nasser) to power, intensified the problems facing the monarchy. The desire of many middle-ranking Iraqi officers to emulate the action of their Egyptian counterparts was palpable from the outset and the political temperature began to rise throughout the country. As the years passed the war cries of Nasserism — anti-imperialism, anti-Zionism, unfettered independence, positive neutrality and non-aligned Arab unity — found a ready echo everywhere in Iraq except amongst the political establishment. Particularly after the creation of the Baghdad Pact in 1955 polarised the Arab world into the 'Westerners' led by Iraq and the 'non-aligned' led by Egypt, and *a fortiori* after the Anglo-French invasion of Egypt in the autumn of 1956, the British connection became an increasingly divisive factor. Domestically the establishment still showed no sign of willingness to share power with the new generation and the brief hope kindled by the coronation of King Fayṣal II in 1953 was extinguished by the refusal of the Regent (now the Crown Prince only) to relinquish the real reins of power. By the late 1950s, although economic prosperity was unquestionably beginning to spread throughout the urban areas and the overall standard of living was rising, the regime was further than ever from securing that degree of popular support which would have deterred any group of men from attempting to overthrow it.

This fundamental fragility was conclusively demonstrated on 14 July 1958 when a handful of troops from the Armoured Brigade led by Brigadier 'Abd al-Karīm Qāsim bloodily swept away in a few hours the structure which had been built up over nearly 40 years. Not a hand, domestic or foreign, was raised in its defence. The Hashemite Kingdom had been destroyed, to be succeeded by a series of republican, socialist regimes.

Nearly 30 years after the event it is intriguing to reflect on the reasons why it was so easy for Brigadier Qāsim to destroy the monarchy in 1958 when it had survived no less than seven *coups d'état* in the 1930s and early 1940s, not to speak of other political vicissitudes. The first significant fact to be borne in mind is that the leaders of the previous military interventions had not attempted to change the constitution of Iraq from monarchy to republic. Indeed, when Prince 'Abdulilāh fled the country in 1941 following the Rashīd 'Ālī *coup*, the latter, so far from proclaiming a republic, moved via the parliament to appoint Sharīf Sharaf, another Hashemite prince, as Regent in his place. The fashion for republicanism had yet to make itself felt in the Middle East. Apart from Turkey and French-influenced Syria and Lebanon, all Middle East states at the time were monarchies. Hence, until 1958 the military *coup d'état* had been used in Iraq as an instrument of political change only, falling short of revolution.

In 1958, the situation was radically different. Nasser had led a movement of socialist, secular, Pan-Arab republicanism which, through propaganda and example, had aroused the people of many Arab states, especially the urban masses and the younger generation, to oppose their traditionalist regimes. In Saudi Arabia and the Gulf states, in Libya and Morocco, above all in Jordan and Iraq, Arab monarchies were embattled and on the defensive. The question being asked by domestic and foreign analysts was not whether the monarchies were likely to evolve and change in the face of new political, economic and social pressures, but simply whether they would survive; even when, not if, the equivalents of the Egyptian Free Officers of 1952 would strike against their respective kings.

In order to have a reasonable chance of survival in the hectic atmosphere of the period 1952–67 (after the June War of 1967 the Nasserist tide ebbed quickly), regimes, particularly if they carried the stigma of close association with Western 'imperialism', needed to possess certain qualities. The morale of their armed forces had to be high and their loyalty assured. These could be achieved by a combination of good pay and terms of service with high social prestige and/or intrinsic ties of allegiance to the national leadership, also satisfaction with national foreign policy, especially towards the Great Powers and the Palestine cause. These conditions, which existed to a great extent in Hashemite Jordan, were almost totally lacking in Hashemite Iraq. Moreover, the political leadership, in the absence of a dominant personality such as King 'Abd al-Azīz ibn Su'ūd or King Fayṣal I, needed to have traditional links with influential elements in the population.

This factor was present in Saudi Arabia where strong Najdī tribes had owed allegiance to the Āl Su'ūd for nearly 200 years; similar loyalties existed in many of the smaller states of the Gulf. There were no analogous ties in Iraq either with the monarchy or with the leading politicians. Economically, vast wealth in relation to size of population could, as in Kuwait, bury dissent under mountains of gold. Iraq's income from oil revenues, although substantial, was sufficient only to promote a slow improvement in what had been a very low general standard of living. Ideologically, the pervasive security and political structures associated with totalitarian creeds, such as Communism, Fascism or Ba'thism, could and still do provide powerful protection against the development of dangerous currents of dissent into open rebellion. Hashemite Iraq was no model democracy and opponents of the regime could expect harsh treatment, but the security apparatus was not highly organised and there was no positive ideology in the name of which the people could be dragooned, mobilised and at the same time closely watched.

Hence, the only strengths in the Iraqi regime lay in the political skills of the leadership in conciliating and balancing the various factions in the country, the Shi'ite south, the Sunnī Arab centre and the Kurdish north, together with the tribal and semi-tribal groupings. Nūrī Sa'īd and his colleagues had richly demonstrated such skills over a period of nearly 40 years and had succeeded in laying the foundations of a modern, unitary state. But they were getting old and complacent and the tide of regional history was flowing strongly against them. A number of factors combined to precipitate the explosion of 14 July 1958. For some time the armed forces, and the country as a whole, had been disaffected at the failure of the monarchy to censure, not to speak of following the example of other Arab states and breaking with, Britain, the partner of Israel and France in the 'Tripartite Aggression' against Egypt in October-November 1956. At the same time the armed forces, far from being a pampered element in Iraqi society, were looking with envy at the enhanced status of their counterparts in the Arab states — the United Arab Republic of Egypt and Syria — who had seized power and freed their countries from the constraints of old-fashioned association with Western European powers. The alignment of the monarchy with President Chamoun of Lebanon against the Lebanese forces of Arab nationalism in the civil war of 1958 added fuel to the flames. The general intoxication with the fumes of Nasserist inspiration provided an atmosphere in which only the opportunity was lacking. This came when the regime lowered its guard and, contrary to practice established since 1941, allowed units of the Armoured Brigade, then in garrison at Khānaqīn near the Iranian border, to pass through the capital with their arms and equipment, en route for Lebanon. The conspirators struck and, with the murder of the King and Crown Prince and the death by his own hand of Nūrī Pasha, the shallowness of the roots of the monarchical regime was quickly and cruelly exposed.

Pahlavī Iran

On the face of it, Iran should have been better placed than all other Middle

Eastern countries to surmount the challenges of modernisation in the conditions of the twentieth century. It was one of a very small handful of Asian states which had avoided absorption by European imperialism in the nineteenth century. Its monarchical system of government had shown considerable stability: with the exception of a chaotic period in the eighteenth century, Iran had been ruled by only two successive dynasties — Safavid and Qājār — since it re-emerged from Islamic medievalism as a nation state in the sixteenth century. In 1906, after considerable travail, the Shāh's more or less absolute rule had been modified by the introduction of a constitution which combined democratic principles with Islamic Shi'ite tradition. In 1908 the first discovery of Middle Eastern oil in commercial quantities was made in south-west Iran. By remaining neutral in the First World War, Iran had avoided the casualties and damage suffered by the Asiatic provinces of the Ottoman Empire and, by 1918, its historical Ottoman rival had been dismembered by the peace settlement, leaving Iran as the only fully sovereign independent state in the region.

However, as is so often the case in matters concerning Iran, the reality behind the facade was very different. The political and military weakness of the later Qājār Shāhs, combined with endemic financial problems, had so debilitated central authority that Iran was not only helpless in the face of British and Tsarist demands — its independence little more than a shadow — but Tehran had effectively lost control of the outlying provinces. By the early twentieth century, the armed forces of the state had declined to impotence and the only operational military formations were the Russian-officered Persian Cossacks in the north and the British-officered South Persia Rifles in the south. The 1906 Constitution had been frustrated by the reluctance of the Shāh to relinquish power. The Anglo-Persian Oil Company was more concerned with negotiating with local Bakhtiyārī and Arab chieftains than with the government of Tehran. Iran's neutrality in the First World War had failed to prevent frequent violations of its territory by the belligerents. At the close of the War, Iran was in a state of virtual collapse with a new threat — from Soviet-sponsored Bolshevik forces — developing in its northern areas.

In 1921, Colonel Rizā Khān of the Cossacks marched on Tehran. After a period as Minister of War and then as Prime Minister — Aḥmad Shāh Qājār had in the meantime left for Europe, never to return — he was crowned as Rizā Shāh Pahlavī in April 1926.

Rizā Shāh set in motion the first Iranian Revolution and drove it forward by sheer force of personality and ruthless power until he was obliged to abdicate following the British and Soviet occupation of Iran in 1941. He had no ideological creed and was not even an avowed monarchist: his original intention was to be President of an Iranian Republic until he was persuaded by the religious hierarchy to maintain the monarchy. His hero was Muṣṭafā Kemāl Atatürk and his objective was to restore central authority, to make Iran independent of foreign domination and to modernise and industrialise the fragmented pastoral and agricultural economy of the country. Given the condition of Iran at the time, this was indeed a revolutionary programme.

Riżā Shāh achieved much in the short time available to him. He created a strong army and gendarmerie with which he brought to heel the overmighty tribal and feudal barons. He opened up modern communications by driving the Trans-Iranian railway from the Caspian Sea to the Arab Gulf. He invoked the United States and Germany to balance British and Soviet pressure. He made a start on industrialisation and negotiated better terms with the oil company. He embarked on a plan of social reform by emancipating women, thus incurring the opposition of the religious leaders. And much more.

However, with Riżā Shāh's departure from the scene, the revolutionary momentum which he had created quickly dissipated. This was due not only to the confusion and disruption caused by foreign occupation in wartime, although this was an important factor. Riżā Shāh's regime had fundamental weaknesses. He had been able to seize power simply because he was an energetic officer in control of the only operationally effective military force in the area of the capital. He had no constitutional mandate to march on Tehran in 1921 nor did he have a popular mandate to lead the country as a national hero, as was the case with Atatürk, the man who had regenerated the Turkish army and nation after the collapse of the Empire, and driven all foreign forces from Turkish territory. Moreover, Riżā Shāh failed to create an ideology and a party organisation to go with it, as in the Soviet Union, which could have mobilised and rallied the people as a whole, thus forming an institutionalised dynamic which would be able to survive the disappearance of its originator. The virtually illiterate Riżā Shāh was not the man to formulate or codify his revolutionary programme into an Iranian equivalent of *Das Kapital* or *Mein Kampf*. He was a hard-driving, practical man, akin to one of the nineteenth-century South American *caudillos*, the main difference being that, having retained the monarchy, there was constitutional provision for his succcession. However, in practical terms, he had been the sole conductor of a more or less submissive but unenthusiastic Iranian orchestra: when the conductor left the stage the orchestra was disposed to revert to the fractious and unco-ordinated *modus operandi* to which it had been accustomed prior to his advent.

Riżā Shāh's successor, his son, Muḥammad Riżā Shāh Pahlavī, came to the throne in 1941 under heavy handicaps. He was only 22 years old and immediately had to function in an environment of experienced and wily politicians; he had grown up in the shadow of a fearsome and ferocious tyrant of a father; and his accession was seen by his people to have taken place under the guns of foreign occupying forces. The omens could scarcely have been less auspicious, particularly since his father's most important creation, the armed forces, had virtually collapsed in the face of the British-Soviet invasion.

For 20 years, Muḥammad Riżā Shāh, although not for want of trying, was unable to achieve the absolute authority enjoyed by his father: he was obliged to manoeuvre and to deploy the monarchy as a balance between different factions — political, religious and military — more or less as his Qājār predecessors had done in the years of Iran's weakness. Sometimes his star waned almost to extinction, as in the period of Dr Muḥammad Muṣaddiq's premiership and the nationalisation of the Anglo-Iranian Oil Company; sometimes he was in the ascendant, as on his return to Tehran after Muṣaddiq's downfall. All the time he was rebuilding the armed forces, constructing fresh foreign alliances, especially with the United States, and promoting economic and social development to the extent permitted by the limited state revenues from oil.

In the early 1960s the Shāh felt strong enough to seize untrammelled power and to launch the second Iranian Revolution. As with his father's programme nearly 40 years previously, the White Revolution of 1963 — later to be known as the Shāh/People Revolution — came from the top, not in response to popular or constitutional demands. However, unlike Riżā Shāh's first revolution, the Shāh/People Revolution was more than a radical programme of modernising reforms, the cornerstone being land reform. Muḥammad Riżā Shāh was possessed of an idealistic vision for his country, which was in due course characterised as the Great Civilisation. The closest analogy is perhaps with Mussolini's Italy. The Shāh saw Iran rising from the ashes of its Islamic past and recreating in a twentieth-century setting the glories of the Achaemenian and Sassanian Empires. Iran was to be a fully modernised, industrial state, with the people participating both in agricultural and industrial development and labour unions co-operating with state capital and private enterprise in the general endeavour. In a nutshell Iran would take its natural place alongside the world of Western Europe, the United States and Japan, the apotheosis of its Aryan origins (the Shāh duly assumed the title of Aryamehr — Light of the Aryans).

There was resistance in certain quarters to the first programme of reforms, promulgated in January 1963. The religious hierarchy, led by Ayatollah Khomeini, aroused opposition to land reform and to the full emancipation of women. The Qashqā'ī tribal chieftains mounted a rebellion. Both movements were forcibly crushed, Khomeini and the Qashā'ī Khāns were exiled, and the Shāh continued his drive forward, supported by a loyal cabinet of non-political, Western-educated technocrats and unhindered by an emasculated parliament.

During my five-year period (1974–79) as British Ambassador to Tehran I was able to observe the sky rocket of the Shāh's ambitions for his country reach the highest point in its trajectory; I was still in Iran when it fell to the ground with the departure of the Shāh and the consummation of the Third Iranian Revolution which brought Ayatollah Khomeini to power. For a short time it began to look as though the Shāh would succeed in leading Iran to a destination approximating to his notion of the Great Civilisation. The trebling of the posted price of crude oil at the end of 1973 — a consequence of the Arab-Israeli war of October 1973, and the Shāh's determination to realise the maximum benefit from Iran's principal natural resource — had removed for the first time since the foundation of the Pahlavī regime the constraint of financial stringency on economic and social development. The country boomed. Industries, services, financial institutions, the infrastructure, education, the armed forces were massively and arbitrarily expanded. A confused and hectic surge of activity flooded the country. A great deal was achieved in a short time but, when serious inflation and a fall in the real value of the oil revenues necessitated a policy of economic retrenchment two years later, the alarming dislocations and disruptions of the boom were clear. The ports and railways were choked; skilled manpower had proved grossly inadequate and huge numbers of foreigners had been brought in to meet this deficiency; there had been a massive influx of the rural population into the capital, creating grim problems of inadequate housing and social deprivation. The distribution system was overstrained and local shortages of foodstuffs and other supplies were commonplace. The scale of corruption in the Court and the government, and in the entrepreneurial class and bureaucracy, had become a scandal even to the tolerant Iranians. By the end of 1976 it was clear that the magnificent expectations aroused in the people by the deafening bombast of government propaganda would not be realised, at least in the foreseeable future. Iran fell into the grip of disillusionment and malaise: the government could find no means to regain the initiative.

None of this would necessarily have proved fatal to the regime. If, on the one hand, the Shāh had been a populist leader (as he believed himself to be) with magnetic personal appeal to the people as a whole, they might have stood by him in hard times as they supported him when the going was good. Such was the case with Nasser when his attempt to resign after the catastrophe of the June War of 1967 was massively and emotionally rejected. But the Shāh was no Nasser. Withdrawn, remote and autocratic, he was as out of touch with the real feelings of the people as they were with him. On the other hand, had he been able to co-opt the people through genuine participation in decision-making or through the creation of a political framework which could at the same time mobilise and monitor public opinion, he would have been in a stronger position first to anticipate serious manifestations of dissent and secondly to rally continuing support for his revolution. But all his attempts to build a valid political structure had failed. By the mid-1970s the multi-party system under the 1906 Constitution had degenerated into a charade. The Shāh's attempt to remedy this by creating a national Resurgence (*Rastakhīz*) Party in 1975 and simultaneously disbanding the existing parties was a fiasco.

Hence the strength of the Pahlavī regime rested solely on two pillars: first the unity and loyalty of the armed forces and the security services (SAVAK), and secondly on the Shāh's ability to satisfy the materialistic aspirations of the people, which his own propaganda had so strongly aroused. At the end of 1977 it was plain to those of us whose task it was to observe and to analyse the Iranian political scene that virtually all important sectors of the population were disaffected. The religious classes had long been alienated by the Shāh's glorification of Achaemenian and Sassanian Iran at the expense of its Islamic tradition, not to speak of certain aspects of his modernisation programme, in particular the increasing penetration of Iran by Western materialist culture. The bazaar merchants, still the backbone of the domestic economy, were apprehensive of their future in the light of the Shāh's encouragement of a modern industrial and financial sector which would ultimately prove fatal to their livelihood. The democratic political groups, including the majority of intellectuals, found unacceptable the Shāh's dictatorial rule and the ubiquitousness and cruelty of the security services. The radicals of the left and right were implacable and had been indulging in sporadic acts of terrorism for years. The principal beneficiaries of the Shāh/People Revolution — the rural peasantry, the workers in the modern industrial sector, and the bureaucratic, entrepreneurial and technocratic upper middle and moneyed classes — were either too scattered (the peasants), too few in number (the industrial workers) or too weakened by luxury (the new elite) to constitute an effective bulwark to the regime.

When, in January 1978, a foolish move on the part of the government — the publication of a newspaper article traducing the religious credentials and personal character of the exiled Ayatollah Khomeini — touched off a cycle of riot and civil disobedience, the regime had no political constituency with which to confront the religious leadership under whom all disaffected elements progressively united. The Shāh was driven to react by a combination of force and appeasement. The force, which took the form of firing on unarmed demonstrators, on occasions involving heavy civilian casualties, fuelled the ardour of the population and swelled the ranks of dissidence. The appeasement — sacking of unpopular Ministers, release of political prisoners, the abrogation of legislation offensive to Islam — whetted the popular appetite for more. In November, in response to a day of widespread arson in Tehran, the Shāh abandoned his attempts to construct a coalition of political moderates untainted by recent association with Pahlaviism, and appointed a military government. This was the signal for a national strike which paralysed the country and left the military power helpless. The morale and discipline of the armed forces declined and, by the time the Shāh left the country in January 1979, the forces of the revolution had taken over most of the provincial centres. A month later, only days after Ayatollah Khomeini's return to Tehran, the victory of the revolution was consummated and an Islamic Republic proclaimed. In retrospect, what was surprising was not that the regime collapsed but that it managed to hold out for 12 months without a split developing in the armed forces leading to a series of military *coups d'état* on the Iraqi model. The principal Pahlavī legacy to Iran — a strong and loyal military machine, created from virtually nothing — very nearly succeeded in preserving the rule of its Commander-in-Chief against the united weight of the civilian population, a rare phenomenon in the modern history of the Third World.

9 One Yemen or Two?

Michael Adams

In the south-west corner of Arabia, where the Red Sea meets the Indian Ocean, climate and geography combined to foster, at least 3,000 years ago, a distinctive pattern of civilisation. Scattered monuments, many of them as yet barely explored and of which the remains of the Ma'rib dam constitute the most remarkable, bear witness to the fact that this civilisation in its time had few rivals. Its foundation was trade, which linked Yemen with the centre of gravity of the ancient world in Mesopotamia and the eastern Mediterranean; but even its commercial partners in Egypt and Syria, in Babylon and Cyprus and Crete, knew little of its true nature. Living always on the periphery, the Yemen acquired a reputation which owed as much to legend as to fact.

The trade which made the Yemen rich was above all the trade in incense, a commodity in constant demand in the ancient world, with its preoccupation with death and the after-life, and of which southern Arabia possessed a virtual monopoly. To this, once its sailors had learned to take advantage of the monsoon winds and so were able to navigate the coast of East Africa and to sail eastward to India and beyond, the Yemen added other precious cargoes: ivory and slaves, silks and ebony and spices. This merchandise was mainly transported by camel trains, along with the incense, over what became one of the most celebrated — and remunerative — trade routes of the ancient world, linking the harbours of southern Arabia by a long and arduous overland route with Gaza and Tyre and Damascus. On the proceeds, a series of small states became wealthy and developed a life-style which was to endure with remarkable consistency through the centuries to come. The dominant state to emerge, in a variety of guises, was the Kingdom of Saba and when the Romans, in 25–24 BC, sent an army under Aelius Gallus, the prefect of Egypt, to conquer South Arabia, the Sabaeans resisted the expedition which ultimately failed, probably as a result of the hostile environment and the treachery of a guide. The Yemen eventually fell victim to internal disorders which were intensified by foreign intervention, itself in part provoked by religious conflict between Christians and Jews, until in the seventh century Yemen became a province in the new empire of Islam.

Out of that early history and through the centuries when the country was a constant battle-ground for the conflicts which divided the Muslim world, the Yemen retained characteristics which distinguished it from its Arabian neighbours and whose echoes still sound strongly today. First and foremost its geographical configuration, with high mountain ranges covering most of the area between the Red Sea and the 'Empty Quarter' of the Great Arabian Desert, imposed a pattern of social and economic organisation inevitably different from that of the surrounding desert areas. Its climate, too, offered advantages which were denied to its neighbours: above all, the relatively plentiful rainfall, which was another element in the Yemen's early prosperity and which the Himyarites and those whom they supplanted learned to husband and exploit with extraordinary skill. Lacking the great rivers which provided the life-blood for the civilisations of Egypt and Mesopotamia, the Yemenis had developed, even before the rise of the Roman Empire, a remarkably sophisticated system of rain-fed agriculture. The Ma'rib dam, which irrigated an area large enough to support an estimated population of 300,000, was the most striking example of this early technology; but equally effective and more enduring was the system of terracing, still practised to this day, which made it possible to grow crops on mountain slopes so steep that without men's intervention they would have been useless for cultivation.

The difficulties of transport and communication among these broken mountain ranges also had a lasting effect on the structure of Yemeni society. Where scattered communities lived in virtual isolation from each other, it was natural that a strong tradition of local autonomy should develop; and it is certainly not surprising to find that over the centuries this crystallised into an almost instinctive rejection of the idea of centralised control. The history of the Yemen is indeed characterised by a constant tug-of-war between the centre and the circumference: between, on the one hand, whatever regime for the time being might claim overall authority at the heart of things and, on the other, the outlying regions or tribes, which might in theory recognise that authority but in practice generally disregarded it and were often in open rebellion against it.

Such, in broadest outline, is the backcloth against which the history of the Yemen has unfolded over the centuries: a backcloth on which geography and climate, interacting with human instincts and inclinations developed to an unusual extent in isolation from the march of events in the outside world, have marked out a distinctive pattern. But the isolation, of course, was never complete. From Abyssinia and Persia, from Egypt and Turkey and the rest of Arabia, at different periods in history, came influences which penetrated it and which, to a greater or a lesser extent, were to shape the eventual outcome, whether in terms of social or economic or political organisation. One of these, in particular, deserves attention.

Once that early period of prosperity had come to an end with the collapse of the Himyarite dynasty, symbolised by the simultaneous collapse of the great dam at Ma'rib, the Yemen turned in on itself, ceasing to play any significant role on the world scene. One ruler after another sought to impose a central dominion, sometimes with the support of this party or that in the wider struggle for power and authority within Islam, sometimes on the purely local scene within the Yemen. Beyond the Islamic confines, the Yemen lost all significance; it was little more than a dream, a legend, a name uncertainly attached to a remote corner of an almost unknown continent. So it remained until, as part of the great stirring of the European imagination which we call the Renaissance, sailors, explorers and traders set out with their mixed bag of ambitions to discover a world which was not their own, but on which they were to set their mark. On some places in that other world, the mark of Europe was to be stamped so firmly as to defy effacement; on others, it was no more than a faint imprint in the margin. On the Yemen, it was in one sense negligible, leaving hardly a trace on the outward surface of a society which continued to go its own way for another 400 years. But in another sense it was crucial, for because of it the Yemen, from being one country with a particular past and a destiny, to all appearances, equally particular to itself and held in common by all its inhabitants, was to emerge into the modern world as two countries, sharing that common past, but set on courses so divergent that it would be difficult to envisage a meeting point for them.

It was late in the fifteenth century when the first Europeans arrived off the coast of the Yemen. The accounts they gave of the country were breathtaking, painting a picture of unimaginable wealth and splendour, so that it was not surprising that the early explorers, sensing opportunities which might rival those of the Americas, were soon jostling each other in the Red Sea to win a share of this wealth. The Portuguese were first on the scene, capturing the island of Socotra in 1507 and making an unsuccessful attack on Aden six years later. Not long after them came the English and the Dutch, whose initial aim was not conquest but trade, in pursuit of which they sought permission to establish 'factories', or trading posts, along the Red Sea coast. They were received with suspicion and another century was to pass before the Europeans were able to establish firm commercial links with the Yemen, which by then was nominally a part of the Ottoman Empire.

For the English, who gained a commanding share of the Red Sea trade, it was not Aden but Mocha which was the focus of attention. It was from Mocha that the Yemenis had begun to export coffee early in the sixteenth century, when the popularity of the new drink began to spread northwards to Mecca and then on to Cairo and Damascus and eventually to Constantinople. From there European travellers carried the taste for it to London, where the first coffee houses were opened in the 1650s, to be followed before the end of the seventeenth century by others in Paris, Amsterdam and Vienna. Soon more coffee was being consumed in Europe than in the whole of the Ottoman empire — and all of it came from the Yemen. As the trade flourished, both exporters and importers became immensely wealthy.

It was all too good to last and when the Dutch, around 1720, began to export not just the crop but the coffee plants themselves, the Yemen's monopoly was broken by growers first in the East and later in the West Indies. Mocha entered on a long period of decline and the great houses of the coffee merchants and the shipping agents, the last of which are still to be seen settling into the sands on the shore of the Red Sea, fell into disuse.

This was in the early years of the nineteenth century and by then other considerations were claiming the attention of the Europeans in what was still thought of as the Near East. The British had established an empire in India, and to secure and maintain the imperial lifeline had become a central objective of British policy. But communications between England and India were extremely slow, and not very sure either. In 1800 dispatches from an official in Bombay could be carried by sailing ship to Baṣra and from there up the Euphrates to Aleppo, then overland through Constantinople and across Europe, to reach London — if all went well — three months later. By sea, the journey might take twice as long.

The introduction of steam navigation in the 1820s changed all this. In 1831 the steamship *Hugh Lindsay*, launched in Bombay, made passage by way of Aden to Suez in 21 days. From Suez a fast courier could reach London in ten days, and the prospect of reducing the journey time between India and England by two-thirds was immensely attractive. But one problem remained: a steamship would need to refuel at some midway point between Bombay and Suez. When the choice fell on Aden, it had a decisive effect on the future of the Yemen.

When the British captured Aden in 1839, with the intention of establishing there a coaling station on the new route to India (a route which was to become one of the busiest in the world after the opening of the Suez Canal 30 years later), they aroused the misgivings of the Ottoman Sulṭān in Constantinople, who reasserted a claim to suzerainty over south-west Arabia which had lain dormant for two centuries. In 1849 Turkish troops occupied the Red Sea port of Ḥudayda, so that there were now two imperial powers established, though precariously, on the fringes of the Yemeni mainland. Their rivalry, which was to continue for 70 years, was also to result in the division of the Yemen into the two independent states we know today.

For a time there appeared to be no good reason why the two should come into conflict with each other. Neither the Turks in the north nor the British in the south were in a position to assert their authority over the turbulent tribes of the interior; nor had the British at first any wish to involve themselves any more in the affairs of the Yemen than seemed necessary for the protection of Aden itself. But imperialism has its own momentum and before long both sides were engaged in treating with or coercing tribal rulers whose allegiances were uncertain, along a border undefined except by informal and often disputed agreements.

The opening of the Suez Canal, which led to an enormous increase in commercial activity in the Red Sea (and at the same time made it much easier for both sides to reinforce their garrisons in the Yemen) helped to differentiate the two zones of influence. In the north, the Turks maintained with difficulty an authority which effectively was confined to the main towns and even there was often only nominal, while in the countryside the population went about its business in ways that had changed little in a thousand years. In Aden, on the other hand, the growth of a modern civil service and the influx of large numbers of shipping agents, accountants, merchants — many of them from Europe and still more from India — altered entirely the shape and size and character of what at the beginning of the century had been an insignificant fishing village with no more than 1,500 inhabitants. Very little of this activity overflowed into the hinterland, but as the British gradually extended their authority inland, its effects began to be felt in remote areas like the Ḥaḍramawt which had had no previous contact at all with the Western world.

In short, the invisible dividing line between northern and southern Yemen became steadily more apparent; and it hardened still more when the Turks were finally expelled from the Peninsula after the First World War and the Imām Yaḥyā was left to pursue without external interference his policy of resolute isolationism. Under him, until his assassination in 1948, and after that under his son Aḥmad, the citizens of what was shortly to become the Yemen Arab Republic were effectively cut off from the political, social and economic tides that were changing the face f the world outside its borders. Meanwhile, only a day's journey away the south, alongside the economic development which had transformed den into one of the world's busiest ports, all sorts of constitutional xperiments were being tried from which the inhabitants of the future eople's Democratic Republic of Yemen derived, however unwillingly, least some acquaintance with the problems of social and political rganisation which would confront them when they snatched their ndependence out of the untidy twilight of imperialism.

So it was that when they emerged, almost simultaneously, on to the orld stage in the 1960s, these two new republics, with their shared heritance of the oldest cultural tradition in Arabia, found themselves ivided in their approach to the overriding problem confronting them oth: the problem of modernisation, of adapting their institutions and eir economies to the requirements of the modern world.

Initially there was a desire on both sides — an instinct, perhaps, as uch as an aspiration — to pursue their goals in unity. Each had helped e other in adversity, providing a refuge for political exiles and much f the impetus for revolutionary activity against the erstwhile rulers of oth north and south Yemen. On the day of his installation as the first resident of the newly-established People's Republic of South Yemen, aḥṭān al-Sha'bī declared that 'the aim of our Revolution has been since e beginning to unite both parts of Yemen. We are all one people.' When e appointed one of the leading political figures in the south as Minister f Yemeni Unity Affairs, the Government of the Yemen Arab Republic the north, at that time still deeply engaged in the civil war which ollowed the revolution of 1962, at once did the same. There was much iscussion of the project for a 'Greater Yemen' and in 1972 the Prime linisters of the two countries met in Cairo and signed an agreement form a single unified state with one executive operating under a ommon leadership from a joint capital and under one flag.

Already, however, the disparities between the two had become too pparent. The roads to revolution in the north and in the south had been o different and the problems of establishing a unified government in ither were difficult enough to resolve without the added complication f trying to accommodate them both within a single framework. In the orth, the civil war had ended in a compromise which preserved the epublican form of government but which took into account the old entrifugal element in Yemeni political life. The revolution had not been nationwide uprising, but a movement sponsored by a minority. Its aim ad been the overthrow of a backward authoritarianism; but its authors ould not count on the co-operation of traditional tribal leaders in substituting for the ramshackle institutions of the Imamate a constitutional framework based on elements which were alien and so automatically suspect. Nor could this co-operation be exacted by force from those who had successfully resisted the republican government for eight years and had now simply withdrawn, undefeated, into strongholds where the central government would not dare to pursue them.

In the south, the revolution had followed a different course. Directed against a foreign, colonialist, enemy rather than a native tyranny, it had a far more coherent national following, even though it too had been accompanied by a form of civil war. But the result of the civil war, as of the revolution, was clear cut. The National Liberation Front, representing the more radical element of south Arabian nationalism, had scattered its enemies, both British and Arab, to emerge as the unchallenged arbiter of the new republic's destiny. And at its party congress at Zinjibar in 1968 the NLF had adopted the most radical programme of state initiative and control over all sectors of the national economy yet seen in the Arab world. Nothing could be more distasteful to almost all sections of opinion in the Yemen Arab Republic to the north.

Nor could the fact that northerners had helped the south, and southerners the north, during the period of revolution and civil war do anything but limit still further the prospects for united action, since the individuals concerned now found themselves in many cases in exile as political suspects in the eyes of the regimes which had gained power in Ṣan'ā' and in Aden.

Because of these differences, the regimes themselves, as they sought to consolidate their position, acquired characteristics which not merely distinguished them one from the other but accentuated the contrast between them. When both adopted new constitutions in 1970, that of the Yemen Arab Republic breathed the spirit of compromise and consultation and made a serious effort to reconcile the latent conflicts between progressives and traditionalists, between the advocates of centralisation in Ṣan'ā' and the tribal and religious leaders whose word was still law for the majority of the population. In the south, where the name of the country was now changed to the People's Democratic Republic of Yemen, the emphasis was on central control by means of 'scientific socialism' and the People's Supreme Council which was the new sovereign body was kept firmly under the control of the dominant NLF.

In their relations with the outside world, as in their domestic attitudes, the two Yemens found themselves gravitating inevitably, by a process of natural evolution, towards quite different alignments. It would not be true to say that they were on opposite sides of the fence, for in its approach to international questions, as in so much else, the YAR remained ambivalent. But if the YAR, officially non-aligned but leaning noticeably to the West (although Soviet aid constituted an important part of the government's resources), sat astride the fence, the PDRY took up from the start an uncompromising position on one side of it. Being itself the embodiment of the anti-imperialist movement, fired by a Marxist ideology and owing its survival through the first difficult years of independence to the support, moral as well as material, of the Soviet Union, the PDRY had little choice but to become a sometimes unruly member of the 'socialist' camp.

For the governments of both Yemeni republics, the most urgent problem was one of legitimacy: of establishing as quickly as possible their credentials as the acceptable rulers of societies caught up in a hasty process of transition. Nor could this be easy when the patterns of social and political organisation which they adopted were unfamiliar, were indeed essentially alien to those societies, owing much to foreign models for which their subjects could not be expected to feel any great sympathy. In the 1970s, a turbulent decade for both north and south Yemen, violence more than once disturbed the attempt to establish the new order. In the YAR the government's lack of any clear ideological basis left the field open for strong individuals to try to set their own stamp on the process. In the PDRY, within the framework of the system of 'scientific socialism' to which the regime had committed itself, a tug-of-war ensued in which rival tendencies sought, not always peaceably, to press for a more dogmatic or a more pragmatic approach to the problems of everyday survival.

For survival, with or without legitimacy, had somehow to be achieved and this was no easy matter for these two impoverished descendants of the legendary Arabia Felix. The old prosperity, built first on the incense trade and later on the monopoly of the export of coffee, was gone; and the Suez Canal, which had brought a new lease of life to Aden, had been closed by the Arab-Israeli war of 1967, less than half a year before the PDRY achieved its independence and while the YAR was still plunged in a bitter civil war. And as if this were not enough, the sharp rise in the price of oil, which brought such unprecedented wealth to their princely neighbours in the mid-1970s, imposed a further burden on the economies of the only two republics in Arabia, neither of which had any oil of its own.

In the statistics of the United Nations, indeed, both the Yemen Arab Republic and the People's Democratic Republic of Yemen were listed (and still are) among the poorest countries in the world, whether in terms of their gross national product or of *per capita* income. Neither possessed any of the minerals or the cash crops — apart from small quantities of coffee and cotton — of which the world had need. The YAR was fortunate in being endowed with the same land and rainfall which had contributed to its ancient prosperity, but while these enabled the rural majority to sustain an adequate standard of living, they contributed little to the cost of the growing quantity of imports for which modernisation and the consequent migration from the countryside to the towns created a brisk demand. The PDRY lacked even these resources and the circumstances of its birth, with commercial activity in Aden suddenly undermined by the removal of the British base and the closure of the Suez Canal, left it on the brink of insolvency. Both countries had to look elsewhere for the income with which to finance development plans which were vital to the achievement of political stability and economic and social advancement.

Both the YAR and PDRY became in fact largely dependent on foreign aid, both from their wealthier Arab neighbours and from governments further afield, which chose to support one or other of the Yemens (and sometimes both at once) for reasons that were seldom disinterested. The YAR benefitted more from this source, because it was successful in treading the tightrope of non-alignment and so received generous amounts of economic and military assistance from both sides, as well as very substantial subsidies from Saudi Arabia, which saw Ṣan'ā' as a useful barrier against left-wing subversion from Aden. In the early 1980s foreign aid to the YAR was on the scale of $5–6 million a year.

The PDRY, with its much clearer ideological orientation, was fo a time so dependent on Soviet assistance that it was in danger of becoming (and was assumed by some Western observers to have become) a Soviet satellite. But the true extent of this dependence varied as different elements jockeyed for power in Aden; as the regime consolidated its position, it was able to attract some development aid from the Western world and even from the more conservative Arab regimes.

It was also from abroad, though not in the form of direct assistance that revenues accrued which for the YAR provided the mainstay of it economy in the 1970s and do so to this day. For the rural inhabitants of the northern highlands, once the growth of the population had begun to exert pressure on the limited amount of agricultural land, emigration in search of work had long been a tradition. During the oil boom of the 1970s, this tradition was revived and expanded, to such a degree that by 1980 one-third of the country's labour force was working abroad mainly in Saudi Arabia and the smaller oil-producing states of the Arab Gulf. The earnings they sent or brought home came to constitute the argest single item on the credit side of the YAR's balance sheet: the 'ive Year Plan for the years 1980–86 is dependent to the extent of nearly 0 per cent on savings and remittances from Yemenis working outside ie country. For the PDRY this was a much more limited source of ıcome, both because of the restrictions placed by the government on ie movement of its citizens and because they were less welcome in the onservative Arab states on account of their government's political lignment.

With these varying resources, and against a background of continuıg political uncertainty in the region of which they form a part, both f the southern Arabian republics have made progress, perhaps even a urprising amount of progress, towards the objectives they set themselves ı the late 1960s. The more dogmatic approach of successive governıents of the PDRY has meant that these improvements have been nposed more often than they have come about as the result of popular emand. Nationalisation, the establishment of state farms, and the asserion of state control over the important fishing industry, have discouraged oreign investment and left little scope for private initiative. On the other and, an infrastructure has been created without which the improvements ı planning, in taxation and in the provision of education and health and ensions services would have been impossible. In the sphere of social eform, some of the legislation enacted has provoked opposition (for ıstance, the attempt to enforce national at the expense of tribal loyalties nd the restrictions on the use of *qāt*), but it is hard to contest the claim ıat the Family Law of 1974, which for the first time secured the rights f women, represents a milestone in the history of social legislation in ıe Arab world.

In the YAR, with its larger resources and its more *laissez-faire* pproach to matters of social and economic development, the advance as been more rapid, although with side-effects in the shape of inflation nd an evident lack of direction in such matters as town planning regulaions. Among the achievements are the rapid development of communicaions in north Yemen, the construction of modern highways, the eopening of the historic port of Mocha, the provision of a country-wide elephone and television service, and above all the remarkable expanion of education, for both girls and boys, at every level from the primary chool to the University of Ṣan'ā', as well as adult education — all vidence of a determination to revitalise a country which for so long ad languished in the margin of history.

To achieve this, without sacrificing the distinctive characteristics of heir common past, is no easy task for the peoples of either north or south Yemen, especially when both countries are relatively unimpo tant players on a field dominated by others more powerful and mor influential than themselves. In both, an enormous amount remains be done before the two Yemens can realistically be considered as moder states, able to support themselves instead of being dependent on the gooc will of this or that outside power or on the generosity of neighbours whor they cannot afford to antagonise.

For the YAR the discovery of oil in 1984 opens the inviting prospec of real progress towards self-sufficiency, but poses also the challeng of how to make this bounty serve as a tool rather than a crutch, a stimulu to fresh enterprise and not, as has happened elsewhere, a substitute fo home-grown initiative.

The discovery of oil has a bearing too on that elusive vision of unit in South Arabia, leaving as it does the PDRY as the only have-not i a world of haves and providing either a potential source of envy an resentment between the two Yemens or, just conceivably, a means c reconciliation. For, whether they remain poor or become rich, mor independent of their neighbours or less, that old instinct for unificatio endures — but remains as far as ever from fulfilment. The relationshi between Ṣan'ā' and Aden is better today than it was — as recently a 1979 the two came briefly to blows, and since then there has been furthe skirmishing along the imperfectly defined border that separates them - but it remains the fragile victim of a lack of confidence on both sides

There have been tentative essays in economic co-operation, a loosenin of border controls, and cultural exchanges, out of which one of the fe tangible results to emerge has been the Yemen Tourism Company established jointly by the two governments in 1980 and which has sinc achieved a modest success in a field where each has much to offer an from which both have much to gain. Tourism may not seem the mo important or the most exciting starting point for co-operation; and y it has its advantages too, if it encourages a systematic and scrupulou concern for the distinctive cultural heritage in whose possession the tw Yemens are as one. In the old city of Ṣan'ā', at the site of the Ma'ri dam (alongside which, in a remarkable enterprise, a new dam is unde construction), in the Wādī Ḥaḍramawt, at Mukallā and Zabīd and Ta'izz and in the crumbling ruins of Mocha, there are monuments of excep tional interest, to whose conservation the two governments have starte to give attention which is long overdue.

To extend this limited co-operation into wider fields is likely to b a slow business, requiring on both sides more self-assurance as well a a calmer political environment and a willingness to compromise of whic as yet there is little sign. But the instinct is there and at the popular level a sense of a common inheritance which has nothing to do with political boundaries — and may yet transcend them.

Postscript

How fragile are the political institutions on both sides was illustrated in January 1986, when a quarrel within the ruling Yemen Socialist Party in Aden touched off a bitter civil war in the PDRY. As factions supporting President 'Ali Nāṣir Muḥammad and his predecessor and rival, 'Abd al-Fattāḥ Ismā'īl, fought a bloody and inconclusive battle in the streets of the capital, the dispute rekindled tribal enmities in the hinterland, while across the northern border emergency measures were taken in the YAR, for fear that the tribes there might be drawn into a conflict which had serious implications for the whole of southern Arabia. As hopes of reconciliation faded, it was the fear of political subversion which was uppermost in Ṣan'ā' concerning the reversion to violence and instability in Aden and the PDRY.

10 Oman: Change or Continuity?

B.R. Pridham

Writers on change in the Arabian Gulf, whether political, social or economic, usually seize with relief on 1970 as a decisive landmark in the affairs of Oman. In other Gulf states there may be arguable cases for change arising from the entry of the West into the area, or from its exit, or from the impact of oil revenues, and so on; but in Oman, it is generally held, all change, and thus all progress, dates from the *coup* on 23 July 1970 by which the present Sulṭān Qābūs b. Saʿīd deposed his father Saʿīd b. Taymūr. The event provoked a flow, which still continues, of publications drawing a stark contrast between the medieval obscurantist regime up to 1970 and the progressive, enlightened government which succeeded it. That a successor regime should seek legitimacy by disparaging its predecessor is probably to be expected, but the same theme has been echoed by others to an impressive degree of unanimity. The aim of this study is to re-examine the conventional wisdom; to see if conditions pre-1970 were as bad as is customarily claimed; to look critically at some aspects of change and performance since 1970; and to decide whether 1970 was truly a watershed or merely an acceleration of flow along an age-old course.

The Conventional Wisdom

Dawn over Oman[1] and *Oman, the Reborn Land*[2] are titles which typify the writing which has appeared since 1970 and in this they follow the lead of the new government's first major publication, *The New Oman*, in 1971. The official view was that Oman had suffered '38 years of medieval and harsh rule'[4] and Sulṭān Qābūs himself said, on his accession, that he had 'marked with mounting concern and intense dissatisfaction the inability of my father to control affairs'. His first aim, he added, would be 'to remove all the unnecessary restrictions that you have been suffering under'.[5] From other official publications we learn that 'it was not until 1970 that oil revenues were used to develop the country. In fact the development of the modern Oman only started in that year'[6] and that 'there was no effort to explore for oil in other than the Petroleum Development (Oman) concession area] parts of the Sultanate'.[7]

All these views were picked up and replayed by later writers as if they were proven facts but without producing any evidence for them:[8] even authors of scholarly works have handed these views on as accepted background to their case work.[9] International organisations, too, are no exception. That UNESCO should contrast the 'sad circumstances' of pre-1970 with the present 'progressive regime' and talk of 'this new era of complete independence' will surprise no one,[10] but for OECD to comment that the word 'development' came to have meaning in Oman only since 1971[11] would normally suggest that evidence was to hand.

Petty Restrictions

In assessing the truth of the conventional wisdom it will be convenient first to clear away the undergrowth of bizarre and multifarious petty restrictions which always seem to be sprinkled over any account of the pre-1970 Sultanate. These restrictions were, it should be remembered, a prime justification for the *coup* and the more serious ones will be considered in relevant later sections.

> His first acts in 1970 — abolishing restrictions on smoking, singing and wearing spectacles — were newsworthy enough.[12]
>
> Automobiles, radios, cement houses, even sunglasses were forbidden.[13]
>
> Sunglasses were forbidden; so, under specific circumstances, were shoes.[14]

These are typical of the petty and incomprehensible restrictions attributed to Sulṭān Sa'īd's regime, and they are, for the most part, the purest nonsense. The Sulṭān himself wore spectacles and sunglasses[15] and, as a glance at *Old Oman* will show,[16] so did many of his subjects. For a completely authoritative view we might refer to Sayyid Thuwaynī b. Shihāb, now Special Representative of the Sulṭān and Governor of Muscat, who has worn glasses daily under both regimes. Radios were not only not forbidden but were surprisingly widespread and popular.[17] A writer in the early 1940s estimated that there were 50–100 sets in the Muscat-Maṭraḥ area,[18] while in the 1950s the new battery portables were avidly sought as gifts by tribal shaykhs visiting the capital (the traditional Lee Enfield rifle by then being considered impolitic).

A leading Omani merchant house owes its early prosperity to a go
trade in radios, radiograms and tape recorders and the Muscat *sūq* carri
ample stocks of records ranging from Lebanese and Egyptian stars
the new rock and roll phenomenon. The sole restriction was, and st
is, commonplace in Muslim countries; during the month of Ramaḍ
music from houses was not to be heard in the streets, although an offici
publication, referring specifically to radios, stressed that news bulletin
talks and the like were unobjectionable during the holy month.[19]

Nor were automobiles forbidden. The rule was that permission fro
the Sulṭān was needed for the import of any vehicle *other than* salo
cars and short-wheelbase Landrovers.[20] John Townsend, usually
admirably balanced observer of both regimes, turns this into no Oma
being permitted to buy a four-wheel-drive vehicle,[21] but the wide
publicised photographs of Sulṭān Qābūs's triumphant arrival in Musc
after the *coup* show the myriad Landrovers owned by Omanis from
over the country. The Sulṭān's restriction grew out of the need to preve
the smuggling of saboteurs, arms and mines during the unrest of the 195
and 1960s; lorries and the larger Landrovers were therefore controll
(not forbidden, except to those deemed security risks).

Cement houses required the Sulṭān's permission in the Muscat ar
(and it was sometimes given) because he cherished the idea of a tow
plan for the capital as soon as funds allowed and did not want rando
permanent construction to impede it. In 1966 therefore, a year befo
oil income began, he invited the firm of John R. Harris to include a tow
plan within a comprehensive development programme to cover al
public buildings, a housing complex, schools, hospitals, water and ele
tricity.[22] In any event, cement houses were 'wholly unfunctional for th
climate', as remarked by the same writer who thought the restrictic
worth mentioning.[23]

The 'specific circumstances' in which shoes were forbidden are le
unspecified but the writer may have seen an extraordinary article in a
Iranian newspaper[24] which claimed that it was forbidden to wear sho
when walking in the shadow of the Sulṭān's palace and, moreover,
unfurl an umbrella near any of the ruling family's palaces. A reign
terror indeed: suffice it to say that both shoes and umbrellas were
fact used at will and as appropriate.

Smoking was certainly banned in public, as it now is in several Musli
countries, but specifically tolerated in private.[25] In this, as in son
other matters, the enlightened attitude is not necessarily the one base
on Western assumptions.

The whimsical restrictions adduced by journalists and scholars alik to add spice to their work are seen to be greatly exaggerated. Those which undoubtedly existed can be equated perhaps with current Omani restrictions on drinking beer in a public place, on Guy Fawkes celebrations, on women swimming in other than a T-shirt and shorts,[26] and on the adoption of Western dress.[27] And in the unfurling of umbrellas class (which nevertheless was untrue), we have the current requirement that for every 20 sheep bought from outside the country Omani farmers must buy one cow from Dhofar.[28] There are, no doubt, good reasons for these 'restrictions' — there always were — and Townsend has shown that the present Sulṭān's *dīwān* is handling just the same level of trivia as his father's.[29]

Education up to 1970

It is under this heading and that of health that the most serious charges of harshness and obscurantism are levelled at Sulṭān Sa'īd. The conventional wisdom is that in 1970 in the whole country there were only three boys' schools containing 30 teachers and 909 pupils,[30] that 'education for girls was considered taboo by the previous Sultans',[31] and that Omanis were thus obliged to seek education abroad and, having done so, were forbidden to return.[32] To this last point is usually added the charge that Omanis who left the country for work were unable to return.[33]

Sulṭān Sa'īd had, in fact, been among the first rulers in the Arabian Peninsula to open schools, in spite of the state's exiguous income. The two government schools opened in 1940 and 1949[34] had become only three by early 1970, but that is not the whole picture. Part of the agreement on civil development made between the Sulṭān and the British Government in 1958 provided for the improvement of educational facilities[35] and by 1963 the first group of students for teacher training were at colleges in Aden and Mukallā.[36] A boarding school for students from the interior was quickly built in Muscat but was never put to its intended use; it became, instead, an institute of Islamic teaching with about 50 pupils.[37] Meanwhile, there were already in operation three schools for ethnic minorities, an American missionary school for about 50 girls in Muscat[38] and, by 1967, the Oman Technical School set up by the oil company, PD(O).[39]

The most interesting aspect of pre-1970 education, however, is probably the existence of at least 50 Qur'anic schools,[40] one in almost every village,[41] and with an estimated enrolment of about 4,800.[42] The

IBRD's own reckoning, therefore, was that there were about 58 (no three) primary schools (grades 1–6) in Oman before 1970. These various schools have been excluded from the official statistics for 1970 bu included from 1971 onwards so as to enhance the impression of a leap forward (the same treatment has been applied to medical statistics).

The Qur'anic schools were attended by girls as well as boys. In 1973 22 per cent of mothers interviewed in Nizwā had attended school,[43] and in 1980 a researcher in Ḥamrā' found that some 50 per cent of adult women of shaykhly status were literate; this rate of literacy remained fairly constant over the generations and compared favourably with the situation in Morocco where 'almost all women over a certain age regardless of their status were illiterate'.[44] In fact, female illiteracy in each of Oman, Qatar and Saudi Arabia was estimated to be 98 per cent in the mid-1970s, and since female education was legalised in Saudi Arabia only in 1960 (when it had existed in both secular and religious forms for years in Oman) there seems to be no justification for singling Oman out for censure.[45] Far from there being a taboo, it must be realised that the first official girls' school was ordered by Sulṭān Sa'īd and opened in 1970.[46]

Although an IBRD estimate of overall literacy in 1972 was 20 per cent[47] (high by many Middle Eastern standards thanks to the Qur'anic schools), a fascinating study by Eickelman[48] suggests that the practical uses of literacy and its value as a means of economic advancement were limited in the interior during Imamate days (up to 1955). Only a small fraction of the Imamate apparatus needed literacy: only 10 out of 56 officials in Rustāq (the second Imamate city after Nizwā), for example. Literacy was not a major avenue of social mobility. We should not, therefore, make the Western assumption that literacy in a society so strongly based on the oral tradition is an absolute good or necessity — (not much has changed — a 1977 estimate was that perhaps half the civil service was unable to read and write).[49] Nor should we forget that until the Sulṭān's rule and peace were both established in the interior in, at the earliest, 1961 there could be no question of any schooling other than Qur'anic in that area. There is, indeed, an instructive description in Ian Skeet's first-class impression of pre-1970 Oman of Ibāḍī opposition (not the Sulṭān's) forcing a private school in Ṣūr to close.[50]

In a unique and honest recognition that education existed in Oman before the 1970 *coup*, the Under-Secretary for Education, Shaykh A. 'Alī 'Umayr, insisted in 1977 that 'Oman before 1970 should not be denigrated . . . Everyone talks as if nothing happened here before 1970' and went on to say that many people learned to read through religious nstruction.[51] They also learned how to behave properly according to ome; bad behaviour was being blamed in 1973 on an insufficient number f Qur'anic schools.[52]

The myth about those educated abroad being unable to return is erhaps best exposed by the fact, mentioned above, that teacher-trainees vere sent abroad for the very purpose of returning and that individuals, uch as Qays al-Zawāwī, now Deputy Prime Minister for Economic and 'inancial Affairs, did precisely that.[53] Nor were there objections to the nflux of educated Zanzibaris from the early 1960s. On the allied quesion of return after work abroad, the official line was that workers were nigrating to the oil-fields of nearby states but 'invariably return and are articular in keeping their Omani passports . . . They make generous emittances . . .'.[54] John Peterson, another of the rare balanced bservers of pre-*coup* Oman, offers confirmation of this.[55] There is no pace in this study to examine the complex questions of who left Oman nd for what purpose; who was refused re-entry and for what reason; vho thought it politic not to try to come back and with what justificaion. We can only say here that those in the last two categories were elieved by the administration, rightly or wrongly, to be enemies of the tate. Up to 1970 Saudi Arabia in particular and the Arab world in general vere committed to the overthrow of the Sulṭān and the establishment f an independent Imamate. In that endeavour they naturally made use f disaffected Omanis, and there was no practical possibility that an)mani student at, say, Cairo University would remain — even if he began y being — loyal to his government.

Education after 1970

Sulṭān Qābūs himself declared early in his reign that 'if education in)man does not proceed along the right track, then the provision of educaion may turn out to be more disastrous than the lack of it'.[56] So it has roved. To balance reasonable criticism of the slowness of pre-1970 rogress many have concluded that subsequent progress has been frenetic nd ineffective.

Before 1972 there was no education policy; decisions were made *ad oc* and were subject to frequent changes, but even the new temporary olicy adopted in that year was 'in the absence of an overall social and conomic plan, after it had been realized that *any* policy was better than *one* at all'[57] (original emphasis). In the laudable rush towards univeral education, numbers, rather than quality, assumed prominence.

One aspect of statistical laundering has been mentioned; another wa
admitted in an official source, 'The number of schools is not the numbe
of buildings. In many cases one building is used for 2 schools mornin
and afternoon':[58] or, in one report, up to four schools.[59] And wh
buildings they were. Tents, huts, private homes, rented buildings, thatc
structures and the shade of trees — 'only a few relatively modern schoc
buildings exist' and even the new ones were 'deficient in ventilation
lighting and sanitation'.[60] In 1974 half the new schools were in tents c
'rented buildings not suited for school use', while most schools lacke
adequate furniture and equipment.[61] By the end of 1985, 94 suc
schools from the early 1970s were to be rehoused.[62]

The numbers game was also being played with teachers. In the earl
years 98 per cent of Omani teachers and 12 per cent of the much mor
expensive expatriate teachers were professionally unqualified: one-quarte
of teachers were not educated even to primary level.[63] Here the poir
should be made that the new government was using tables of figures an
Westernised concepts of education against the previous regime's recor
and therefore invites judgement in those terms.[64] Teaching method
were widely condemned. It was doubtful in 1972 if more than half th
pupils were provided with textbooks and writing materials, and the black
board was normally the only teaching aid available.[65] Up to 1978
least (when an 'Omanised curriculum' was introduced) teaching had bee
by rote memorisation of whole texts.[66] (UNESCO even cites, with som
distaste, the requirement to recite the names of the Arabian poetess, Al
Khansā', up to the eighteenth ancestor).[67] Since such methods were sti
in use and since many teachers in those early 1970s had an educatio
which was 'mostly classical and religion based'[68] the Qur'anic school
(from which they came) could reasonably be counted to the old regime'
credit.

The international organisations concerned with education did not minc
their words when surveying the general scene. In 1972 the IBRD note
that no part of the educational system was without problems; unclea
goals and policy, lack of organisation and proper staffing in the Ministry
no statistics and no plans to compile them, no national curriculum
unqualified teachers and no plans for training them.[69] We may note th
most of these problems were not inherited. A year later the IBRD sti
found an 'education system of poor quality and with little relevance t
the national needs'.[70] By 1974 it was still condemning inadequat
teaching qualifications, rote memorisation as the basic teaching techniqu
and the lack of local textbooks and curricula. Administration and plan
ning of education were 'virtually non-existent'.[71] At this stage

was ironic to note that the teacher/pupil ratio had gone from 1:30 in 1970 to 35, 36 and 42 in the three subsequent years.[72] This particular statistic is not used by the present regime. As late as 1977 the IBRD found that six out of every ten Omani children were not at school,[73] while in 1979 it considered that many schools were still housed in unsuitable physical facilities and much remained to be done to meet the population's needs adequately.[74]

UNESCO was no less scathing about the general situation. The education offered in the schools, it said in 1974, was unsatisfactory. There had been rapid expansion without due concern for planning and there was a 'misfitness to cultural, social and economic needs and characteristics of the country'. How, it asked despairingly, can you plan education when there are no population statistics?[75] There still are none, and the curious avoidance of a population census by the new regime is mentioned again later. Sulṭān Qābūs, to his credit, admitted some of the mistakes: 'In the first five years we did everything in such a rush . . . But there was waste here and there and things of dubious quality. Some schools were thrown up too quickly so we had to build them again.'[76]

Notwithstanding all of the above, however, the most deleterious aspect of post-1970 education is probably the impact of the enormous preponderance of foreign teachers at all levels. The alienation from national values of a whole generation has been well documented in the case of the Yemen Arab Republic,[77] and the problem in Oman is very similar. In 1977/78 expatriates were 88 per cent of teachers[78] and even as late as 1983/84 there were only 1,384 Omani teachers out of 8,658: of the remainder, 5,231 were Egyptian.[79] The UNESCO concern for 'misfitness' arose from this imbalance, and a sociologist in the mid-1970s believed the modern education available to be an indirect attack on Omani self-pride and the identification of children with their own traditions. In an exact echo of the Yemeni findings he saw the expatriate teachers as having 'quite negative attitudes toward everything local and traditional, and thus Omani'.[80]

It seems fair to conclude that education before 1970 was not as bad as normally represented, that after 1970 it has been a good deal worse than claimed by the government, and that the continuation of Sulṭān Sa'īd's laboured pace might have produced results which, taken in the round, would have been at least as successful.

Health

Although the general charge against Sulṭān Sa'īd is that medical services barely existed until 1970, there have been varying estimates of the scale of deprivation. We have statements that there were only two hospitals in the country,[81] that there was only one,[82] and that there was none at all 'run by the Ministry of Health'.[83] Estimates of health centres similarly ranged from nil upwards.[84] Hospital beds were thought to be as few as 12,[85] although even that figure seems excessive from a source which believes that there were no hospitals or health centres. It is also maintained that there was no preventative medicine or public health facilities.[86]

The reality was rather different. Only one post-1970 official publication out of many came closer to the truth by recording that in 1970 there were five hospitals, 39 clinics and dispensaries, 276 beds, 33 doctors and 132 ancillary health workers.[87] American missionaries of the Dutch Reformed Church opened their first hospital in Oman in 1892 and continuously maintained one after 1907. By 1954 their hospital in Maṭraḥ had 150 beds and their women's hospital in Muscat 75 beds.[88] There were, in addition, the British Consulate hospital in Muscat with 12 beds (a charitable foundation providing treatment to all), the hospital of the Evangelical Mission in Buraymī, two military hospitals and the oil company hospital with 20 beds.

The official health service began only after the development programme financed by Britain began in the late 1950s. By 1963 the personal representative of the UN Secretary-General was able to say that he was impressed with what was being achieved with modest means, after visiting the Rustāq health centre.[89] There were then nine health centres, each with a doctor, 14 dispensaries, each with a medical assistant, and an anti-malarial unit. Other spraying units were soon added and toured the country, and a maternity centre was built at Samā'il; some of the doctors were continually touring the remoter areas with mobile clinics as soon as security conditions allowed.[90]

Whatever view is taken of the state of health services in Oman before 1970, certain factors must come into the reckoning:

(a) The Imām refused to allow doctors to visit the interior even though the people themselves were keen. The head of the American mission records how difficult it was to obtain permission from the Imām's acolyte to visit the Sharqiyya, whereas the Sulṭān's permission was given without delay.[91]

(b) After the Imām's deposition in 1955 guerrilla operations continued to make normal civilian life and movement impossible in much of the country. The inhuman blowing-up in 1962 of the new dispensary at Bahlā (the medical assistant was badly wounded) is a measure of the difficulty facing the Sulṭān. Shooting, sabotage and mining of roads continued into 1963.[92]

(c) Revenues from oil sufficient to enlarge the modest official health programme started accruing only in 1967. By the time of the *coup* a start had already been made on three new government hospitals at Ruwī, Tan'am and Ṣalāla.[93] It is therefore a distortion of the truth to claim for the new regime the credit for these (for example, after Qābūs's accession 'within a matter of months a hospital was set up in Salala'),[94] as it is to omit or insert statistics of non-governmental health facilities so as to show the old regime in the worst light.[95]

Given the universally bad impression of medical conditions under Sulṭān Sa'īd, it is curious to note that infant mortality in Nizwā and Ṣuḥār was thought to be lower than that in Saudi Arabia and similar to that in Iraq.[96] And in spite of the long years of high oil income in Saudi Arabia, that country's crude death rate in 1970 was higher than that of Oman and its life expectancy lower.[97] As for the extent of improvement after 1970, there is some evidence that the reputed change of direction and commitment was not equal to the magnitude of the problem — even with the vastly increased revenues of the 1970s. Nutritional levels in the middle of the decade reached only 86 per cent of the standard average in Arab countries in calories and 91 per cent in proteins. Health studies showed that children and pregnant women were suffering from malnutrition, even though there had been a more than five-fold increase in the value of food imports from 1970 to 1975, and a later, 1978, study found over 67 per cent of children suffering from anaemia.[98] As the IBRD observed in 1979, to meet the health needs of the population adequately 'much remains to be done'.

Roads

The mileage of available roads is another favourite yardstick for demonstrating the retrogression of Sulṭān Sa'īd and the enlightenment of his successor. The seemingly impregnable statistics show that by 1970 there were 'only a few kilometres of tarmac road in the Sultanate; there are now [1980] over 12,000 km of tarmac and graded roads.'[99] We should, however, once again make allowances for certain factors:

(a) The newly-appointed Development Secretary in 1959 found that the Sulṭān was 'really keen' about roads[100] and by 1963 his department had made and was maintaining 400 miles of graded roads.[101]

(b) Mining of roads continued until 1963, and possibly later. There were 17 mine explosions in 1962 and 101 other mines were recovered safely.[102]

(c) Before the *coup* contractors had already been engaged to survey the roads to Ṣuḥār and Nizwā — a total of 242 miles — and work had started. Firms had also been invited to tender for the new Maṭraḥ corniche.[103]

(d) The statistical presentation was slanted. In 1970 there were already 1,817 km of graded roads while the 1980 ratio of graded to tarmac was 7:1.[104]

Moreover, the significance of the statistics can be questioned. Did Oman, at that stage, need tarmac roads? The IBRD found, in 1972, that over 90 per cent of villages could be reached with four-wheel-drive vehicles because the terrain permitted cross-country driving. Most roads were over-designed and neglected to use local materials (unlike, in both respects, the pre-1970 roads). The construction of roads to the current standards was not needed to provide access for motor transport but more to reduce its costs and improve service. As for the figures, the listed road network exceeded 2,400 km but 'about half of this length represents roads in the sparsely populated southern two-thirds of Oman, which are used very infrequently and almost solely by the PD(O) or the military' (a reference to the Dhofar province and the strategic roads built to assist the campaign against the rebels there). So, concluded the IBRD, for the next few years Oman should not embark on major new transport investment.[105]

Judged by its own standards, the ones used to denigrate its predecessor, the post-1970 regime failed for many years in its road building policies. It seems remarkable that the important village of Ḥamrā', the capital of the 'Abriyyīn and with a population of 2,500, was reached by a graded road only in 1976 and a paved one in 1979.[106] There were unwelcome results too: the development of paved roads killed off Ṣuḥār as a port[107] and the more than doubling of road accidents from 1971 to 1973[108] challenges Western measures of what constitutes progress. But the truth is that the IBRD was right and the previous Sulṭān was going ahead at the right speed and in the right way. After all, the Trucial States, where oil income began much earlier, where there were no internal security problems, and where cross-country driving was generally more difficult, had only eight miles of paved roads in 1968.[109] No one, however, seems to find this deplorable — and quite rightly so.

Isolationism

The closed, unknown and secretive nature of Oman before 1970 is commonly contrasted with the 'new Oman', open to the world.[110] Let us straightaway lay his due share of the responsibility for the earlier record on the Imām and his supporters. In the area of the Imamate there was a complete ban on non-Muslims and most strangers.[111] After the Imām's exile there were at first security problems and later on the need, as the Sulṭān saw it, not to offend the reactionary inhabitants of an area where the extension of his writ was just beginning to run. As the official line had it,[112]

> It should be remembered that it is the people themselves, though naturally hospitable and possessing delightful manners, who are suspicious and sometimes resentful of the intrusion of foreigners, and that is why the Sultanate out of respect for their feelings is so careful about introducing strangers.

Other considerations which came into play were the complete absence of hotel accommodation — making it necessary for every visitor to have a sponsor who would put him up — and the Sultanate's bad experience with visiting writers and journalists, most of whom were obsessed with unfurling umbrellas and the like. This latter factor became a vicious circle as journalists who could not get in fantasised from a distance and so reinforced the Sulṭān in his opinions.

Not much seems to have changed, especially given the ample hotel accommodation and the long-standing stability in the north of the country. Until 1983 Oman remained officially closed to tourists and even then the first group of 14 had to be strictly organised under trustworthy leadership. The usual reason given for this reserve is the lack of tourist infrastructure and also 'intrusion into a strict Muslim community' — an echo of pre-1970.[113] The attitude of the regime is the same for any other visitor: immigration formalities are strict and visitors require a sponsor resident in Oman who can acquire the necessary 'No Objection Certificate' which, with luck but not always, can be used to obtain a visa.[114] These realities are no match for a brisk dose of statistics, however: 'With about 84,000 visitors in 1983, the government sees tourism . . . as a big development area.'[115] Note the rolling up of tourists (14) with other, mainly commercial, visitors (the rest). A more honest approach, and one making the continuity since 1970 more apparent, comes from the Minister concerned. Tourism, he said in mid-

1985, has to be approached with caution because Oman has many traditions and customs it would like to maintain. 'What we're talking about is controlled tourism.'[116]

Political isolation is a more complex matter and one which requires a separate study in the context of the dispute pitting the Sultanate and Britain against the Arab supporters of the Imamate. Since Sulṭān Sa'īd was regularly assailed in the United Nations by countries whose ideological animus against Britain was matched only by their total ignorance of the facts (with the unique exception of Saudi Arabia whose desire to control potential oil-producing areas exceeded both), he was not inclined to join that organisation.[117] For the sake of the development to which he was alleged to be opposed, however, applications were made to join FAO and WHO.[118] The applications were voted down and it must be pointed out that the politically-inspired criticisms of internal conditions in the Sultanate which marked every UN debate on Oman during the 1960s came from precisely those who stood in the way of progress.[119] An application to join OPEC in 1967 was also turned down, although Abu Dhabi was accepted at the same meeting. Since Abu Dhabi was demonstrably not a fully sovereign state, the Sultanate's rejection was presumably politically motivated.[120] The ready acceptance of Oman into international organisations after 1970 (only the PDRY voting against and Saudi Arabia abstaining)[121] may indicate Arab relief at being able to avoid supporting the by-now discredited Imamate movement. There were certainly no objective reasons for the switch: the British role in the Sultanate was unchanged in nature and scale, while the new Sulṭān's internal regime duplicated his father's (see below).

Development before 1970

Some aspects of development work before 1970 have already been dealt with, but there is a great deal more evidence that the new regime's claim to have begun the country's development in that year is nonsense. In the earlier days of oil exploration the PD(O) representative recorded his understanding that the Sulṭān proposed to spend his oil royalties on educational and health services[122] and a year later the agreement on military and civil development between Britain and the Sultanate was signed.[123] A Development Secretary began work in 1959 when the British Government sent a new member of its Consulate-General's staff to Muscat with the specific task of supervising the administration of the military and civil development subsidies.[124] Between that year and the advent of oil revenues in 1967 development went ahead under the agreed heads of health, roads, education and agriculture. Progress was as much as could reasonably be expected, given the smallness of the subsidy (ranging up to £250,000 a year) and the limitations imposed by the Sultanate's enemies. In agriculture, two experimental farms with extension services were set up in Nizwā and Ṣuḥār and great impetus was given to the installation of motor pumps. Customs duty was waived on pumps and by 1964 about 5,000 were believed to have been installed.[125] In all of these developmental fields full use was made of the experts in the British Middle East Development Division (based in Beirut) and of their parent body, the Ministry of Overseas Development.

The 1966 development plan by John R. Harris already referred to was soon followed by action. This has been well described by Townsend and Peterson[126] and some of it incorporated above, but major points are worth making here. Plans for the new airport and port were drawn up in Sulṭān Sa'īd's time; the plans for the latter were ready in 1968 and the Phase I contract for £2 million was awarded in April 1970[127] (that it should later be named after Qābūs is curious). Contractors arrived in force in 1968[128] and work began in that year on large contracts for the Muscat/Maṭraḥ water and drainage system,[129] and the power station and lighting system in Ṣalāla.[130] Other projects under way or completed by 1970 were three new hospitals, a girls' school, the major roads to Nizwā and Ṣuḥār, a new electricity supply for Muscat/Maṭraḥ, a government office block, a Post Office, the Muscat-Maṭraḥ corniche, recreation areas, drainage and water supplies in the capital, a new Currency Authority building (with a new currency to administer) and a housing complex. The Sulṭān had expressed interest in setting up a radio station in the early 1960s and a feasibility study had determined the site of the transmitters, but he called for a full consultancy in 1967, to cover also the possibility of providing a television service.[131] An IBRD estimate that $7.2 million was spent on development projects from 1967 to 1970 must certainly be too low.[132] A measure of the increased tempo is that Gulf Aviation decided to increase their Muscat service to three flights weekly from October 1968.[133]

The United Nations Development Programme was thus well justified, even though it got the date wrong, in saying in 1974 that some attempt had been made as early as 1968 to draw up plans for the country's development, whereas the new regime had not prepared a development plan up to then (1974).[134] The first development plan in fact began in 1976. The IBRD admitted that 'the new Government was able to increase development expenditure so quickly because the design of some big projects . . . had already been commissioned by the former Sultan' and because he had left behind 'accumulated public savings'. Anyone hoping to understand this question properly should study the public statement made in 1968 by the Sulṭān and usually known as 'The Word of Sultan Sa'id bin Taimur, Sultan of Muscat and Oman, about the history of the financial position of the Sultanate in the past and the hopes for the future, after the export of oil.'[135] An open-minded collation of that policy statement with what actually happened up to 1970 should serve to clear the former Sulṭān of the charge of being opposed to the development of his country.

One more aspect of pre-1970 development remains for scrutiny. It is commonly held that the Sultanate's resources, even before oil, would have permitted a greater pace of development but were being stored away. Views ranged from a belief in private reserves of between $30 and $40 million by 1966[136] to the more moderate accusations that the former Sulṭān was careful to spend the British developmental subsidy but not his revenues from customs and duties,[137] and that, in his 'Word', he 'neglects to mention the Canning Award payments which continued until 1956 of 40,000 Maria Theresa dollars which probably went into his privy purse'.[138] These Canning Award payments or Zanzibar subsidy, to use the more usual title in this century, had originated as compensation to the Sulṭān for the loss of his East African territories in 1861 and were made by the British Government until 1967 at the rate of £6,500 a year.[139] Whether such sums lodged in the privy purse or not may be thought trifling but every Arab state in the Gulf shows the same lack of distinction between privy purse and public treasury. This is still the case in Oman where about ten per cent of the 1985 recurrent, capital and development budgets is allocated to the Dīwān of Royal Court Affairs (more, for example, than Health or Agriculture and Fisheries).[140]

The implication that Sulṭān Sa'īd spent none of his state revenues could be sustained only if there were no state outgoings. But apart from a country-wide system of *wālīs, qāḍīs* and their retainers, and the armed forces (before British help), there was a reasonable range of central administration. There were departments covering Interior, Development, Petroleum, Public Works, Justice, Customs, Defence, Capital Area, Police, Finance and Audit, Foreign Affairs and Schools.[141] The administration may have been minimal but so were the revenues. Part of the British Consulate-General's function was to monitor Sultanate finances as closely as possible so as to determine how much aid Britain needed to give, and for how long. That the 1958 civil development and military payments and the Zanzibar subsidy continued until 1967 tells its own story. The Sultanate's exiguous finances are well covered by Peterson (although he exaggerates four-fold the size of the civil development subsidy) and Skeet.[142] Here, we may simply note the bald statement by the IBRD that until 1967 revenues did not cover expenditures[143] and give, as an example, the financial year 1962/63. In that year exports were valued at about £334,000 and imports at just under £3 million.[144] Bearing in mind that customs dues represented up to 90 per cent of state income[145] and that plant and equipment for the oil company, the armed forces and development projects were duty-free (more than half of the total),[146] we can dismiss the Arabian Nights fantasy of secreted riches which was common journalistic usage in the 1960s. A 1967 estimate put state income at about £900,000 and expenditure at about £450,000.[147]

Political Development

This is the last important heading under which the conventional wisdom attacks Sulṭān Sa'īd. He was commonly characterised by such words as harsh, autocratic, cruel, despotic and absolute, whereas the new regime, while not addressing these specific issues, presents a generalised image of itself as enlightened and inaugurating a new era in every field. Sulṭān Qābūs's accession statement (p. 132 above) carried a strong connotation of freedom being given to the people.

Sulṭān Sa'īd was undoubtedly an absolute ruler. He appointed advisers and at times accepted their advice, but in the end he did what he judged best. Because the informal shaykhly council or *majlis* system scarcely existed in Oman and because his family counted for nothing in his counsels, Sulṭān Sa'īd was actually more autocratic than rulers further up the Gulf. Until 1958 it was possible for tribal leaders — not the general populace — to visit the Sulṭān and express grievances but his removal to Ṣalāla in that year put an effective end to that, as it was designed to do. By any objective measure Sulṭān Qābūs is just as absolute. His equivalent of going to Ṣalāla is the dīwān, which works as a buffer beween Sulṭān and people;[148] he believes that majlises are an inefficient and time-wasting way of running a modern state;[149] he is the sole source of legislation and the highest judicial authority; he continued to disregard his close family — even though his uncle Ṭāriq was made Prime Minister, Qābūs ordered that he should not have access to financial matters.[150] In one respect Qābūs is actually more autocratic than his father because it is his policy to increase the authority of the wālīs and ministers (all appointed by him) over that of the tribal shaykhs.[151]

In another respect it can be argued that Qābūs has made some movement towards popular participation in the establishment of the State Consultative Council (SCC) in 1981. He had previously announced on National Day in 1980 that in the succeeding five years the process of consultation with his people would be extended and developed.[152] Since then the only other development has been the increase in SCC membership from 45 to 55 in 1983, after which the Sulṭān was asked whether he foresaw any further political progress and replied 'Not for the moment.'[153] The nature of the SCC is therefore important.

The purpose of the SCC was defined as giving 'the people a greater voice in the planning and development of the economy and social services'.[154] This rather restricted remit is even less than it appears to be because the Ministry of Petroleum and Minerals is not represented in the Council, which cannot, therefore, discuss mineral resources and their revenues (i.e. almost the whole economy).[155] Of the original 45 members (appointed for two years) 17 were government representatives and eight of the regional and private members also worked for the government:[156] of the present 55 members 19 are government representatives.[157] The decrees setting up the SCC guaranteed its members freedom of speech during its meetings (there is no written constitution in Oman so this freedom is not guaranteed elsewhere) but only if they adhered to the approved agenda, obeyed the laws of the land and respected the state.[158] The SCC may perhaps be regarded as a useful meeting ground rather like a top people's majlis, but since it has no powers whatever it remains closer to bureaucracy than democracy.

In talking of the SCC Sulṭān Qābūs said that it would be a very happy day for him when more people would take responsibilities off his shoulders: 'But we have to take into consideration the situation of our culture, our religious heritage and guidance, our traditions . . .'[159] It must be said that most of these run counter to the concept of absolute monarchy. *Shūrā*, taking counsel, is recognised as being the very basis of Ibāḍī government (and thus of the Imamate),[160] and institutionalised or absolute power was anathema to the Kharijite sectarians who founded Ibadism.[161] We can perhaps sum up the issue of absolutism by saying that the present position is remarkably similar to that of pre-1970 and that the former Sulṭān would approve of his son's statements. It is not surprising that the US Congress should list the absence of increased opportunities for political participation by an increasingly educated population among its negative factors with regard to Omani stability.[162]

How the power is used is another matter. Part of Sulṭān Sa'īd's reputation for cruelty rested on his uncompromising, vindictive attitude towards former rebels, part on the apparently medieval petty restrictions already touched on and part, no doubt, on the conditions of imprisonment in Fort Jalālī, the Muscat gaol which seems to have made a deep impression on many writers. It was disturbing indeed to Westerners to see shuffling lines of shackled prisoners chained together and to sample, even briefly, the terrible conditions inside.[163] Even so, it is interesting to reflect that the inmates were accorded regular medical attention and diet control unlike, according to the opposition, most people in the country. It certainly surprised this writer to be told by some convicted murderers released after eight years in Jalālī that they had no complaints.[164] More objective measures are hard to find. We might note that political opponents were merely imprisoned under Sulṭān Sa'īd, whereas for the first time death sentences were carried out for sedition in 1972 and 1974.[165] However, it seems fair to conclude that the new regime, executions apart, has a mass of evidence to show that it is infinitely more benign than its predecessor and that this is the area of most emphatic discontinuity between the two eras.

Performance since 1970

Lack of space precludes a detailed analysis of how the new government has handled the economy and development planning but, in short, it has been poor and would have been absolutely disastrous but for a continued run of good luck.[166] The good luck has been the unexpected and unplanned-for continued rise in oil production instead of the expected tailing off, plus the movement of oil prices. Throughout the first three years of oil exports until the *coup* the oil price was $1.820 per barrel, but within six months of the *coup* it had risen by over 20 per cent and in early 1974 shot up to $12.298. From 1971 there was an increase at least once a year until the present decade.[167] The references will show how the immensely increased revenues were spent in profligate and dubious ways to such effect that Oman started incurring huge debts — the first for 40 years. They also show how the delicately interlocking structure of agriculture, water and social organisation was ruined[168] and an expatriate population of over 257,000 brought in by 1983.[169] Significantly, in view of the last fact, they record how the Omani Government refuses to conduct a census although urged on all sides to do so.[170]

Among the wealth of material showing the poor performance since 1970 let us focus on some evocative figures which have special relevance for Oman's post-oil future. Non-oil exports (almost exclusively from agriculture and fisheries) ranged from OR 648 million up to OR 965 million in Sulṭān Sa'īd's last five years: in the first three years of Qābūs's reign the figures were 381 m., 430 m. and 394 m., and it was only in 1975, by which time inflation exceeded 20 per cent, that pre-1970 figures were exceeded.[171] These figures exemplify the general observations of the IBRD that a sector which supports roughly 80 per cent of the population and which is supposedly the king-pin in current economic strategy has been grossly ignored or ill-treated.[172]

The Legacy

Sulṭān Sa'īd inherited a country so heavily in debt that its sovereignty was impaired;[173] one effectively cut in half by the semi-autonomous existence of the Imamate; and one torn apart by internal feuding.[174] What his son took from him was a country with healthy accumulated public surpluses, permitting a rapid build-up of an existing development programme; one whose complete independence was in no doubt; one without the running sore of the Imamate; and one settled in its metropolitan area,[175] although disaffection reigned in Dhofar. The balance was hugely in Sulṭān Qābūs's favour; the general conclusions of this study must be that conditions before 1970 were not nearly as bad as painted, that some aspects of the era since 1970 are, equally, not as good as we are usually told, and that there is a strong theme of continuity in governmental matters which refutes the 'new Oman' image.

Notes

1. Pauline Searle, *Dawn over Oman*, (Khayat, Beirut, 1975).
2. F.A. Clements, *Oman, the Reborn Land*, (Longman, London, 1980).
3. Ministry of Information, Labour and Social Welfare, *The New Oman*, (Muscat, 1971).
4. Ibid., p. 24.
5. Ibid., p. 7.
6. Sultanate of Oman Development Council, *The Five-Year Development Plan 1976–1980*, (Muscat, 1976), p. 2.
7. Ministry of Information and Youth Affairs, *Oman in 10 Years*, (Muscat, 1980), p. 118. For a typical, and easily accessible, refutation of this see D. Hawley, *Oman and its Renaissance*, (Stacey International, London, 1977), p. 178.
8. Chosen simply because it was the most recent at the time of writing, see Roger Scruton in *The Times*, 20 August 1985: 'until 1970 . . . virtually without hospitals, roads or schools'.

9. For a recent example see Christine Eickelman, *Women and Community in Oman*, (New York University Press, New York, 1984), pp. xv–xvi.
10. A.M. Yousuf, *Education in Oman*, (UNESCO, Beirut, 1971), p. 2.
11. OECD, *A Preliminary Estimate of Foreign Exchange Absorptive Capacity of the Sultanate of Oman*, (Paris, March 1974), p. 7.
12. MEED, 21 November 1980, p. 6.
13. Unni Wikan, *Behind the Veil in Arabia: Women in Oman*, (Johns Hopkins University Press, Baltimore, 1982), p. 6.
14. Liesl Graz, *The Omanis: Sentinels of the Gulf*, (Longman, London, 1982), p. 16.
15. James Morris, *Sultan in Oman*, (Faber and Faber, London, 1957), pp. 50, 157.
16. W.D. Peyton, *Old Oman*, (Stacey International, London, 1983).
17. Unreferenced statements or opinions such as this rest on the author's personal observation or involvement.
18. Paul W. Harrison, *Doctor in Arabia*, (Robert Hale, London, 1943), p. 283.
19. *The Sultanate of Muscat and Oman*, (Sultanate Printing Press, Muscat, n.d. but probably 1964), p. 11. This publication, incidentally, gives the lie to the claim that the first printing press was set up after the *coup*: see Ministry of Information and Youth Affairs, *Oman in 10 Years*, p. 62.
20. *The Sultanate of Muscat and Oman*, p. 12.
21. J. Townsend, *Oman: the Making of a Modern State*, (Croom Helm, London, 1977), p. 68.
22. London Chamber of Commerce, *Report of the Trade Mission to Muscat and Oman*, (LCC, London, April 1967).
23. Wikan, *Behind the Veil*, p. 12.
24. *Kayhan*, 14 August 1968.
25. Morris, *Sultan in Oman*, p. 120.
26. MEED, *Oman: A MEED Practical Guide*, (London, 1981), p. 61.
27. F. Barth, *Sohar*, (Johns Hopkins University Press, Baltimore, 1983), p. 210.
28. MEED, 15 June 1985.
29. Townsend, *Oman*, p. 134.
30. *Development in Oman 1970–1974*, (National Statistical Department, Ministry of Development, Muscat, n.d.).
31. An Omani Government advertisement placed in *The Financial Times* of 17 November 1972; see also *Middle East*, No. 8, (May 1975), p. 24.
32. Graz, *The Omanis*, p. 16.
33. Ian Skeet, *Muscat and Oman: The End of an Era*, (Faber and Faber, London, 1974), p. 196.
34. Clements, *Oman*, p. 59.
35. *Exchange of Letters between the Government of the United Kingdom of Great Britain and Northern Ireland and the Sultan of Muscat and Oman concerning the Sultan's Armed Forces, Civil Aviation, Royal Air Force Facilities and Economic Development in Muscat and Oman, London July 25th 1958, Cmnd. 507*, (HMSO, London).
36. United Nations General Assembly, Document A/5562, 8 October 1963, p. 17; J.E. Peterson, *Oman in the Twentieth Century*, (Croom Helm, London, 1978), p. 84.
37. *Oman*, (Department of Information, Muscat, 1972), p. 53.
38. Ibid; UNESCO, *Sultanate of Oman; Present Situation of Education*, (Paris, 1972), p. 1.
39. Yousuf, *Education*, p. 6.
40. IBRD, *The Economy of Oman*, (Report No. EMA-55a, 12 September 1972), p. viii.
41. Yousuf, *Education*, p. 2.
42. IBRD, *Current Economic Position and Prospects of Oman*, (Report No. 393a-OM, 31 May 1974), p. 13.
43. UNICEF, *Beliefs and Practices Related to Health, Nutrition and Child Rearing in Two Communities of Oman*, (Abu Dhabi, December 1973), First draft, Vol. 1, p. 15.

44. Eickelman, *Women and Community*, p. 199.
45. F. Allaghi and A. Almana, 'Survey of Research of Women in the Arab Gulf Region' in *Social Science Research and Women in the Arab World* (UNESCO and Frances Pinter, London, 1984), pp. 22, 30.
46. Townsend, *Oman*, p. 170.
47. IBRD, *Economy of Oman*, Country data p. 1.
48. Dale F. Eickelman, 'Religious Knowledge in Inner Oman', *Journal of Oman Studies* (Ministry of National Heritage and Culture, Oman), vol. 6, Part 1 (1983), p. 166.
49. James Buxton, *Financial Times*, 17 November 1977.
50. Skeet, *Muscat and Oman*, p. 184.
51. Stewart Dalby, *Financial Times*, 17 November 1977.
52. UNICEF, *Beliefs and Practices*, vol. 4, p. 4.
53. MEED, *Practical Guide*, p. 68.
54. *Sultanate of Muscat and Oman*, p. 10.
55. Peterson, *Oman in the Twentieth Century*, p. 205.
56. UNESCO, *Present Situation*, p. 21.
57. Ibid., p. 17.
58. *Statistical Year Book 1983*, (Development Council, Oman), p. 15.
59. *Financial Times*, 13 January 1983.
60. IBRD, *Economy of Oman*, pp. viii, ix; *Oman '83* (Ministry of Information, Muscat, 1983), p. 74.
61. IBRD, *Current Economic Position* (1974), p. 14.
62. *Oman '83*, p. 74.
63. UNESCO, *Present Situation*, p. 10.
64. See, for example, *Oman in 10 Years*, possibly the most inaccurate and wilfully tendentious book about Oman ever published.
65. IBRD, *Economy of Oman*, p. 33.
66. *Oman '83*, p. 73; IBRD, *Current Economic Position* (1974), p. 14.
67. UNESCO, *Present Situation*, p. 11.
68. IBRD, *Economy of Oman*, p. 33.
69. Ibid., p. ix.
70. Townsend, *Oman*, p. 158.
71. IBRD, *Current Economic Position* (1974), p. 14.
72. Ibid., Table 9.1.
73. IBRD, *Oman: Transformation of an Economy*, (Report No. 1620-OM, 25 October 1977, 3 vols.), vol. 1, p. 18.
74. IBRD, *Oman: Current Economic Position and Prospects* (Report no. 2528-OM, 16 October 1979), p. i.
75. UNESCO, *A Report on Oman's Strategy for Educational Development*, (Regional Office for Education in the Arab States, Beirut, 1974), p. 14.
76. *Financial Times*, 13 March 1984.
77. Horia Mohammad al-Iryani, 'The Development of Primary Education and its Problems in the Yemen Arab Republic' in B.R. Pridham (ed.), *Economy, Society and Culture in Contemporary Yemen*, (Croom Helm, London, 1985), pp. 184–8.
78. IBRD, *Current Economic Position* (1979), p. 5.
79. *Statistical Year Book 1983*, p. 23.
80. Barth, *Sohar*, p. 200.
81. UNDP, Report DP/GC/OMA/R.1, 3 September 1974, p. 4; Frauke Heard-Bey, 'Social Changes in the Gulf States and Oman', *Asian Affairs* (Journal of the Royal Central Asian Society), vol. 59 (New Series vol. III), Part III, (October 1972); *Oman in 10 Years*, p. 93.
82. *Arab British Commerce*, (Arab-British Chamber of Commerce, London, June/July 1985), p. 27.
83. UNDP, Report DP/GC/OMA/R.2, 17 October 1978, p. 9.

84. Ibid., for nil.
85. Ibid.; *Arab British Commerce*, p. 27; *Oman in 10 Years*, p. 93.
86. Townsend, *Oman*, p. 68.
87. *Development in Oman 1970–1974*, p. 67.
88. MEED, *Oman; a MEED Special Report*, November 1982, p. 21.
89. UN General Assembly, Doc. A/5562, p. 17.
90. *Sultanate of Muscat and Oman*, p. 8.
91. Harrison, *Doctor in Arabia*, pp. 198, 200, 217.
92. UN General Assembly, Doc. A/5562, pp. 12–13; Hugh Boustead, *The Wind of Morning*, (Chatto & Windus, London, 1971), p. 224.
93. Clements, *Oman*, p. 81; *Oman*, (Department of Information, Muscat, 1972), p. 52.
94. *Oman in 10 Years*, p. 93.
95. Ibid.; UNDP (1974), pp. 4, 14; UNDP (1978), p. 9.
96. UNICEF, *Beliefs and Practices*, vol. 1, p. 41.
97. IBRD, *Transformation of an Economy*, vol. 1, p. 1 (Social Indicators).
98. United Nations, Economic Commission for Western Asia (ECWA), *Food Security in Gulf States* (Report No. E/ECWA/AGRI/79/8), Rev. 1, English translation, September 1979), Part 1, *Oman*, pp. 7–8, 23.
99. *Oman in 10 Years*, p. 129.
100. Boustead, *Wind of Morning*, p. 219.
101. UN General Assembly, Doc. A/5562, p. 17.
102. Ibid., pp. 12–13; Boustead, *Wind of Morning*, p. 224.
103. Board of Trade, *Export Services Bulletin*, 16 April 1970.
104. *Statistical Year Book 1983*, p. 83; Development Council, *Oman: Facts and Figures 1979*, (Directorate General of National Statistics, Muscat, August 1980), p. 3.
105. IBRD, *Economy of Oman*, pp. vi–vii, 25.
106. Dale F. Eickelman, 'Omani Village: the Meaning of Oil' in J.E. Peterson (ed.), *The Politics of Middle Eastern Oil*, (Middle East Institute, Washington, DC, 1983), p. 212; Christine Eickelman, *Women and Community*, p. xi.
107. Barth, *Sohar*, p. 197.
108. *Development in Oman 1970–1974*, p. 74.
109. Heard-Bey, 'Social Changes', p. 315.
110. Clements, *Oman*, p. 68; *Oman in 10 Years*, pp. 22, 104.
111. Barth, *Sohar*, p. 248; W. Thesiger, *Arabian Sands*, (Longman, London, 1959), pp. 255, 290, 300–6.
112. *Sultanate of Muscat and Oman*, p. 12.
113. MEED, *Oman* (A Special Report, November 1983), p. 8.
114. J. Robb, *Financial Times*, 13 March 1984.
115. *South*, April 1985.
116. MEED, 27 July 1985, p. 25.
117. See, as a random example, UN General Assembly document A/RES/2302 (XXII) of 14 December 1967.
118. Peterson, *Oman in the Twentieth Century*, p. 105, n. 26.
119. A typical example is UN General Assembly document A/5492 of 11 September 1963 and its Addendum of 16 September 1963.
120. *The Times*, 3 October 1967; *Arab Report and Record*, Issue 19 of 1967, 1–15 October 1967, p. 314. Although this report quotes OPEC's Secretary-General, the records of the subsequent OPEC conference which considered the application do not mention it.
121. IMF document EBD/71/367, Supplement 1 of 15 December 1971; IBRD document R71-278 of 17 December 1971; IBRD, *Economy of Oman*, p. 3 (for Arab League); UN General Assembly document A/RES/2754 (XXVI) of 8 October 1971.
122. *Daily Mail*, 25 July 1957.
123. *Exchange of Letters* (Cmnd 507).
124. Boustead, *Wind of Morning*; the new member of staff was the present writer.

125. Sultanate of Muscat and Oman, p. 7.

126. Townsend, *Oman*, pp. 69, 170, 192; Peterson, *Oman in the Twentieth Century*, pp. 58, 84–5, 205.

127. *Oman*, (Department of Information, Muscat, 1972), p. 49; *Financial Times*, 20 April 1970.

128. MEED, *Practical Guide*, p. 98.

129. Middle East Association, *Information Digest*, 23 August 1968. The contract was for £500,000.

130. Ibid., 1 November 1968. This contract was for £300,000.

131. IBRD, *Economy of Oman*, p. 8; Board of Trade, *Board of Trade Journal*, 17 November 1967; *Arab Report and Record*, Issue 14 of 1967, 16–31 July 1967, p. 244.

132. IBRD, *Transformation of an Economy*, vol. 1, p. 29. Heard-Bey estimates £1.8m. was spent on major projects in 1969 alone ('Social Changes', p. 310); a Taylor Woodrow press release gave the Ruwī hospital contract value as £570,000.

133. Middle East Association, *Information Digest*, 15 November 1968.

134. UNDP (1974), p. 4; UNDP Recommendation DP/GC/OMA/R.1 of 5 September 1974, p. 2.

135. English original in Centre for Arab Gulf Studies, University of Exeter. Text reproduced in Townsend, *Oman*, pp. 192–8.

136. Patrick Seale, *Daily Star* (Beirut), 4 September 1966.

137. Clements, *Oman*, pp. 56–7.

138. Townsend, *Oman*, p. 56.

139. See the annual *Civil Estimates* (HMSO, London) under Class II.

140. Royal decree no. 1/85 summarised in MEED, 8 February 1985, p. 26.

141. Townsend, *Oman*, p. 69; Peterson, *Oman in the Twentieth Century*, pp. 79, 84; Skeet, *Muscat and Oman*, p. 35.

142. Peterson, *Oman in the Twentieth Century*, pp. 86–90, 106, n.48; Skeet, *Muscat and Oman*, pp. 64, 185–90.

143. IBRD, *Economy of Oman*, p. 7.

144. *Sultanate of Muscat and Oman*, p. 10.

145. Peterson, *Oman in the Twentieth Century*, p. 88.

146. Board of Trade, *Board of Trade Journal*, 17 November 1967, p. 1269; London Chamber of Commerce, *Report*.

147. London Chamber of Commerce, *Report*.

148. Clements, *Oman*, p. 76.

149. *Financial Times*, 28 January 1980.

150. Townsend, *Oman*, p. 81.

151. Clements, *Oman*, pp. 70–1; Graz, *The Omanis*, p. 150.

152. MEED, *Practical Guide*, p. 2.

153. *Financial Times*, 13 March 1984.

154. *Oman '83*, p. 7.

155. Dale F. Eickelman, 'Kings and People: Oman's State Consultative Council', *Middle East Journal*, vol. 38, no. 1, (Winter 1984), p. 58.

156. Ibid., pp. 57, 59.

157. British Bank of the Middle East, *Sultanate of Oman*, (Business Profile Series, 3rd Edition, April 1985), p. 4.

158. Articles 3 and 51 of Decree 82–86 dated 18 October 1981, cited in Eickelman, 'Kings and People', p. 57.

159. *Financial Times*, 13 January 1983.

160. UNESCO, *Present Situation*, p. 11; Dale F. Eickelman, 'From Theocracy to Monarchy: Authority and Legitimacy in Inner Oman, 1935–1957', *International Journal of Middle East Studies*, vol. 17 (1985), pp. 3–24.

161. T. Lewicki, art. 'Al-Ibāḍiyya', *EI*², vol. 3, pp. 648–60.

162. US Congress, *US Security Interests in the Persian Gulf*, (US Government Printing

Office, Washington, DC, 1981), p. 186.

163. P.S. Allfree, *Warlords of Oman*, (Curtis Books, New York, 1967), pp. 173–5. The vividness of its writing risks obscuring the solid worth of this excellent book.

164. The murderers and their crime are described in Ibid., pp. 11–13, 174. It bears reflection that the Sulṭān's prison facilities were judged more suitable than any available in the Trucial States in the early 1950s.

165. Townsend, *Oman*, p. 135.

166. Even a complete list of references containing adverse judgements would be too long. The following are a sample: IBRD, *Economy of Oman*; IBRD, *Current Economic Position* (1974); IBRD, *Current Economic Position and Prospects of Oman* (Report No. 934-OM of 10 February 1976); IBRD, *Transformation of an Economy*; IBRD. *Report and Recommendation of the President of the International Bank for Reconstruction and Development to the Executive Directors on a Proposed Loan to Oman Telecommunication Corporation (Omantel) for a First Telecommunication Project* (Report No. P-2782-OM, 4 June 1980; IMF, *Staff Report for the 1977 Article VIII Consultation*, 25 January 1978; IMF, *Staff Report — 1974 Article VIII Consultation*, 31 May 1974; IMF, *Oman — Recent Economic Developments* (Report No. SM/79/81), 28 March 1979.

167. *Statistical Year Book 1983*, p. 126.

168. Again, only a sample can be given: Dante A. Caponera, *Report to the Government of the Sultanate of Oman on Water Resources Policy Administration and Legislation*, (FAO, Rome, 1975); R.W. Dutton, 'The Agricultural Potential of Oman' in May Ziwar-Daftari (ed.), *Issues in Development: The Arab Gulf States*, (MD Research and Services, London, 1980); *Financial Times*, 28 January 1980, articles by James Buxton, Dr. Bill Donaldson, Prof. H. Bowen-Jones and Dr. John Wilkinson; Townsend, *Oman*, p. 163; FAO, *Report of FAO/UNDP Programming Mission to Oman*, (Rome, 1975), p. 12.

169. *Statistical Year Book 1983*, pp. 43, 50. This huge figure excludes the armed forces, police, the General Telecommunications Organisation and the Central Bank of Oman.

170. IBRD, *Economy of Oman*, p. 2 of main report, p. 7 of Annex; IBRD, *Current Economic Position* (1976), p. 2 of main report, p. 4 of Appendix I; IBRD, *Transformation of an Economy*, vol. 1, p. vii; FAO, *Programming Mission*, p. 3; ECWA, *Food Security*, p. 30.

171. *Statistical Year Book 1972* (General Development Organization, Muscat), p. 96; *Statistical Year Book 1983*, p. 131.

172. There are many instances: see, for example, IBRD reports already mentioned from 1974 (p. 11), 1976 (pp. i, 7, 26), 1977 (pp. vi, 62) and 1979 (pp. 8, 20). See also IMF, *Oman — Recent Economic Developments* (Report No. SM/73/64), 12 April 1973, p. 10.

173. For general background on this see Peterson, *Oman in the Twentieth Century* and R.G. Landen, *Oman Since 1856: Disruptive Modernization in a Traditional Arab Society*, (Princeton University Press, Princeton, 1967).

174. How torn apart may be judged from an engaging entry in Sheila A. Scoville (ed.), *Gazetteer of Arabia* (Akademische Druck — u. Verlagsanstalt, Graz, 1979), p. 21: 'The inhabitants of Adam are too remote to take much part in the faction wars of Oman and maintain feuds among themselves instead.'

175. UN General Assembly, Doc. A/5562, p. 15.

11 Kuwait, Qatar and the United Arab Emirates: Political and Social Evolution

Glen Balfour-Paul

Any attempt by a Western outsider to evaluate the political and social experiences, recent or not, of an Arab society is by definition presumptuous, exposing him to the dreaded charge of 'orientalist' misreading. The extent of his first-hand knowledge is necessarily limited to externals. What went on, or goes on, in the *psyche* of an Arab society is something he can only guess at. However intrigued he may be by the subject under study — in this case the response of the Gulf States to sudden and previously unimaginable wealth and independence — it remains for him a spectacle. The rest is speculation. The only valid account of what has been happening to the Arabs of the Gulf must come from the Gulf Arabs. They too, like all of us, are prisoners of their own presuppositions; but they are at least entitled, as the rest of us are not, to identify behind the acts and facts of their own recent history the springs of action and faction.

None the less, after a brief description of the state of Gulf society before wealth and independence descended on it and a rather longer account of their visible consequences, this essay will speculate unashamedly, if interrogatively, on the less visible effects of the Gulf's whirlwind experience and on the extent to which the transformation has been absorbed into the social metabolism.

One other preliminary admission is necessary. The geographical entities allotted to this contribution are too disparate for generalisation to be wise. What may be true of Kuwait at one end of the Gulf may well not be true of Fujairah (Fujayra) at the other. No one, of course, would deny that all Gulf States — Bahrain included, though it lies outside this essay's terms of reference — have much in common. (Parenthetically, one common feature not always recognised by commentators is that throughout their recent history they have all in essence been urban societies centred on coastal towns, however small. The bedu element within them, though never till today insignificant, often fractious and always to be husbanded, has played a distinctly minor and now vanishing ole in the evolution of state and society.[1]) But in many respects, as een today — in their demographies, their natural endowments, their xposure to external threat, their development policies, their life-styles nd their chosen roles on the world stage — Kuwait, Qatar and the United rab Emirates visibly diverge.

Whether their history, as a group or individually, would have onspicuously differed had nineteenth-century Britain not incorporated hem, however marginally, into its imperial system is now of little oncern. There are only two features of that curious episode which may eed re-stating here. Firstly, by signing individual treaties with whatever haykhly figures were dominant at the time along the route through the Gulf to the Indian empire, Britain's policy had the effect, wittingly or ot, of 'legitimising' and perpetuating the fragmented political system which happened then to prevail. Secondly, the extraordinary nature of hose treaties deliberately restricted the extent of Britain's interference n a colonial sense in the internal affairs of the Shaykhdoms. Whether colonial relationship, which this was not, would have been an advantage to either side is debatable.[2] As things were, it may be argued that ll Britain (as distinct from geology) bequeathed to the area was a respect or law and law-enforcement, a recognition of the value of local stability nd an embryonic concept of structured administration in a Western and erhaps irrelevant sense. Certainly the consequence of Britain's imperial nconcern for internal affairs — coupled, rather oddly it may now seem, vith its insistence on excluding everyone else — was that the Gulf States vere ill prepared for the almost simultaneous arrival of oil wealth and ndependence.

Indeed, the life-style of the Shaykhdoms had remained virtually nchanged until the Second World War. The shaykhly system was barely questioned. Under it each ruler continued until death (by whatever gency) to exercise comprehensive power, subject only to the vague lemocracy of the *majlis*, the acquiescence of his near relations and his bility to maintain, by whatever instruments he could muster, the loyalty of his sometimes troublesome subjects. The idea of a voluntary merger nto a larger grouping — still less of forcible incorporation by a bigger regional power — was unthinkable, or at least unthought. Within this nchanging political framework every man's role was, as it were, preordained: the son of a pearl-diver assumed he was to dive for pearls, he son of a merchant worked unquestioningly in his father's shop, the son of a bedu took it for granted that his future lay with the family camels, the son of a ruling shaykh grew up naturally to play some part in the running of public affairs — and the perspectives of the daughters of all of them were pre-ordained even more narrowly. It was this which maintained throughout the area a stable, socially-determined and unchallenged life-style with all that followed in the context of family and tribal cohesion, the network of area loyalties, the hierarchical chain of control and the generalised understanding of the individual's rights and duties in the community. If the prospects of socio-political change were at that stage improbable, so too were those of socio-economic betterment. The pearl industry had collapsed by the 1930s and, despite the whiff of oil, no alternative source of an improved livelihood in a general sense had presented itself.

So superficial a summary may suggest total immobility. That would be misleading. Well before oil and independence there were signs of movement, economic, social, educational and even political. But such neologisms as 'social infrastructure' and 'political mobilisation' were not yet translated, so to speak, into the Gulf vernacular. The two revolutionary developments we are considering changed all that. The approach of oil-rigs meant the possibility of accelerated change: the approach of independence its certainty. What was less clear was the *direction* of change — economic, social and political; and it remains even today uncertain.

Oil started flowing from Kuwait in 1946 (having done so in Bahrain on a small scale 22 years earlier), from Qatar in 1949, from Abu Dhabi in 1962, from Dubai in 1969, and as a final (post-independence) bonus from Sharjah in 1974. The visible and material effects of the resulting bonanza, as demonstrated first in Kuwait, included on the credit side the rapid transformation of living standards, massive infrastructure development, the elaboration of welfare-state provisions, an educational leap forward, essays in industrial initiative, and so on. On what may be thought the debit side, the process involved a huge influx of immigrant labour skilled and unskilled, an internal drift to the towns and the adoption of an increasingly consumerist life-style. Despite minor differences in emphasis the pattern repeated itself everywhere else, as the money came.

To some outsiders at any rate this was and is a disappointment. There is, they feel, nothing particularly adventurous in converting patches of sea-side desert into undifferentiated high-rise concrete jungles sprouting cornucopiae and television aerials, particularly when there will be nothing to fertilise them in the post-oil era. From this dyspeptic view, what should have been done in the interests of posterity is the exact reverse of constructing urban phantasmagoria for the sands to bury in 50 years' time: the sensible policy would have been to enable the few genuine residents of the area to provide themselves, gradually and by their own effort, with such services — educational, medical, recreational, etc. — as poverty had previously denied them, and to dump the whole of the rest of the windfall in profit-bearing investments abroad, securing thereby a state income of an adequate and predictable kind in perpetuity and preventing the flooding of the national landscape by waves of immigrant aliens. A more desperate alternative, advanced in the 1960s,[3] was that the proceeds from oil should be exclusively used to remove the whole population from these desolate shores and re-locate them in an agreeable bit of Switzerland or somewhere. But for better or worse the chance of adopting either of these alternatives was missed and the cities of the Gulf have mushroomed. Their critics can at least take comfort from the fact that from the beginning of the oil boom in Kuwait it was Shaykh 'Abdullāh al-Sālim's rule-of-thumb policy, with an eye to the future, to invest a third of the state's oil revenues in the industrial West;[4] and in 1976 a specific Reserve Fund for Future Generations was set up with annual allocations. By now Kuwait's income from foreign investments is as high as its income from oil, so that in its case perhaps the post-oil era may pose no serious financial threat. The long-term future of the smaller City-States, even if they pursue a similar policy, may prove for demographic reasons much less manageable. But this is to divert from our immediate theme.

As the oil boom took its course, Britain's withdrawal of protection and the ending of exclusivity (1961 in Kuwait, ten years later elsewhere) meant not only a confrontation with the question of national identity (and an international role for it) but equally a head-on exposure to alien cultures and perhaps physical threats.

In adjusting themselves to the international limelight the Gulf States showed few misgivings and much enterprise. Quite apart from formal entry and active participation in the UN's manifold activities and in joint Arab organisations,[5] the sense of responsibility with which they have used some of their wealth for the benefit of needier peoples has been conspicuous. Kuwait's Fund for Arab Economic Development (founded in 1962) — a pattern followed by other oil states — is a rightly admired model.[6] Internally, meanwhile, the governments have taken pains not only to institutionalise the machinery of administration in a general way but also to develop a conscious pride in their respective identities, or at the very least in that of their respective rulers.

An effective response to the invasion of alien cultures was and remains less easily formulated, given the singular tolerance of the Gulf peoples and the universal human inclination of those hitting the jackpot to enjoy instantly whatever material benefits the world offers. After the first flush of excitement they were soon faced with the impalpable problem of reconciling all this with the preservation of traditional values. And if on independence the possibility of physical (as opposed to cultural) threats from abroad may have seemed a more palpable and immediate problem, an effective response in that field is little easier. The protection provided by a rapid build-up of armed forces equipped with the best that money can buy can scarcely be seen as more than symbolic: and in view of the mercenary nature of the composition of some of them, perhaps not even that.[7] In terms of internal security, however, they may perhaps be regarded as effective.

Meanwhile, a less visible effect of oil and independence, but one of growing concern to the ruling establishments, was the reaction of the commonalty to this heady brew and the gradual dislocation of traditional acceptances. If continued economic prosperity in the longer term (the age-old problem of survival in a desert environment) was not already seen as something to worry about, continued political stability — an accommodation with the rising expectations of the people — certainly was, whatever the hesitations of the ruling groups to come to grips with it.

All the above considerations are general to the area. Since the individual States did not all have to grapple with them from the same starting-points, in time or in other respects, we must now particularise.

Kuwait not only took off in terms of wealth and development ahead of the others but differs from them in terms of geographical location, of population and even of traditional political structure. This is not the place to re-examine the ambiguities of its former relationship with the Ottoman Empire or with its local successor state Iraq,[8] beyond drawing attention to the nervousness so engendered and the sensible Kuwaiti policy of being no man's enemy, not even Iraq's. (Bahrain, though not the concern of this essay, has had equal or greater cause for political nervousness but has adopted a different technique for survival.) Kuwait's population, in terms of national citizenry, being bigger than that of the other individual Emirates, also set it somewhat apart and has made it marginally easier for it to digest the influx of foreigners. Its political structure also was historically distinct, for although the Ruler (like those of the rest) has always been from a single family, there is no parallel elsewhere for the traditional importance, on the socio-political as well as the economic scene, of half a dozen other influential families with whom the ruling Āl Ṣabāḥ have always needed to reach an accommodation. Obviously, however, what most distinguishes Kuwait from the others is its precedence in the oil stakes, leading to earlier and more advanced development; and this in turn doubtless explains why Kuwait (in 1961) spontaneously demanded full independence, whereas the others (in 1971) had independence thrust upon them.

A catalogue of the internal achievements of Kuwait and of the other States is not the purpose here. Still less intended is a statistical presentation of them — if only since responsible statistics differ from source to source (and sometimes within a single one). To illustrate a consciously selective theme, however, various facts and figures for Kuwait, alongside the corresponding ones for Qatar and the UAE, are set out in Table 11.1. The population explosion since the coming of oil is in itself so startling that the detailed records are shown in graph form in Figure 11.1. Within the totals shown, and even more in the relevant work-forces, the proportion of non-nationals is such that the formal determination of policies, social, economic and political, has long been recognised as a problem of nightmare quality. (In Kuwait's case the much higher ratio of Arab to Asian immigrants may be regarded as a mitigating factor, though the reverse is equally arguable.) The course of history is unlikely to make solutions easier. In brute terms the alternatives are either to retain national discrimination and view the immigrants as a temporary embarrassment or to liberalise substantially the nationalisation laws — the former risking economic collapse, the latter a non-national 'take-over'. But this is to jump ahead, and we turn instead to a backward look at Qatar and the UAE.

Before oil (on stream since 1949) Qatar's sparsely populated peninsula had been something of a backwater. It had never enjoyed the commercial importance of Kuwait as an entrepôt; nor had it matched the earlier maritime potency of the Qawāsim at the mouth of the Gulf, or the later commercial sparkle of Dubai. Its population was no more than 20–25,000 and, pearl-banks apart, it had no evident natural resources. The British themselves saw no compelling reason to bring Qatar into their treaty system until 1916, though it may have drawn a certain strength from its status as the only Gulf Emirate to have embraced the Wahhābī doctrines of the Saudi Kingdom, with which it has consequently had closer links. This may indeed be one reason why the complete dominance of the Āl Thānī in Qatar's body politic has never been challenged. If Kuwait can be described historically as a merchant oligarchy, the Āl Thānī ran Qatar as a family business. Even since its emergence as an affluent and independent member of the comity of nations, Qatar has remained somewhat out of the mainstream, adopting a more relaxed attitude to world affairs than Kuwait and quietly concentrating on its own measured internal development. This caution has not spared it the familiar

Figure 11.1: Population Explosion Since the Coming of Oil in Kuwait, Qatar and the UAE

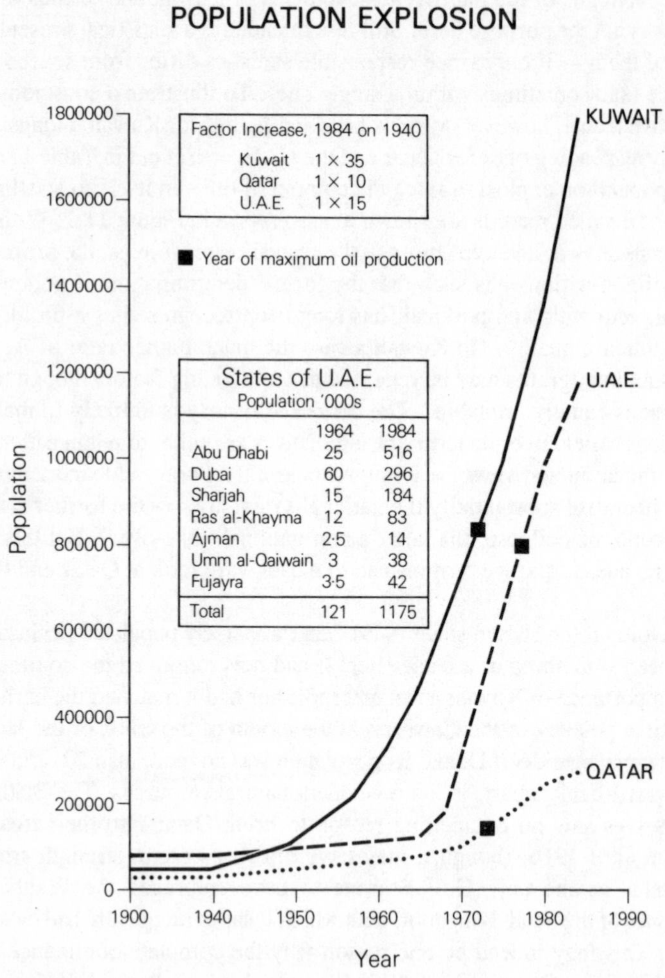

Sources: See Appendix B following Notes, p. 174.

Table 11.1: Selective Data

	Demography				Crude Oil					Education			Armed Forces	
	1	2	3	4	5	6	7	8	9	10	11	12	13	14
		Immigrants (1980)								Students 1982				
	Total pop. (1984) 000s	% of pop.	% of work force	Est. Shi'ite	Date first prod.	Peak prod. (& year) mbbl	Peak prod. mbbl	Years left	Oil as % of exports	Pre-secondary	Secondary	State univ.	Manpower 1983	Expenditure per head of pop. 1982
Kuwait	1,787	59	78	20	1946	1,200 (1972)	300	162	88	249,936	62,683	14,389	12,500	$735
Qatar	272	74	83	15	1949	208 (1973)	120	25	94	36,464	5,084	3,237	6,000	$2,486
UAE	1,175	76	90	8	1962	729 (1977)	456	72	79	115,117	11,639	3,779	49,000	$3,690
			Abu Dhabi		1962	603 (1977)	329							
			Dubai		1969	132 (1978)	125							
			Sharjah		1974	14 (1975)	2.5							

Sources: See Appendix A following Notes, p. 173.

demographic dilemma, whereby its nationals have become a minority in their own country, outnumbered four to one or so by the army of immigrant helots.[9] About this too they have shown less perturbation, although a special committee (*Lajnat al-Istiqdām*) was set up by the Ministry of the Interior in 1975 to monitor the subject.

Turning to the seven small States which now comprise the United Arab Emirates, these were (at least until their union) the prime example of the political fragmentation of the area confirmed, though assuredly not caused, by Britain's treaty system. Oil came to them late and in singular maldistribution;[10] and development had barely started when Britain left them to their own devices. It is arguable, if barely sustainable, that if the expectation of oil concessions had not obliged the British in the 1950s to undertake the formidable task of defining boundaries between them, unification would have occurred by force of circumstance, since their continued political separatism would otherwise have proved impracticable. Be that as it may, these seven Emirates (Fujairah having been recognised by the British as the seventh one in 1952) were individually of such diminutive size in terms of population — varying at the time from 60,000 to as little as 2,500[11] — that their separate transformation on independence into individual members of the United Nations was recognised as unthinkable. There were of course more compelling, if less formal, reasons for some kind of merger, the maldistribution of oil being one, the special need for a new sort of protection being another.

So far as there had ever been historically a unifying force native to the area, this was perhaps the pre-eminence of the Qawāsim before the arrival of the British enlarged the other ruling shaykhs to uniform 'trucial' status. But the most conspicuous feature of the scene, ended neither by Britain's arrival nor by Britain's departure, was the complexity of the inter-Emirate and inter-tribal friction and jealousy, compounded historically by differing views of who owned which well, palm-tree or grazing area. The fact that jealousies survive the unification of the States is unremarkable: what *is* remarkable and encouraging is that unification survives the jealousies. The production of oil has so far been vouchsafed to only three of the seven: the material benefits resulting from it have spread through all of them, though not of course uniformly. Maybe this would have happened whether or not the seven had united, since the rich — in Arabia if not everywhere else — see advantage as well as merit in helping the poor. But material interdependence ought surely to induce a corresponding habit of mind.

Once again the processes of headlong development have presented the UAE with the same demographic dilemma as we have noted further up the Gulf. According to one calculation,[12] as much as 90 per cent of the UAE labour force is now expatriate. Even more pregnant is the fact that 85 per cent of the army is mercenary.

In all the Gulf States institutional and infrastructural development has been well publicised and documented.[13] The point has been reached when there is not much more in the way of public services, in quantitative terms, that money can provide. Their maintenance is of course costly; but as long as oil lasts (and despite the current slump and current deficit budgets)[14] there should be ample national income to cover this reduced need and at the same time to invest on the Kuwaiti model against an oil-less future.

Industrial options lie outside the scope of this essay, but two obvious *caveats* may be in place. First, industries dependent on cheap petrochemical feedstock can scarcely outlast its local supply and are therefore no substitute long-term economic base. Second, non-oil based industries, however desirable as providing an alternative source of livelihood, face plenty of problems of their own, not least the paucity of local markets, the difficulty of competing outside them with mass production elsewhere, and the shortage of foreign exchange in African and Asian markets. Moreover, the capital-intensive kind require advanced and continually advancing technology unlikely in the relevant time-scale to be available locally, while the labour-intensive kind are almost wholly dependent on imported labour, which in a sense defeats the object. Much thought has been given to the problems of industrialisation, but there is clearly no easy answer of long-term benefit to small states of this unusual kind.[15]

Problems even more acute face the achievement of self-sufficiency in basic food, an obvious (and declared) *desideratum* in a dangerous world. Agricultural expansion in sub-desert conditions, however advanced the technology, is hampered by the serious and growing inadequacy of water for irrigation. The authorities in Abu Dhabi, where irrigated agriculture has gone relatively furthest, are alarmingly aware of the rate at which fossil water is being exhausted.[16] Moreover, even the wealthiest governments cannot happily envisage producing food crops at a cost astronomically above world rates.

Though such basic economic considerations are obviously relevant to the future viability of the States and to their political and social evolution, it is to the latter that we must now revert. These have understandably been the subject of much less public airing than developments of a more material kind.

What then has been the response of these States to pressures for political evolution, which are, as already observed, inseparable from th rapid spread of education (Table 11.1, cols. 10–12) and the emergenc of a politically sensitive 'middle class' (though that term should be use with caution in a society happily free of Western class consciousness) To many Western observers the continued near-monopoly of power b the ruling families seems either ideologically improper or pragmaticall unwise or both. A number of counter-observations are current. First Western democracy has taken no more root in Arab countries wher socialist revolutions have occurred than in traditionalist ones where the have not. Second, to quote one shrewd inside social analyst, wherea in the West authoritarianism *causes* neuroses, in the Arab world prevents them.[17] Third, the expanding bourgeoisie in the Gulf seems fo the most part to be more interested in profiting from the existing orde than in subverting it.[18] Western experience of the political consequence of an expanding middle class may be irrelevant. Fourth, it was widel regarded in the West as probable that, when British protection wa withdrawn, the shaykhly system would rapidly crumble. It has not. It survival suggests that it remains something far more readily *understoo* by the people of the Gulf, whatever its failings even in their view, tha any alternative mode of government which Westerners declare woul be better for them.

All that said, the need for at least gradual accommodation wit emergent political aspirations in the citizenry has certainly bee recognised by the ruling classes. The question is not whether chang is inevitable but how fast. The first experiment with constitutional elec tive government in Kuwait (1962) was suspended after 14 years; tha in Bahrain (1973) after only two — in both cases broadly on the ground that opposition elements were obstructing the executive.[19] Kuwait' second and apparently more successful move (1981) to legitimise bu restrict the paramountcy of the Āl Ṣabāḥ encourages the belief that suc attempts to balance political modernity and political tradition will sprea down the Gulf, where conciliar government is still embryonic. Th Advisory Council decreed in Qatar in 1971 and formally set up in 197 after the take-over by the present Ruler, has made at least some progres towards establishing itself as a political sounding-board. In the UAE th elective National Assembly ordained by the Provisional Constitution o the Union in 1971 seemed initially to hold greater promise of popula participation in the affairs of state; but its one conspicuous initiative – the submission of a memorandum in March 1979[20] urging political an social change of an evolutionary kind and greater 'federalism' — wa side-stepped by the Supreme Council.

Meanwhile, the response in organisational terms of the nine Gulf Emirates (i.e. all save Kuwait) to the imminence of British withdrawal had been the subject of prolonged debate. The initial proposal to unite all nine, from Bahrain to Fujairah, which had British as well as Saudi and Kuwaiti backing, was discussed at a series of meetings between rulers or their deputies between early 1968 and October 1970.[21] It foundered largely on the particularist considerations of Bahrain and Qatar. The union of the remaining seven 'trucial' States, despite the hesitations of Ras al-Khaima (Ras al-Khayma), thereupon went forward under the joint urging of Abu Dhabi and Dubai, whose pre-eminence the Provisional Constitution of 1971 (still unchanged) implicitly endorsed.[22]

One of the prime concerns of the UAE, as of the other states, on the withdrawal of British protection was to contrive their own. The extent to which their respective armed forces have been rapidly expanded (or, in Kuwait's case, better equipped) has been documented elsewhere.[23] In the case of the UAE, most of the individual rulers were permitted under the Provisional Constitution to build up separate forces, the pre-independence Trucial Oman Scouts (re-named the Union Defence Force) being envisaged as the nucleus of a single federal army when amalgamation should prove possible. Such amalgamation was indeed decreed in May 1976; but the extent of effective integration remains doubtful. Moreover, the mercenary element, particularly in the case of the dominant Abu Dhabi part, is formidable. Despite the UAE's miliary expenditure being the highest *per capita* in the world,[24] and despite fairly sophisticated armament, no one has ever supposed the Union's forces, any more than those of Kuwait or Qatar, to be capable of defending the national territory against a major aggressor.

Indeed, the awareness on the part of all Gulf States of their military weakness was perhaps the principal, if unstated, motive for the next and wider move towards unification which led to the foundation in May 1981 of the Gulf Co-operation Council.[25] This brought for the first time all the smaller Gulf States together with Kuwait and Saudi Arabia into a formal relationship — faced as they were with the successive implications of the Iranian revolution, the occupation of the Great Mosque in Mecca and the Soviet occupation of Afghanistan (all in 1979) and the outbreak of the Iran-Iraq war in September 1980. (Although the explicit aims of the GCC were initially limited to co-ordination in every field except defence, any doubts that joint defence was an implicit aim were removed when the Defence Ministers of the constituent States began in January 1982 a regular series of meetings. Joint army manoeuvres have been held since.) Though resented by some of the citizenry in the States we are considering as exposing their more liberal ethos to domination by the more rigorous Saudis, the GCC — like the UAE itself — has been careful to avoid interference in the internal administration of individual States. Paradoxically, the very looseness of both their structures may prove (in contexts other than the purely military) an element of strength.

This is not the place to examine the responses of our three States, or of the GCC as a whole, to the alarming developments already mentioned in 1979 and 1980, the implications of which — most directly, of the Iranian revolution and the Iran-Iraq war — were heightened by the presence in each State of varying proportions of potentially disaffected Shi'ite minorities.[26] Sober and sensible as their responses have been, they are only relevant to the theme of this essay as signs of the increased maturity of these newly sovereign States and of their ability to collaborate quietly in a number of important fields. We must now return to internal affairs, social and political.

To marshal the indicators of social evolution simply in terms of material welfare and infrastructural services is to stop where the real questions begin. And these of course concern the effect of the whirlwind changes resulting from oil and independence on the *psyche* of the ordinary Gulf citizen. The evolution taking place in a social organism is not something which can be scientifically demonstrated or reduced to statistics. But some attempt is inescapable.

A key phrase in the third Saudi Development Plan may be borrowed as rubric. The aim is there[27] stated as 'trying to ensure that the new conditions in which people live will not force unwanted social change' — the term 'unwanted' being left carefully undefined. (Indeed it may well mean one thing to a government and another to the ordinary citizen.) The same Saudi plan bravely declared that 'the extended family, neighbourhood groups and traditional relationships are still the dominant features of the social structure . . . the people essentially retaining their customary life-style, values and personal networks'. But even if this is true of Saudi Arabia, where the scale is different, it looks improbable that, in the small Gulf States, the 'customary life-style, values and personal networks' of traditional society can withstand the onrush of the centralised welfare state.

Perhaps the best this essay can usefully do in this context is to identify the sort of questions to which Gulf sociologists should surely be addressing themselves. For instance: Has the 'socialisation' of the young in the parental *majlis* been virtually abandoned? Is this once standard mode of social indoctrination now left to the processes of free state education for all, and if so with what results? Can Gulf society digest the personal desire for self-fulfilment that equal education must inspire in the (unequal) female half of the rising generation? Do the large number of school leavers who pursue higher education in the West, where liberalism, individualism and pushfulness are the dominant social motifs, reimmerse themselves without strain on their return into the disciplines of a society where structural hierarchies and group loyalties are traditional? Even in the case of those who stay at home the effect on their social thought processes of regularly listening, as large numbers do, to foreign broadcasts cannot be negligible and is barely open to control. And does not the new mobility of labour, aided by the ease of transportation over the new network of roads, contribute to the dislocation of the old elaborate cat's-cradle of social behaviour? What effect have changes in the style of housing — whether we are thinking of low-cost housing areas, bedu settlement or segregation into city apartment blocks — had on social cohesion? Is the progressive break-up of the extended family and its replacement by an anti-social nuclear substitute a fact, and is it reversible? And how are all these processes affecting the status and welfare of the aged, which were so conspicuously assured under the traditional life-style? In a society which has always regarded the services of a *waṣta* (the next man up) as deserving payment, what are now the accepted limits of bribery? Does the common man regard the new life-style of the wealthy elite with indifference or resentment, admiration or anger? Does not the tendency of governments to ensure the contentment of nationals (and their keen sense of superiority over immigrants) by turning so many effectively into state pensioners for life discourage effort and sap the national vitality? Must the injection of unprecedented sums into the economy have the consequences foreseen centuries ago by Ibn Khaldūn in that famous passage from the *Muqaddima*:[28]

> The things that go with luxury and a life of ease break the vigour of group feeling, which alone produces superiority. When group feeling is destroyed, the tribe is no longer able to defend or protect itself, let alone press any claims. It will be swallowed up by other nations.

Ruminations of this sort, the stock-in-trade of Western observers, have certainly aroused the concern of home-based, if not home-trained, sociologists. It is, one commentator has declared,[29] within Gulf societies themselves that the study of them 'is now focused and that outside theories of social change, development and modernisation are being systematically tested, modified, expanded and in some cases discarded for the future of the so-called Fourth World'. To the present writer the published evidence is less than conclusive and seems better at recognising the problems than at solving them.[30]

The trouble in truth is that everything summarised in this essay has been happening too fast for any alternative conception of the individual's role in the community to establish itself. The question is often asked whether the ruling elites can harness the aspirations of the common man to a share in the framing of evolving society without arousing the syndrome of the sorcerer's apprentice. This may, for the reason indicated at the beginning of this paragraph, be putting the cart before the horse. But pressures, rationalised or not, exist. Let us hope they lead to the emergence of a Gulf-wide consensus on the nature of the society its people wish to see prevail. The one certainty is that no amount of patronising advice from outsiders can or should do it for them.

We have endeavoured to show that in some respects, especially in the external context, the Gulf States have adapted themselves so far with skill to the challenges of wealth and independence. It remains to be seen how they will adjust their internal (political and social) life-style to the mixed blessings of modernity. And in the longer term a problem of a starker kind will have to be addressed. For by what sort of social engineering will a society so starkly dependent on immigrant workers refashion itself when the approaching spectre of an oil-less future heralds their disappearance — or indeed well before that day, if those immigrant workers become politicised?

Notes

1. In the case of the UAE, F. Heard-Bey observes that, because the *Pax Britannica* enabled the coastal shaykhs to prosper, the power struggle between them and the inland tribes was settled in the former's favour. F. Heard-Bey, *From Trucial States to United Arab Emirates*, (Longman, London, 1982), p. 290.

2. An unusual gloss was put to the writer by a prominent Gulf Arab in the mid-1960s: 'Our great misfortune (he said) was that you people never colonised us. If you had, you would at least have spent some effort on our development and we would then have had the pleasure of finally throwing you out.'

3. Blueprint presented by a Lebanese engineer, the late Maurice Gemayel (brother of Pierre), to the British Embassy in Beirut in 1962.

4. R. Hewins, *A Golden Dream: The Miracle of Kuwait*, (W.H. Allen, London, 1963), p. 239.

5. For one detailed account see F.H. Beseisu, *Pragmatic Approach to Arab Gulf States Development Cooperation*, unpublished PhD. thesis, Durham University, 1982, Pts II III and IV.

6. For a succinct analysis of these Arab Funds see R.S. Porter, 'Arab Economic Aid', *Development Policy Review*, (March 1986). A fuller account of the KFAED is R. Stephens, *The Arabs' New Frontier*, (Temple Smith, London, 1976).

7. The mercenary (largely Omani) element in the UAE armed forces is put at 85 per cent by A. Plascov, 'Modernization, Development and Stability' in S. Chubin (ed.), *Security in the Persian Gulf, 3*, (Gower, for IISS, London, 1982), p. 102, and in MERI Report, *United Arab Emirates*, (Croom Helm, London, 1985), p. 7. No published estimate of the mercenary element in those of Kuwait and Qatar is traceable. Plascov, 'Modernization', p. 103, states that Kuwait's include 'many ill-educated Sa'udis, Iraqis, Iranians and Asians'; but in view of the small size of Kuwait's armed forces (12,500) and of the introduction in 1976 of national conscription, this seems questionable — though A.H. Cordesman in his *The Gulf and the Search for Strategic Stability*, (Westview, Boulder, Colorado, 1984), p. 573, declares that conscription has been a 'corrupt failure' and echoes Plascov in saying that the Kuwaiti army is largely of 'former Iraqi Shi'ite bedouin . . . Sa'udi bedouin and some Asians'. On Qatar, (in 1980) Plascov says its 5,000 armed forces, though officered by nationals, contain a large number of non-Qatari other ranks. Since the strength has risen to at least 6,000 and according to one estimate to nearer 12,000, the number of non-Qataris must have increased at least *pro rata*. See also Note 23.

8. A convenient account of the Iraqi claim to Kuwait (and of the perceived threat of 1961), is given by J. Bulloch, *The Gulf*, (Century Publishing, London, 1984), pp. 62–5.

9. The ratio in 1977 was put at 3:1 by R.S. Zahlan, *The Creation of Qatar*, (Croom Helm, London, 1979), p. 119, quoting British press reports. The UN ECWA *Demographic and Related Socio-Economic Data Sheets*, (Beirut, 1982), p. 131, produce much the same ratio for 1980. (See Table 11.1, col. 3.) It has certainly worsened since, by virtue of the population increase. Bulloch, *The Gulf*, Appendix A, estimates the immigrants in 1982 at 82 per cent. The proportion of non-nationals in the labour forces of the three states is still higher. See Table 11.1, col. 4.

10. See Table 11.1, cols. 5, 6 and 7. Prospects of oil in commercial quantities are entertained also by Ras al-Khaima and possibly Fujairah.

11. Figure 11.1 inset.

12. MERI, *United Arab Emirates*, p. 9.

13. There is in fact no recent comprehensive academic study in English. Bulloch, *The Gulf*, gives a general rundown of a 'popular' kind. Earlier general works include D.E. Long, *The Persian Gulf: An Introduction to its Peoples, Politics and Economy*, (Westview, Boulder, Colorado, 1978); and sections of A.J. Cottrell (ed.), *The Persian Gulf States*, (Johns Hopkins University Press, Baltimore, 1980), are useful. On specific states, see for Kuwait J.F. Ismail, *Kuwait: Social Change in Historical Perspective*, (Syracuse University Press, New York, 1983), Chs. 3, 6 and 7; H.A. el-Ebraheem, *Kuwait and the Gulf*, (Croom Helm, London, 1980); and of a popular kind, Hewins, *A Golden Dream*. On Qatar there is rather more, e.g. Zahlan, *The Creation*, pp. 118–34; Z.A. Nafi, *Economic and Social Development in Qatar*, (Frances Pinter, London, 1983), pp. 39–117; R. al-Mallakh, *Qatar: Development of an Oil Economy*, (Croom Helm, London, 1979); M.A. al-Kubaisi, *Industrial Development in Qatar*, unpublished PhD thesis, University of Durham, 1984. For the UAE, Ch. 9 of Heard-Bey, *From Trucial States* is useful; see also MERI, *United Arab Emirates*; A.M. al-Khalifa, *The UAE: Unity in Fragmentation* (Westview, Boulder, Colorado, 1979), pp. 57–86; R. al-Mallakh, *The Economic Development of the UAE*, (Croom Helm, London, 1981), Chs. 2, 3 and 4.

For statistical detail, see Kuwait Ministry of Planning, *Annual Statistical Abstract 1984* and *Social Statistics 1984*; Qatar Ministry of Information, *Year Book 1981/82* (and presumably later years); UAE Ministry of Planning, *Statistical Abstract 1983*.

Relevant Special Supplements in the British press are too many to mention.

14. Kuwait and the UAE moved into deficit budgeting in 1982/83.

15. 'I would hate to see a series of white elephants draining the economies of the oil exporting countries under the guise of industrialisation', 'Alī Khalīfa Āl Ṣabāḥ, Under-

Secretary, Ministry of Finance, Kuwait, quoted in MEED, 4 November 1976. For useful insights on the problem, see J.S. Birks and A.C. Sinclair, *Arab Manpower*, (Croom Helm, London, 1980), pp. 48–55.

16. As demonstrated at the UAE Conference on Water Resources held at al-ʻAyn in May 1984.

17. L.H. Melikian, *Jassim: A Study in the Psychosocial Development of a Young Man in Qatar*, (Longman, London, 1981), p. 82.

18. This is the view of R.H. Magnus, 'Societies and Social Change in the Persian Gulf' in Cottrell (ed.), *The Persian Gulf States*.

19. A.T. Baaklini, 'Legislatures in the Gulf Area: The Experience of Kuwait, 1961–1976', *Journal of Middle East Studies*, vol. 14, (1982), pp. 359–79, examines the Kuwait case in detail. For a shorter account, see Arnold Hottinger, 'Political Institutions in Saudi Arabia, Kuwait and Bahrain' in S. Chubin (ed.), *Security in the Persian Gulf 1: Domestic Political Factors*, (Gower for IISS, London, 1981), pp. 1–14.

20. Summarised by John Whelan, 'The Emirates at Odds', *MEED Arab Report*, 1979, Issue 7, 25 April 1979, pp. 6 and 7.

21. For a detailed account, see Heard-Bey, *From Trucial States*, pp. 341–62.

22. The text of the Provisional Constitution is reproduced in *Middle East Journal*, vol. 27, No. 3 (1972), pp. 307–25.

23. Notably in the annual issues of *The Military Balance*, (Gower for IISS) and in A.H. Cordesman's somewhat unsympathetic *The Gulf and the Search for Strategic Stability*, esp. Ch. 15. See Note 7 above for the 'mercenary' aspect.

24. MERI, *United Arab Emirates*, p. 23. See also Table 11.1, Col. 14 and *The Military Balance* (1984/5), pp. 140–2, where the 1982 UAE defence expenditure *per capita* is shown as about ten times the average in Western Europe. In 1978, according to the *New York Times* of 20 September 1981, quoted by el-Ebraheem in *Kuwait*, p. 8, the *per capita* defence expenditure was then even higher in Qatar ($1,194 as compared to $836 in the UAE and $636 in Kuwait).

25. El-Ebraheem, *Kuwait*, pp. 68–86, gives a useful account. The initiative for the GCC idea came from Kuwait, though till recently Kuwait has been less than enthusiastic about co-operation in defence matters.

26. The figures are nowhere officially documented. For estimates, see Table 11.1, col. 3. The Shiʻite proportion in Bahrain (about 56 per cent) accentuates the possible risks elsewhere. Many Gulf Shiʻites are reportedly responsive to the calls of the agency set up in Iran for the export of Khomeini's Islamic Revolution. For this 'Gulf Office', now directed by Hujjatulislām Hādī Mudarrisī, see *Defense and Foreign Affairs Daily*, (Perth Corporation, New York), 16 July 1985, p. 1.

27. *Third Development Plan 1980–85*, (Ministry of Planning, Saudi Arabia, 1979), p. 54.

28. Ibn Khaldūn, *The Muqaddimah*, tr. F. Rosenthal, 2nd ed. (3 vols., Routledge, London, 1976), vol. 1, p. 287.

29. J.S. Ismail, 'The Politics of Social Change in the Arab States of the Gulf: The View from Within', *Middle East Journal*, vol. 32, no. 3 (1978), p. 354.

30. One Gulf sociologist who discusses some of the obstacles (from an anti-establishment viewpoint) in M.Gh. al-Rumayhī, e.g. in his *Obstacles to Social and Economic Development in Contemporary Communities of the Arab Gulf*, (Dār al-Siyāsa, Kuwait, 1977 — in Arabic). The psychological problems of self-estrangement and loss of personal identity amongst the young are usefully discussed by F. al-Salem, 'Bureaucracy and Alienation in the Arab Gulf States', *Journal of Economics and Administration*, (King Abd al-ʻAzīz University, Jidda), No. 14 (1982), pp. 81–4. See also Melikian's admirable *Jassim*, throughout.

Appendix A: Notes and Sources for Table 11.1

Col. 1	See Figure 11.1
Col. 2	All figures based on UN (ECWA) Data Sheets 1982. Birks and Sinclair's figures for 1975 were 52%, 70% and 69%. Cordesman (1984), p. 590, puts Qatar's figure at 80% ('virtually all sources agree') and, p. 596, the UAE's at about 80%.
Col. 3	K.ASA 1984, Table 97; Kubaisi, p. 42; MERI Report, p. 97. Birks and Sinclair's figures for 1975 were 70%, 81% and 85%.
Col. 4	No official figures published. Percentages chosen here are somewhat above the average of the widely varying estimates seen. The *Defense and Foreign Affairs Handbook* (Perth Corporation, Washington, 1984) declares that 23% of the Qatar population are Iranian; Cordesman, p. 579, puts the Shi'ites at about 17%.
Col. 6	K.ASA 1984, Table 158; QYB 1982, p. 118; UAE ASA 1983, Table 75. For individual UAE States, MERI Report, p. 79, and UAE ASA 1983, Table 75.
Col. 7	K.ASA (as in Col. 6); QMA, p. 3; UAE ASA (as in Col. 6).
Col. 8	Estimates vary widely and are subject to many imponderables. Field, pp. 56 and 57, puts them at 97, 23 and (Abu Dhabi) 57 years in 1981; Bulloch, Appx. C, at 49, 20 and 35. The higher ones for 1985 shown here are thought as reliable as any.
Col. 9	K.ASA, 1984, Table 176; QYB, p. 109; MERI Report, p. 107.
Col. 10	K.Soc St. 1984, Table 4; QYB 1982, p. 45; UAE ASA 1983, pp. 354–357. Pre-oil education was in all cases negligible.
Col. 11	As for Col. 10.
Col. 12	K.Soc.St 1984, Table 42; UN(ECWA) Table 12, for Qatar (in 1980); UAE as for Col. 10. In 1982, 2,683 Kuwaitis were in universities abroad, K.Soc.St. 1984, Table 274; 722 Qataris a few years earlier, Birks & Sinclair, p. 60.
Col. 13	*The Military Balance* (1984/85) (IISS, London), p. 125. The 1982/83 edn. recorded Kuwait as having 18,000 paramilitary forces as well, a figure dropped to 2,500 in the 1984/85 edn.
Col. 14	As for Col. 13. In the case of Qatar the figure shown represents 2/3 of the 18-month budget 1982/83.

Full Titles of Sources

UN(ECWA):	UN(ECWA), *Demographic and Related Socio-economic Data Sheets*, 1982.
Birks and Sinclair:	J.S. Birks and C.A. Sinclair, *Arab Manpower*, (Croom Helm, London, 1980).
Cordesman:	A.H. Cordesman, *The Gulf and the Search for Strategic Stability*, (Westview, Boulder, Colorado, 1984).
K.ASA 1984:	Kuwait Ministry of Planning, *Annual Statistical Abstract*, (1984).
Kubaisi:	M.A. al-Kubaisi, *Industrial Development in Qatar*, unpublished PhD thesis, Durham University, 1984.
MERI Report:	Middle East Research Institute, University of Pennsylvania, *United Arab Emirates*, (Croom Helm, London, 1985).
QYB:	*Qatar Year Book, 1982*, Qatar Ministry of Information.
UAE ASA 1983:	UAE Ministry of Planning, *Annual Statistical Abstract 1983*.
QMA:	Qatar Monetary Agency fact sheet, *Qatar Economy in Figures 1979–83* (n.d.)

Field:	M. Field in S. Chubin (ed.), *Security in the Persian Gulf, 1: Domestic Political Factors*, (Gower for IISS, London, 1981).
Bulloch:	J. Bulloch, *The Gulf* (Century Publishing, London, 1984).
K.Soc.St. 1984:	Kuwait Ministry of Planning, *Social Statistics 1984*.

Appendix B: Sources for Figure 11.1

	KUWAIT		QATAR		U.A.E.	
Year of Estimate or Census	Pop. 000s	Source	Pop. 000s	Source	Pop. 000s	Source
1900–10	50	Lorimer, p. 1074	27	Lorimer, p. 1732	80	Lorimer, pp. 53, 408, 455, 1475, 1759
1940	50	Ebraheem, p. 71	28	Zahlan (Q), p. 111	80	Zahlan (TS), pp. 11–16
1949	100	Ismail, p. 117	—	—	—	—
1957	206	K.ASA, p. 25	—	—	—	—
1961	322	K.ASA, p. 25				
1965	467	K.ASA, p. 25	80	Fenelon (TS), p. 242	121	Fenelon (TS), p. 79
1968	—	—	—	—	180	Fenelon (UAE), p. 132
1970	739	K.ASA, p. 25	100	Zahlan (Q), p. 111	—	—
1975	995	K.ASA, p. 25	170	Zahlan (Q), p. 111	656	MERI Report, p. 4
1977	—	—	200	Zahlan (Q), p. 111	862	UAE. ASA, p. 43.
1980	1,358	K.ASA, p. 25	245	UN (ECWA), p. 179	983	UN (ECWA), p. 179
1984	1,787	K.ASA, p. 25	272	Bulloch, Appx. A	1,175	Bulloch, Appx. A

Full Titles of Sources

Lorimer:	J.C. Lorimer, *Gazetteer of the Persian Gulf, 'Omān and Central Arabia*, (6 vols., Superintendent Government Printing, India, Calcutta, 1908–1915), vols. IIA and IIB.
Ebraheem:	H.A. el-Ebraheem, *Kuwait and the Gulf*, (Croom Helm, London, 1980).
Zahlan (Q):	R.S. Zahlan, *The Creation of Qatar*, (Croom Helm, London, 1979).
Zahlan (TS):	R.S. Zahlan, *The Origins of the United Arab Emirates*, (Macmillan, London, 1978).
Ismail:	J.S. Ismail, *Kuwait: Social Change in Historical Perspective*, (Syracuse U.P., New York, 1982).
K.ASA:	Kuwait Ministry of Planning, *Annual Statistical Abstract*, (1984).
Fenelon (TS):	K.G. Fenelon, *The Trucial States*, 2nd edn. (Khayat, Beirut, 1969).

Fenelon (UAE):	K.G. Fenelon, *The United Arab Emirates: An Economic and Social Survey*, 2nd edn., (Longman, London, 1976).
MERI Report:	MERI (University of Pennsylvania) Report, *United Arab Emirates*, (Croom Helm, London, 1985).
UAE. ASA:	UAE, *Annual Statistical Abstract*, (1983).
UN (ECWA):	UN (ECWA), *Demographic and Related Socio-Economic Data Sheets*, (1982).
Bulloch:	J. Bulloch, *The Gulf*, (Century Publishing, London, 1984).

12 Bahrain in Transition

Anthony Parsons

When I was appointed British Political Agent in Bahrain in 1965, it did not occur to me that, only a few years later, Bahrain would be a full member of the Arab League and the United Nations following the termination of the series of nineteenth-century treaties which had given Britain responsibility for Bahrain's external defence and for the conduct of its foreign relations. At the time neither side was contemplating so radical a change. On the contrary: the Government of Bahrain felt no diminution of the need for British protection so long as Iran continued to claim the islands as the fourteenth province of the Iranian Empire. On the British side, the requirement to maintain the *status quo* in the Gulf and thus to safeguard the flow of Arab oil to the industries of the West was as strong as ever, while it looked as though, with the forthcoming independence of Aden and the Aden Protectorates, the centre of gravity of the British system of military communications to and from the Far East would move to Bahrain, thus augmenting the British presence there.

Twenty years ago British public opinion, apart from those few specialists in government, trade and industry who were directly concerned with the area, was disposed to see the Arab states of the Gulf as an undifferentiated collection of romantic nomads, comprising archaic societies which, on account of their new-found oil wealth, were in the process of exchanging their camels for Cadillacs, but were otherwise still anchored to a medieval way of life. This perception had as much, or rather as little, relevance to Bahrain as to any of the urbanised Arab states such as Egypt or Syria: only the scale was smaller. Bahrain had for thousands of years been a settled centre for entrepôt trade and had continued as such since the Āl Khalīfa, the present ruling family, coming from the Arabian mainland, had taken over the islands in 1783. In addition, Bahrain's material prosperity had, since time immemorial, been bolstered by the pearling industry which only began to decline in the 1920s with the competition of Japanese cultured pearls. Fortunately for the islands, oil shortly thereafter became an alternative source of wealth, with production (the first in the Arabian Peninsula) beginning in 1933.

In the 1920s the then Ruler, Shaykh Ḥamad b. 'Īsā Āl Khalīfa, had embarked on a major programme of social and economic modernisation. Free health and education services were established, internal communications were improved and, with the availability of substantial funds from oil, amenities such as electricity and piped water were progressively projected to towns and villages. Hence, 30 years later, at the time of my arrival, Bahrain exhibited the characteristics of, and was experiencing the problems common in, a sophisticated urban society. After a generation of welfare services, the population was young in demographic terms and increasing rapidly. Endemic killer diseases such as malaria and tuberculosis had been eradicated and the infant mortality rate had fallen to European levels. Universal education up to secondary standard had virtually eliminated illiteracy and had produced a new generation of Bahrainis who combined high economic and social expectations with acute political awareness.

The Bahrain Government faced daunting problems in meeting these popular aspirations. Bahraini oil production had declined to about 70,000 barrels a day and most of the crude which was fed into the Sitra refinery came by under-sea pipelines from Saudi Arabia; prospects for further discoveries of oil were bleak. The domestic market was too small to sustain major industries, urbanisation had already seriously reduced agricultural output — abandoned date gardens were a common sight — and the large Bahraini private, mercantile sector was traditionally disposed to employ Indians and Europeans rather than Bahrainis. On the face of it Bahrain was geographically the ideal centre for multinational or international enterprises wishing to conduct operations throughout the area. But these potential benefits were denied to Bahrain owing to the refusal of the Iranian Government to do business with anyone located in what they regarded as their usurped fourteenth province.

Hence the economy was stagnating and the prospect of widespread unemployment lay ahead with all its social and political implications. The British presence was a further complication. Admittedly the 3,000 or so British service personnel and their families in the army, naval and RAF installations were a significant employer of labour, and injected a substantial quantity of foreign exchange into the economy. Admittedly the Arab people of Bahrain genuinely feared an Iranian invasion and realised that, without a foreign military presence, the islands would be defenceless. However, Britain had for many years been the prime target for Arab nationalist attack: in the Arab political vocabulary deployed so vividly by the Egyptian public media and by their lesser counterparts in Baghdad and Damascus, the words 'British' and 'imperialist' had become, if not synonymous, inseparable the one from the other. The young Bahrainis, many of whom had received their university education in Egypt, Syria or Iraq, were particularly susceptible to the fulminations emanating from Nasser's Egypt and perceived themselves as being frustrated and humiliated by living under an old-fashioned regime which was still in an anachronistic relationship with the arch-imperial power. The violence which was attending Britain's attempts to dragoon Aden and its hinterland Shaykhdoms into a federation was already beginning to cast its shadow up the Gulf, particularly in Bahrain. The political outlook was far from promising and I arrived on the heels of serious labour unrest which had strained the exiguous security forces to their limit.

On the other side, the Bahrain Government had a number of assets to counterbalance its liabilities. The population of Bahrain was divided more or less equally into Sunnīs and Shi'ites, the latter being the indigenous inhabitants and, generally speaking, the rurally based element in the population. Divisions between the two ran deep and had in the past caused considerable turbulence and bloodshed. It was equally the case that the Shi'ites probably looked for their political inspiration more to revolutionary Iraq (not Iran) than to Nasser's Egypt, the focus of young, Sunnī admiration. And yet a generation of standardised, modern education had blurred the distinction between Sunnīs and Shi'ites at least in the younger generation, and the problem was no longer regarded as serious in terms of internal security (this was of course some years before the renaissance of militant Shi'ism following the Iranian revolution of 1978–79). Furthermore, by regional standards, the Bahrain Government at the functional level was efficient and honest. Even in the gossip-laden atmosphere of the capital there were few allegations of corruption and the talent and competence of a number of senior government officials, Sunnīs and Shi'ites, Āl Khalīfa of the younger generation and people from non-shaykhly origins, was freely recognised.

Above all, the traditional style of Arab rule practised at the political level by the Ruler, Shaykh 'Īsā b. Salmān Āl Khalīfa, who had succeeded his father in his early thirties in 1961, was well suited to a geographically small and demographically compact society. Shaykh 'Īsā's *modus operandi* was the reverse of the single-party based, bureaucratic and highly structured versions of republican Arab socialism which were functioning in Cairo and elsewhere in the Arab world. But his style had the great merit of openness and accessibility. Yes, the ultimate decisions rested with him alone, but he sat in open Council (*majlis*) three times a day for seven days a week and anyone in the population could attend these sessions, present his petition and air his grievance. Thus Shaykh

'Īsā kept in close touch with his people and could feel the pulse of the island before deciding on a course of action. It may not have been parliamentary democracy Western-style, nor people's democracy Eastern-style, but it created a kind of cosiness and intimacy which promoted consensus and smoothed down the roughest surfaces of opposition.

Throughout 1966, although there were no mass outbreaks of violence, I was conscious of an underlying tension and malaise. The unremitting drumfire of Cairo's *Voice of the Arabs* and *Voice of the Arab Gulf*, coupled with the mounting opposition to the Federation in Aden, were having their effect. Subversive organisations such as the Arab Nationalist Movement, the National Liberation Front and the Popular Front for the Liberation of the Arab Gulf became active and there were car bomb attacks against expatriate officers of the Bahrain State Police. The old Irish Commandant had a stroke and departed, to be followed by the (British) Head of the Special Branch. It began to look as though an Aden situation was developing in Bahrain, and the Ruler's security screen was thin. There were no Bahraini armed forces, only the State Police of about 1,000 men, a mixture of Omanis, Baluchis and Bahrainis. There was no question of the British forces in the island being deployed in an internal security role.

The Bahrain Government sensibly concentrated on trying to revive the economy and to create employment for the growing body of school-leavers. In 1965 they commissioned an Economic Survey from the British Ministry of Overseas Development. The results of the survey generated little optimism: the recommendations for the establishment of small, cottage-type, industries, if implemented, would do little to alleviate the problem of finding work for thousands of young men and women. The Government then turned to the American-owned Bahrain Petroleum Company (BAPCO) for a second survey. The Company, conscious that political stability was central to their own operation, applied themselves to the task on a broader canvas than that on which the Ministry of Overseas Development had worked. They took as their thesis three elements favourable to Bahrain: first, the existence of large and untapped supplies of cheap, 'associated', natural gas; second, Bahrain's central location on the East/West communications network; third, the passage of large numbers of oil tankers close to the islands. In late 1966 their recommendations were submitted to the Government. Amongst a host of subsidiary projects, such as the extension of the airport runway to accommodate the new generation of jumbo jets on the Far East run, two major projects stood out. The first was the construction of a graving dock offshore to service super-tankers. The second was an aluminium smelter to be based on natural gas, with the raw alumina coming in otherwise empty tankers from Australia *en route* to fill up with crude oil at Gulf terminals, and a world-wide market for the finished product. (Both these projects are now well-established features of Bahrain's economic landscape.) In a nutshell the BAPCO report offered realistic prospects of economic expansion in labour-intensive areas and the pessimism of the Bahraini development planners began to lift.

As the year 1966 ended in an atmosphere of relative tranquillity, none of us could have anticipated the seismic shocks which lay ahead over the next twelve months, nor could we have forecast their far-reaching consequences. In the first months of 1967, tension rose between Israel and Syria and there were serious clashes between the two sides in which the Syrian Air Force suffered losses. In May the Syrians got wind of an almost certainly non-existent Israeli military build-up in the north. They called for Egyptian help to prevent a possible invasion. President Nasser, although large Egyptian forces were bogged down far away in the civil war in the Yemen, responded by re-occupying Sinai. The United Nations Emergency Force (UNEF), which had been monitoring the demilitarisation of Sinai since 1957, withdrew; constitutionally it could only remain if acceptable to both parties. The Egyptian Government made clear that this was no longer the case. Nasser then closed the straits of Tirān to Israeli shipping. To all of us who were acquainted with the Arab-Israeli dispute, this action meant one thing — war. The Israelis would not tolerate being bottled up and denied their only access to the outside world on their southern border. The salvos of threat and bombast being bellowed from Cairo Radio indicated that Nasser had no intention of climbing down diplomatically. Excitement in Bahrain rose to feverish heights. In the last weeks of May and the first days of June there was never a time when groups of people were not clustered round radio sets listening to the anti-Israeli fulminations of the commentators. The tension became palpable. On 6 June the news broke that war had erupted between Egypt and Israel.

The following five or six days surged past as in a dream. After Arab radio stations had mendaciously reported that British and American aircraft had been flying alongside the Israeli Air Force in its attack on Egyptian airfields, a large crowd gathered outside the Political Agency, one of the most prominent buildings in the business quarter of Manāma, and continued to chant and demonstrate almost without respite, night and day. The atmosphere grew confused and ominous. The people of Bahrain were being exposed to contradictory information. The Arab radio stations, up to the moment of the cease-fire, were dramatising the battle in such a way as to give the impression that the Egyptian army was at the gates of Tel Aviv. The Western public media, including the BBC Arabic Service, were reporting the truth, namely a catastrophic defeat for Arab arms. When this fact became incontrovertible, the mood of the crowd outside the Agency began to worsen. One evening, it must have been about 12 June, we were told that, the following morning, the Agency would be stormed and burnt down. I was determined that there would be no shots fired from a diplomatic mission, whatever the circumstances, and refused an offer of help from the British forces. I equipped my small guard from the Bahrain State Police with sticks, not rifles. Our plan was to do our best through persuasion to prevent the building from being occupied but, if the worst came to the worst, to retreat into the garden and let the crowd get on with it.

In the event, Shaykh 'Īsā got wind of what was afoot. Just at the moment when the crowd was on the point of breaking into the building — they were coming over the wall and my staff and I were preparing to argue them out of advancing any further — Shaykh 'Īsā's car drove slowly into the middle of the assembly. The Ruler, who was unescorted, climbed on to the bonnet and addressed the people. I was just out of earshot but he was clearly speaking with some vehemence and considerable effect. The denouement was as dramatic as the climax. The Ruler re-entered the car and drove slowly away: the whole crowd of, say, 2–3,000 people followed him. Half an hour later the open space in front of the Agency was empty. The crisis had passed.

In the following weeks a profound change came over the Bahraini political scene. National morale was, of course, low and a general air of gloom prevailed over the Arab defeat and the Israeli occupation of Arab territory, particularly Jerusalem and the other remaining parts of what had been Mandatory Palestine. By the same token we had received confirmation of what we had already suspected, namely that the Bahrainis, although remote from the geographical confrontation between the Israelis and the Arabs and although the Palestinian community in Bahrain did not exceed 40 or 50 souls, felt as strongly and as deeply about the Palestine cause as did any Arabs from any part of the Arab world. But this was not the heart of the matter so far as the internal situation in Bahrain was concerned, although the government must have absorbed the lesson for the future that they could not afford to lag behind their own people in regard to the Palestine question. What was decisive was the fact that, within days of the cease-fire, the flow of hostile propaganda directed from Cairo against the Gulf regimes and the British presence in the Gulf dried up. *The Voice of the Arabs* dropped the subject and, so far as I can remember, *The Voice of the Arab Gulf* was closed down. Egyptian support for organisations such as the ANM, NLF and PFLOAG stopped. The Bahraini exiles in Cairo and Damascus fell silent. It appeared that the revolutionary Arab governments had decided that they should do nothing to upset the *status quo* in the Gulf in order not to endanger the free flow of oil with all that this meant in financial terms for the rebuilding of the shattered Egyptian and Syrian armed forces. For the first time since the early 1950s, an all-embracing Arab consensus, comprising secular and republican as well as traditional and monarchical regimes, was beginning to emerge. The disaster of the 1967 war had, it seemed, at least temporarily stilled the inter-Arab quarrels which had characterised the previous decade and which had created such serious problems for the smaller states, vulnerable as they were to the blandishments or the objurgations of their larger and more powerful neighbours.

Almost overnight the malaise drained out of the Bahraini political scene and, particularly with some more favourable indicators showing for the economic future, a calmer and more relaxed atmosphere characterised the islands than at any time for many years past. Perhaps the most striking illustration of this transformation was the fact that the transfer of a substantial British military headquarters to Bahrain following the British departure from Aden and the Protectorates passed off almost unnoticed; certainly there was no hostile reaction.

However, more drama was in store. Following the chaotic finale to Britain's long-standing presence in Aden and the subsequent loss of the naval and air communications facilities there, rumour began to circulate in the Gulf that British withdrawal was imminent. This was fuelled by the current which was flowing in certain circles in London to the effect that, for a combination of financial and general political reasons, Britain should give up all its commitments 'East of Suez', and that its future lay, not in policing the communications of a virtually defunct Empire, but in a European role. By the autumn anxiety was growing amongst the Gulf rulers and the late Mr Goronwy Roberts, then Minister of State at the Foreign and Commonwealth Office, toured the Gulf in November to reassure the rulers. In Bahrain he made public statements to the BBC Arabic Service and to the editor of the only Arabic language newspaper, *Al-Aḍwā'*. His message was in all cases the same. Britain had no intention of withdrawing from the Gulf. Britain would stay in the Gulf so long as its presence was necessary to maintain peace and security in the area and thus to ensure economic and social development. The Gulf relaxed, but not for long.

In January 1968 we were told that Mr Roberts was paying us another visit. His purpose was not revealed in advance but the Bahrain Government was under no illusion that he was coming, after so short an interval, to wish them a Happy New Year. On this occasion he remained in the islands for only a few hours. His instructions were short and to the point. On his last visit he had been unable to give the Ruler a date for the termination of the British presence. He could now tell him that it had been decided (apparently for financial reasons) that the treaties would be terminated at the end of 1971.

This news came as a bombshell to the Bahrain Government, particularly after the reassurance given only two months previously. It was not that the Āl Khalīfa had any intrinsic wish to remain indefinitely under the protection of a foreign, non-Arab power. But they were acutely conscious of the turbulence of the region, of their lack of any defensive capability, of the continuing absence of co-operation amongst the nine states of the Lower Gulf and, above all, of the threat posed to the integrity of Bahrain by the unsettled Iranian claim. Furthermore, until the new economic projects could be translated into reality, the British military presence was making a major contribution, both in terms of employment, business activity and foreign exchange, to an economy which was still in a precarious state.

Once the first shock had passed, the Bahrain Government addressed its problems vigorously. The economic development programme was accelerated and the British Government agreed to provide financial assistance to extend the airport runway, thus enhancing Bahrain's attraction as a global centre of communications. In 1967, anticipating a change in British policy, Shaykh 'Īsā had laid plans for the creation of a small Defence Force. These were now put in train. On a regional basis, the British announcement stimulated a hitherto unrealised degree of co-operation. In February 1968 the nine Lower Gulf Rulers (Bahrain, Qatar, Abu Dhabi, Dubai, Sharjah, Ras al-Khaima, Ajman, Umm al-Qaiwain, Fujairah) met (in Abu Dhabi) for only the second time in history (the first ever meeting took place in 1965), and it was announced that agreement had been reached in principle to establish a Union of Arab Emirates comprising all nine states.

This development touched off a major public debate in Bahrain. Broadly speaking the younger, more pan-Arab generation were in favour of the projected Union of the Nine. They believed in unity as a principle and also thought that Bahraini membership of the Union would facilitate access to the wealth of Abu Dhabi as well as providing a wider area of employment for the Bahraini labour force; they also hoped that union would heal the rift which had estranged Bahrain and Qatar for so many years. The older generation felt otherwise; my personal views were closer to theirs. I found it difficult to imagine that a union between Bahrain and the seven so-called Trucial States would work. Bahrain was far away: its history, demography and economic base were totally different from those of the Trucial States. My view was that Bahrain should go it alone when the time came and seek full membership of the Arab League and the United Nations. The problem was the Iranian claim. I had no doubt that a Bahraini application for UN membership would succeed. None of the Permanent Members of the Security Council would be likely to veto such an application, which would receive overwhelming support in the General Assembly. However, such a consummation, although it would provide an element of deterrence against an Iranian move against Bahrain, would be far from satisfactory. Most important, it would not solve the problem of Iran boycotting commercial enterprises which were based in Bahrain, thus vitiating economic growth in the islands. The dilemma seemed insoluble.

In December 1968 the then Shāh of Iran turned the key in the lock. While on a state visit to India he made a statement at a press conference to the effect that, although he had no doubt that Bahrain was part of Iran, the population might have changed over the years; he would therefore be prepared to accept their verdict on their future provided that their views could be freely expressed and independently verified. This statement, with its overt acceptance of the principle of self-determination for Bahrain, changed everything.

The British Government (acting for the Government of Bahrain) and the Government of Iran then had recourse to the good offices of the Secretary-General of the United Nations. Intensive confidential negotiations took place with the Under-Secretary-General concerned, Dr Ralphe Bunche, throughout 1969 and early 1970 in order to formulate a scenario acceptable to all parties for the ascertainment of Bahraini opinion on their future. In the event, terms of reference were agreed and Dr Winspeare Guiccardi, an Italian official of the UN Secretariat, visited Bahrain. He spoke to individuals, to community leaders, to representatives of clubs and associations, to village headmen and many others. In April he submitted his report to the Secretary-General who transmitted it to the Security Council. The recommendation, which was adopted unanimously the following month by the Council, was clear: Bahraini opinion was overwhelmingly resolved that Bahrain should be an independent Arab state. The ancient claim had at last been laid to rest. In 1971, with the termination of the British treaties, Bahrain, along with Qatar, the UAE (of seven states) and Oman were admitted to membership of the United Nations. Two years later, in 1973, the price of crude oil rose more steeply and suddenly than at any time in the history of the exploitation of hydrocarbons and great wealth came to the Gulf region.

Now, 15 years later, it is difficult to imagine Bahrain as a protected state facing high unemployment and a bleak economic future, a target for the rhetorical thunderbolts of revolutionary Arab nationalism. Bahrain is a member in good standing of the Non-Aligned Movement and is in the mainstream of the Arab League and the Gulf Co-operation Council. The Foreign Minister, Shaykh Muḥammad b. Mubārak Āl Khalīfa, is one of the longest-serving and most experienced of Arab Foreign Ministers. Economically the islands have prospered beyond the most optimistic forecasts. The settlement of the Iranian claim, the collapse of Beirut, and the relaxed and amenable conditions of life, combined with the oil boom of the 1970s, have helped to turn Bahrain into a regional centre of communications, commerce and finance. So far from there being unemployment, the foreign community has increased substantially: there are now more British subjects living and working in Bahrain, many of them employed by Arab enterprises, than there were in the days when Britain had a military presence there.

The problems and uncertainties confronting Bahrain are totally different from those of 20 years ago. The most immediate preoccupation is the Iran-Iraq war and the danger of escalation to the Lower Gulf, already present with the attacks on tankers and other shipping which began in 1983. Economically, the problems are more complex. Bahraini oil production has declined to negligible proportions and government revenue may prove inadequate to continue to provide the welfare and public services on which the growing population has come to depend. Resort to significant taxation to fill the gap would alarm the private sector and could reduce Bahrain's regional attraction. These factors could be compounded by a degree of recession arising out of the relative slump in the international oil market.

The subject which has aroused the most controversy amongst the people of Bahrain is the long-term effect of the combined bridge and causeway which will link the islands to the mainland of Saudi Arabia, about 20 kilometres away. There are many viewpoints, some favourable, others more apprehensive. It is generally accepted that the causeway will have a positive effect on the integrity of Bahrain in that it would facilitate the passage of Saudi and other GCC forces in the event of external threat. From the economic point of view, some fear a damaging impact on the

Bahraini market because the lower Saudi tariff on imports will encourage Bahrainis to jump into their cars and do all their shopping on the mainland. Others look to a major inflow of foreign exchange from increased numbers of Saudi visitors escaping from the austerities of the Kingdom to the fleshpots of Manāma. Others fear that closer proximity to Saudi Arabia may eventually lead to the imposition of Saudi-style restrictions on, for example, the sale of liquor and the intermingling of the sexes, with the consequence of a decline in national morale — there is no Wahhabism in Bahrain — and the exodus of numbers of foreign enterprises. Whatever the advantages and disadvantages may prove to be in the years to come, one thing is certain. Bahrain's wholly independent and idiosyncratic island character is bound to come under greater pressure than hitherto from its large and, by Gulf standards, somewhat overwhelming neighbour.

At present, the principal threat to Bahrain's internal stability derives from the renaissance of militant Shi'ism, stimulated by the Iranian revolution and by the new dynamic in the Shi'ite community in the Lebanon. This phenomenon has manifested itself in sporadic plots against the regime, inspired and in some cases directed from outside. So far the security services have nipped these attempts in the bud. The Shi'ite community, like their Sunnī compatriots, have benefitted from Bahrain's prosperity, but their historical perception of themselves as a depressed class and their emotional reaction to the achievements of their co-religionists in Iran, allied to the fundamentalist wave which is permeating the whole Islamic world, make them susceptible to agitation. So long as this tide continues to flow it is difficult to see what pre-emptive policies the Government can reasonably adopt, other than strict security measures against conspiracies.

In this context, many Western commentators argue that the Gulf States must, if they are to preserve stability, modernise their political systems and introduce some representative institutions in order to enable the educated majority of the population to feel a sense of genuine participation in governmental decision-making.

It is easy for outsiders to make facile suggestions of this kind. The historical fact is that the traditional, patriarchal regimes of the Arabian Peninsula have shown greater staying power than have the 'modern' political structures elsewhere in the Arab world. The adaptations of multi-party parliamentary systems, as practised in, for example, monarchical Egypt and Iraq, were swept away by military *coups d'état* as was the case with the equivalent regimes of Syria. Nasserism itself, for all its emotional appeal in terms of 'anti-imperialism' and pan-Arab nationalism, failed to find a satisfactory political base to replace military rule. The Ba'thist regimes in present-day Syria and Iraq can hardly be described, in terms of their treatment of and relationship with their own peoples, as improvements on the open, accessible system which operates in Bahrain and which has not changed over the past 15 years, except in so far as pressure of work has slightly reduced the frequency with which the Amīr sits in open *majlis*. Bahrain did indeed experiment with a parliament in the 1970s, but it degenerated into sterile faction and was dissolved. It is difficult in small states for political parties or even individuals to remain immune from external or internal factional influence, and representative institutions in such circumstances tend to fragment into patchworks of squabbling pressure groups. Modernisation may be necessary, but the experience of the past 20 or 30 years has demonstrated that there is no simple panacea for the problem of adapting existing political systems in the light of social and economic change. Precisely how and when to accomplish this is best left to the Bahrainis themselves; they need no gratuitous help or advice from outsiders, however well-meaning.

13 Human Resources in the Gulf

Roger Webster

Development in any part of the world is conventionally linked to the capacity to exploit with greater efficiency the key resources of land, labour and capital. The technological advances in Western Europe culminating in the Industrial Revolution generated wealth and political power which in turn were fuelled by the appropriation of ever larger tracts of land and the application of the labour of subjected peoples to its exploitation, a process manifested in its most ruthless form in the transportation of African slaves to the seemingly endless territories of the American colonies. Colonialism and slavery, one must believe, are not prerequisites of development, which these days is coupled with the more benign ideas of aid, transfer of technology, and self-help. While in much of the developing world it is the third element, capital, that is lacking and which hampers the efficient utilisation of abundant labour and in some cases also abundant land, in most of Arabia the situation is reversed. The discovery of huge hydrocarbon deposits in the territories of the Arab Gulf States has all but eliminated poverty in the crude sense of a theoretical *per capita* income, but it does not in itself make up for the lack of manpower, particularly skilled manpower, nor the paucity of other natural resources that is equally characteristic of the region. The Arab Gulf States are in this respect an anomaly. As 'rich developing countries' they have both opportunities and unique problems that distinguish them from the more general 'poor developing countries', but they share with them many of the same obstacles to social and economic progress: high rates of illiteracy, infant mortality and disease, low rates of participation in development tasks, and the social and economic dislocation caused by the juxtaposition of a small but energetic modern sector, employing up-to-date, often imported, technology, ideas and personnel, with a larger but stagnant and dispirited traditional sector. To cite but one illustration of this, a farmer in Oman recently pointed out with much concern and astonishment that he can now go to the *sūq* in Nizwā and buy fresh European-grown tomatoes of a more reliable quality, and at a cheaper price, than he can afford to produce himself on his small family farm. How can such a man persuade his children to devote the same patient care to tending the crops, the soil, and the *falaj* irrigation channels as their forebears have done over many generations, particularly when more prestigious and much better paid opportunities exist in the army or civil service? Such employment might even allow for an Indian labourer to be hired who could keep the farm just about ticking over for weekend recreational use.

It is hardly surprising that Arab writers on development draw parallels not with the European colonial experience but with the roots of Western cultural and scientific transformation in the Renaissance. Such terms as *al-nahḍa* (Renaissance) or *al-izdihār* (flowering) have for some time been commonplace enough to require no explanation by the Arab writer to his reader. What is implied by such words is not simply a revitalisation of moribund ways of thinking, whether in the artistic, scientific, intellectual or economic spheres, but a radically new outlook. The pace of development may be measured, up to a point, by monitoring the numbers of schools and pupils, the building of hospitals, the spread of roads, air and sea ports, and the establishment of new industries. Any regular visitor to the Gulf cannot fail to be impressed by the rapid strides that have been made in all these fields, while the newcomer to the region, no matter how diligently he has pursued his preparatory background reading, is invariably astonished at the scale of material development, its pervasiveness, and the contradictions highlighted by the remaining gaps. Yet development clearly cannot be equated with concrete, glass and steel nor the other paraphernalia of modern living. The transition from traditional to modern life involves a fundamental change of attitude; it is not simply that the old games can be played with more efficiency and therefore with more success, but that the rules of the game itself are reinterpreted, new goals are set, and fresh criteria for judging success or failure are employed. What is implied, above all, is a new self-consciousness, the awareness of choice at all levels from the everyday options of the individual — which soap powder to use and whom to marry — to policy decisions at national government level.

Recognition of the existence of valid alternatives — the acceptance of pluralism — brings with it many challenges. There is the challenge to the authority of social norms, which suddenly appear not as inevitable, self-evident and immutable rules, but as inherited habits whose perpetuation may or may not be desirable. There is the challenge to religious authority, which in the eyes of many of a fundamentalist persuasion, whether in the Muslim East or Christian West, is and must always be opposed to the dangers of free choice. A real reconciliation of secular, speculative science with religious precept, as distinct from an exercise in fudging the issues, demands intellectual exertions on both sides which traditional thinkers have by and large not been required to make. While it is easy to state baldly, as development plans in the Gulf States often do, that development must not and need not contravene established religious and social values, yet such harmony is not easy to achieve in reality. We in the West, for whom the clash of science and religion is barely a live issue, owe our present complacency to a line of heretics, outcasts and dissidents who could not afford to dismiss the question lightly. Again, one must believe that violent persecution and martyrdom are not necessary accompaniments to the reshaping of religious and social thinking, although events in Iran, Egypt and Mecca, to mention but a few instances, give grounds for pessimism.

Then there is the challenge to political authority posed by the opening up of debate and the desire for wider public participation in decision making. Complacent despotism even of the benign kind — if there can be such a thing — is inadequate for satisfying the expectations of an increasingly aware populace. In times of such far-reaching change, the art of government in translating the possible into the actual is severely taxed. Since the onset of oil-inspired development, rulers in four Gulf States — Oman, Abu Dhabi, Qatar and Saudi Arabia — have suffered the consequences of their incapacity to meet this challenge. We might add to the list of modern Arabic clichés, *al-thawra* (revolution), although in the cases mentioned there was, of course, no question of a general popular uprising.

Perhaps this sounds like a call for unrestrained individualism or Westernisation of the social and political institutions of the Gulf. How to separate modernisation from Westernisation is a question raised with increasing frequency in the Gulf. A general tightening of belts, after the boom years of the 1970s, allows time for reflection on the goals of development, a reflection no doubt encouraged by the fate of the overtly Westernising imperial regime over the water in Iran. How often in the Gulf one hears Japan cited as an example of a non-Western country that has succeeded in playing and beating the West at its own game while retaining its cultural integrity. One is much exercised to find significant parallels between Japan and the Gulf States, whether in their respective historical experiences or modern industrial capacities. Nevertheless Japan stands as a source of moral encouragement for the developing Gulf States; proof that success is possible, even if it cannot be a model.

Definitions of development in general, or human resources development in particular, differ more in the range of criteria embraced than in the content of each measure. A very narrow definition in economic terms would be to take *per capita* national income as a yardstick, but in reference to the 'hot-house, forced-growth environment of the Gulf'[1] this and other conventional analyses are clearly inadequate. Broader definitions embrace less easily pin-pointed attributes: social and psychological elements, spiritual qualities that promote citizenship,[2] 'enriching the cultural specificity of the society'.[3] Reverting again to the thesis that it is the awareness of a broader spectrum of choice, both for the individual and for society, that distinguishes a modern from a traditional society, then development can be defined as the process of exploiting such options effectively so as to achieve a sustained improvement in the material and spiritual well-being of the people concerned. As one writer has put it, 'development *is* human resources development'.[4]

This essay, representing the thoughts of a layman, cannot pretend to comment with authority on the growing volume of literature concerned with demography, manpower and education in the Gulf which are the raw materials of the study of human resources, much less to add substantively to this body. A more limited and, I hope, legitimate objective would be to review some of the issues that are central to the debate as they might appear to a visitor to the Gulf in the late 1980s, bearing in mind the underlying notion of development as a broadening of choice. To what extent, the visitor might ask, have changes in population structure, employment patterns, educational provision and so forth opened up new opportunities for the people of the Gulf, and how successfully are these opportunities being exploited to promote material and spiritual well-being?

The one fact that dominates all other considerations of the development of human resources in the Gulf is the influx of vast numbers of foreign workers into the region, to the extent that by 1980 foreigners outnumbered nationals in the labour forces of all Gulf countries except Oman (37.3 per cent) and Saudi Arabia (47.4 per cent), and in Kuwait, Qatar and the UAE the immigrants also comprised a majority of the total population.[5] [See Tables 13.1 and 13.2.] There is no doubt that the massive investments in infrastructure undertaken by all the states would not have been possible without recourse to importing labour — the native populations lacking both the numerical strength and the skills required. The range of opportunities in employment, education, consumer goods, leisure facilities, health and welfare services now available to the people of the Gulf would not have existed without this wholesale purchase of foreign labour. Yet the costs, both material and social, of supporting this large immigrant population are raising fears up and down the Gulf. The sobering effect of recession in the oil-exporting countries has encouraged a more critical examination of the economic costs and benefits

Table 13.1: Total and foreign population and labour force in labour-importing Arab countries, 1980

Country	Total population (in thousands)	Foreign population (in thousands)	% population foreign	Total labour force (in thousands)	Foreign labour force (in thousands)	% labour force foreign
Bahrain	344	107	31.1	119	65	54.6
Kuwait	1,356	794	58.6	453	342	75.5
Libyan Arab Jamahiriya[a]	2,430	532	21.9	782	332	42.5
Oman	984	179	18.2	303	113	37.3
Qatar	243	178	73.3	130	116	89.2
Saudi Arabia	9,229	2,150	23.3	2,375	1,125	47.4
United Arab Emirates	1,043	794	76.1	554	502	90.6

Note: a. Figures are for 1975. J.S. Birks and C.A. Sinclair, *International Migration and Development in the Arab Region*, (Geneva: International Labour Organisation, 1980).

Sources: Calculated on basis of data in United Nations, ECWA 1982.

Table 13.2: Per cent distribution of foreign labour force by area of origin in labour-importing Arab countries, 1980

Country	Arabs	Asians	Europeans and Americans	Other
Bahrain	6.4	85.1	8.3	.2
Kuwait	82.2	16.8	0.9	.1
Libyan Arab Jamahiriya[a]	93.4	4.5	2.1	—
Oman	1.9	94.2	3.6	.3
Qatar	33.2	63.3	3.4	.1
Saudi Arabia	57.3	35.9	5.6	1.2
United Arab Emirates	28.4	68.5	2.4	—

Note: a. Figures are for 1975. Birks and Sinclair, *International Migration*.
Source: Estimated by R. Tabbarah from national sources (censuses and statistical abstracts) using data on stocks of migrants, entry and exit, residence permits and working permits.

of their development strategies, while also focusing attention on the impact of development on the quality of the physical and social environment.

A recent attempt to quantify the relative costs and benefits of the foreign labour force in one Gulf state found that the pros and cons, even in purely economic terms, are surprisingly finely balanced.[6] While foreign workers were estimated to generate 26 per cent of total GDP, after accounting for local consumption and transfer of remittances abroad, the state is obliged to spend an estimated 30 per cent of GDP in sustaining this workforce. The benefits of the immigrants to their host country are fairly clear; not only do they provide a mobile and responsive pool of labour from which to make up severe deficiencies in national human resources, they also stimulate domestic consumption of goods whose supply is in the hands of local merchants, from the importer of luxury limousines to the owner of the corner grocery store.[7] Costs, far the most difficult side of the equation to evaluate, are made up of salaries (of which an estimated 10–15 per cent is channelled back to the countries of origin in remittances) and the extra burden placed by the foreign population on the educational and health services, roads and communications, and, most visibly, housing.

There is general agreement that the employment of expatriates has been of benefit to both parties, and thus worthwhile at least as an interim measure for establishing the Gulf States in the modern world. It has in any case been unavoidable. A worrying development however, is that labour migration on this scale appears to move forward under its own momentum; the swollen population places demands on infrastructure which can only be met by importing more construction workers, teachers doctors and clerical staff, who in turn require housing, schools, roads and so on. Reliance on foreign labour began as a means of realising the ambitions of the national populations, but has come to determine in its own right the course of development. Blocks of flats, high-density housing developments, barrack blocks for construction gangs, whole streets of shops, restaurants and cinemas inhabited, managed and patronised solely by immigrants now dominate large areas of the principal cities of the Gulf from Kuwait to Muscat. Planners are confronted with the dilemma of whether they should be planning for the needs of the national population alone, or for the whole society including the foreign residents Since both parties are so inextricably dependent on one another, the outcome must always involve compromise dressed in the appropriate colours to placate each faction in what is potentially a dangerous juggling act.

As in all such symbiotic relationships, there is the risk of mutual benefit turning to mutual suspicion, each party fearing that the other is a parasite exploiting a weakness or need in its host. Immigrants may believe, and not without cause, that they are exploited for their skills or simply their willingness to undertake work that nationals prefer to avoid, while being denied the right to social and political participation High salaries may be adequate compensation for the deprivations and boredom endured by the short-stay, skilled contract worker, but the pill is a bitter one for those long-term residents of Arab, often Palestinian origin. Having contributed a lifetime of service to their adopted country they are still denied citizenship with its concomitant rights to property ownership, welfare benefits and such limited exercises in public consultation as the Gulf regimes permit. On the side of the national populations there is the suspicion that immigrants may be lining their own pockets at the expense of their trusting hosts, whether by demanding too high a price for their services at the top end of the professional scale,[8] or among the lower echelons of craftsmen and technicians, by taking on jobs for which they are not adequately trained.

A pervasive fear among the indigenous peoples of the Gulf is provoked by the spectre of cultural domination as the numbers of foreign residents rival or exceed the natives. The very striking effects of large immigrant enclaves on the physical appearance of the cities has already been mentioned. Lighthearted references to 'Little India' in Muscat or 'the Third Yemen' in Riyadh abound among the wits on street corners up and down the Gulf, but the underlying anxieties are in earnest. Open racial conflict of the kind seen in the United States, Britain and France has mercifully not materialised in the Gulf. No doubt this is due in part to the measures that might be employed to contain such outbursts, and to the evident need for the co-operation of the foreigners in realising development targets, but much credit must also be given to the traditions of tolerance and hospitality that are a feature of traditional Gulf society.

The history of migration between countries and cultures bordering the Gulf is as old as the history of trade, and certainly antedates the oil era. Baluchi soldiers, Indian pearl merchants, Persian craftsmen and traders have a long tradition of residence in the Arab states. This, coupled with the British imperial umbrella that for the first half of the present century linked the Gulf to the Indian subcontinent, made India and Pakistan a natural source for supplying the sharp rise in demand for additional manpower during the first decades of industrial development. Since about 1970 the story of labour migration has evolved rapidly through three phases.[9] First was the growth of migration from other Arab states, especially Egypt, Yemen and Jordan (including the displaced Palestinians). The second phase was ushered in by the rise in oil prices of 1973 when ambitious new development projects created further demands. This new scale of need prompted the formation of manpower agencies in India, Pakistan and Sri Lanka capable of supplying 'from stock' skilled and tested manpower to the employers' specification. Human rights abuses caused the Governments of India and Pakistan to intervene in this system in 1977 and 1978, so that in the third phase, from 1978, manpower agencies in the Far East have taken over a large share of the traffic, often in association with engineering companies in these Asian countries which have won construction contracts in the Gulf. This latest wave of Asian immigrants does not share in the history of contact that formed a bridge, however shaky and over-extended, between the Gulf and India, nor in the common heritage of Arab language and culture that unites the Gulf peoples with their Egyptian, Palestinian and Yemeni guests. The barriers of language, religion and culture that separate the two parties are reflected in barriers of wire that surround the barrack-like compounds built by and for the Asian workers, while the Arab employer's uniform of sparkling white *thawb* and headdress is mirrored by the Asian employee's uniform of hard hat and overall bearing the company crest.

These outward signs of mutual exclusion merely reinforce a feature of the relations between the indigenous population and the immigrants that has existed since the earliest stages of the process: namely that such relations have barely existed outside the context of the workplace. F.

Barth, a social anthropologist, has given us a number of studies of ethnic and cultural identity, and the effects of two or more disparate cultures coming into regular contact. He points out that such contact does not necessarily lead to assimilation; cultural differences and ethnic identities may be maintained despite interaction, or even strengthened, for 'interethnic encounters have their own rules which need not extend beyond situations where they are needed'.[10] Ethnic boundaries may persist even despite the 'conversion' of individuals from one group to another; the categories of ethnic ascription may be maintained in spite of changing participation. Cultural traits, but not necessarily ethnic identity, may be accentuated or diminished according to the degree of security, or the lack of it. Under a strong, centralised administration such as a colonial power cultural differences may be minimised, but in less secure circumstances internal cohesion and conformity are stressed so fortuitous cultural differences may be retained.[11] In the Gulf context we need look no further than the Huwwala Arabs — those who migrated to the Persian shore, remained there for several generations, then turned back to be re-admitted into the Arab fold — for evidence of the persistence of ethnic identity despite prolonged residence in an alien environment and a change of nationality. The town of Ṣuḥār (Sohar) on the Oman shore of the Gulf is the setting for a recent study by Barth[12] in which he describes how nuances of dress, language, behaviour, residential and occupational patterns perpetuate the diversity of cultural and ethnic affiliations that give the town its unique identity. Here it is not immigration that threatens to erode the traditional social fabric — the mechanisms for peaceful co-existence are well established — but ironically the new prestige attached to Arab identity as opposed to Baluchi, bedouin, Indian, Ṣuḥārī or Omani.

Barth's study of Ṣuḥār focuses on ethnicity in a small-scale traditional society. A comparable anthropological investigation of more recently established expatriate communities in the Gulf has yet to be undertaken and would make fascinating reading. Has the British community, for example, been significantly Arabised by its experience? I doubt it very much; here, if anywhere, are to be found the last undiscovered tribes preserving intact antique customs only dimly remembered in Britain itself. The scale and, to some extent, the nature of immigration in the traditional society of Ṣuḥār and the modern Gulf States are, of course, rather different. One would not wish to dismiss the fears of cultural dilution too lightly, yet it would seem that the threat may be exaggerated. No doubt some specific issues do call for caution and, if necessary, intervention on the part of Gulf governments. There is the fear, for example ıat the large immigrant population poses a threat to security, both ecause of its uncertain political allegiance and the potentially crippling ffect if it were suddenly withdrawn. There is also the fear of the linguistic nd cultural impoverishment of children raised by foreign domestic staff nd taught by foreign school teachers. (Since parental neglect of children ardly seems a necessity in a society where very few women work outside ıe home, this appears to be a case of wanting to have the cake and eat .) Government intervention has too often consisted of drastic reaction fter the event, with the aim of allaying public fears rather than producıg long-term solutions. Periodic purges of immigrants working illegally nd the draconian proposal to take fingerprints of all foreign residents ı the United Arab Emirates are two such measures which risk driving ı further the wedge of mutual suspicion between the national and foreign ommunities.

The extraordinary degree of segregation between the communities has self impeded the enrichment of Gulf society, both culturally and in the ield of education and training. A recent study makes the point that echnical training is often best undertaken in the working nvironment:[13]

> In the oil-rich countries, this working environment is being built from the ground up. Its construction and operation are largely in the hands of highly qualified expatriates who have the experience to manage substantial numbers of workers, the know-how to instruct subordinates about the technology employed, and access to site and facilities needed for demonstration. In many cases, these highly qualified expatriates are surrounded by barely skilled Arab subordinates or associates. With few exceptions, the process of learning-while-doing is not being developed and extended to them.

ather than taking full advantage of the foreign presence with its diverity of skills, there has been a general pattern of sending national mployees abroad for their training — in theory as a stop-gap measure ntil adequate training institutions can be developed in the Gulf — while ıaintaining at home an aloofness that has been described as a 'siege ıentality'.[14] This closing of ranks gives the national populations the ppearance of a privileged group *vis-à-vis* the foreigners, with many of ıe attributes of a middle class. Although great disparities in wealth and evel of education exist among the indigenous people, nearly all share ıe privileges of guaranteed income and propery ownership, and have ıe status of employers of domestic and commercial labour.[15]

It is often claimed that the Gulf Arabs have a culturally ingraine reluctance to engage in manual labour, amounting almost to a phobi This is one of those sweeping generalisations that make one immediatel uncomfortable; it is all too easy to find rational justification for one' own prejudices while perceiving the preferences of others as produc of blind traditionalism. Who in any society chooses a career in refus collection when there are vacancies for property speculators? In so fa as there is some truth in the claim, the cause may be sought in historica circumstances. In the traditional world of the past, those engaged in pai manual labour — craftsmen, share-croppers, sailors and pearl divers - bore a disproportionate share of the risks associated with these activiti in a hostile, parsimonious environment, while the elite group o landowners, boat owners, employers of labour and larger merchants we shielded from these risks by their dependent employees. Boat owne received a guaranteed fee each pearling season regardless of the succe or failure of the venture, but the hired crewmen who received only small share of the proceeds were trapped in a spiral of indebtedness fro which only an exceptionally favourable season could free them. Manua work has thus usually entailed subservience, dependence, and exploita tion. Much of this work was performed by slaves or low-status minori groups — foreigners, negroes, tinkers of dubious origin, members o the Shi'ite peasant communities in eastern Saudi Arabia and Bahrain wh are the only section of the national workforce who can still be seen i for example, municipal road gangs in Ḥasā. In nearby villages of sem settled nomads, the bedu point out the ruined cottages once occupie by the *ṣunnā'* — the client smiths and tinkers of the tribe who produce pots and pans and metal utensils for their patrons. When oil camps fir appeared in the region, the ṣunnā' were quick to learn welding and th operation of lathes, and soon turned from the production of tent peg and horse shoes to motor maintenance, construction and light enginee ing. Now they have forsaken their former masters and are the prosperou proprietors of engineering workshops in Hufūf. The bedu have broug in Pakistani and Egyptian labourers for constructing the village hous and tending the gardens, and have turned their own hands to vehic maintenance. As one bedouin commented, 'People who are incapab of repairing and maintaining their own cars should stick to riding camels In one village the ṣunnā' have left as a parting gift a welded steel fram for hoisting camels on to the back of a pick-up truck — a most fittin monument.

If technical training has so far failed to attract significant numbe of nationals, then the cause is to be found in the lack of economic incentiv rather than in some mysterious psychological fixation. The welfare state, the burgeoning bureaucracy, the spectacular profits to be made through import agencies and property development simply offer too many more lucrative and glamorous alternatives for the more prosaic trades and professions to be attractive. As so often in developing nations, particularly when finance is not a major constraint, political will rather than technical feasibility is the limiting factor. Who can blame the people of the Gulf for seeing in the miraculous 'opening of the gates of prosperity'[16] a providential compensation for the centuries of poverty that went before? For the near future there is little prospect of rapid solutions to the problems of dependence on foreign labour, low participation by nationals in the skilled technical fields, and the ensuing social dislocations. Growing financial, social and political pressures must in the end force the issues. Education in all its forms lends flexibility to the social edifice, which is essential if it is to withstand the shock waves of change. In addition to the increasing numbers of schools, technical institutes, adult literacy classes, and universities, a significant contribution is made by less formal education through newspapers, radio and television and travel abroad, whether for study, recreation or medical treatment. All of these continue to play a crucial role in removing the veil of traditional prejudices that hampers participation in the modern world.

There are two reservoirs of human resources which so far remain largely untapped, and whose exploitation in the future may prove as significant as the discovery of fresh oil and gas deposits. The role of women in UAE Gulf society is treated elsewhere in this volume. Suffice it to say that the traditional limitations on women's participation in public life can no more be assumed to be immutable facts than the other cultural habits discussed above. In essence, the problem here is that whatever apologists may say about the legal rights accorded to women by Islam, or the hidden power of the woman behind the man in traditional society, nevertheless the power to apply, withhold, grant or retract these rights has usually in reality been the monopoly of men. The opportunities for abuse are legion. Development for many ordinary women in the Gulf has meant the loss of their former economic roles and stricter confinement within the stereotype of respectable seclusion.[17] In the past, seclusion was an ideal that acquired kudos because it was unattainable except by the very wealthy. Now that it is available to all it must lose its allure. There is nothing attractive about enforced boredom. A fact that is striking in many of the published accounts of women's lives, attitudes and aspirations is that not only young educated women but their uneducated and outwardly more traditional mothers and aunts are strongly in favour of a freer and more energetic role for women in the future.[18]

The second untapped resource is the rural sector, which is significantly large only in Saudi Arabia, Oman, and parts of the United Arab Emirates. Agricultural and pastoral development has its own problems of technology and manpower, amongst which is the demoralisation mentioned at the beginning of this chapter. In the larger Gulf countries there is a noticeable disparity between the gleaming modern cities and the still largely traditional hinterland where perhaps 40–50 per cent of the population live and work. Some of the general regional problems are also felt in quite remote corners: in Oman, Indian workers are increasingly replacing nationals as agricultural labourers, while in Saudi Arabia even the nomads now occasionally employ Indian shepherds and Egyptian or Yemeni camel herders. The traditional enclaves serve to some degree as a counterbalance to the cultural alienation of the cities, which is one justification for the generous subsidies which some ruling families pay, in various guises, to the bedouin and villagers. If the malaise of these rural areas is to be tackled seriously — the ills include depopulation, declining productivity in the majority traditional sector, water wastage and water shortage, poor educational opportunities, environmental degradation — then they need to be treated as more than an ethnographic museum. The implantation of prestigious high-technology projects in such areas arguably only adds to the hopelessness of small traditional producers.

The growing body of research on manpower and human resources in the Gulf is unanimous in calling for an integrated regional planning approach to replace piecemeal reactions by each country individually. There is growing insistence too from the labour-supplying countries that they are included in these deliberations, since the depletion of skilled labour causes problems in Jordan, Egypt, Yemen and India just as its acquisition raises difficulties in the Gulf. The harmonisation of employment policies between the member states of the Gulf Co-operation Council should lend some coherence to the debate. Certainly the issues mentioned in this essay are given growing prominence in the planning documents of all the Gulf States. The most recent Five Year Plan for Saudi Arabia, for example, gives high priority to developing indigenous human resources and predicts a 22.6 per cent reduction of the foreign labour force by 1990, involving the shedding of some 600,000 workers.[19] The same document forecasts an addition of 40,000 women to the Saudi workforce by 1990, an increase of 30 per cent. Co-operation among GCC member states will not on its own suffice, since all of these countries share very similar deficiencies and surpluses and so are unable to help each other directly. A clarification of objectives and co-ordination of

:ffort among the Gulf States would, however, facilitate the development of wider manpower strategies for the region, embracing other countries vith differing and complementary needs and assets. While GCC co-operation should help the development of locally-based training institu-ions, and in strengthening incentives for national participation, it is :ertain that the need for supplementary foreign labour will remain for ome time to come. A question that is likely to be prominent in future lebates is whether the Gulf States should continue to look towards Asia or their manpower needs, or to concentrate on the development of pan-Arab co-operation. The latter option has obvious ideological attractions is a long-term goal, but in the shorter term the flexibility and respon-iveness of the turnkey package approach to development projects is likely o remain important.

Notes

1. John Townsend, 'Philosophy of State Development Planning' in M.S. El Azhary ed.), *The Impact of Oil Revenues on Arab Gulf Development*, (Croom Helm, London, 984), pp. 35–53.

2. Riad Tabbarah, 'Population, Human Resources and Development in the Arab World' n *Population and Development in the Middle East*, (United Nations Economic Commis-ion for Western Asia, Beirut, 1982), pp. 19–52.

3. Nader Fergany, 'Manpower Problems and Projections in the Gulf' in El Azhary, *'he Impact of Oil Revenues*, pp. 155–69.

4. Ibid., p. 156.

5. Tabbarah, 'Population, Human Resources and Development', pp. 36–7.

6. Abdulrasool Al-Moosa and Keith McLachlan, *Immigrant Labour in Kuwait*, (Croom lelm, London, 1985), p. 95.

7. Ibid., p. 97.

8. A perhaps positive outcome of this suspicion has been the encouragement given o the domestic private sector in bidding for government contracts against foreigners.

9. J.S. Birks and C.A. Sinclair, 'Contemporary International Migration and Human esources Development in the Arab Region: Background and Policy Issues', in UNECWA, *'opulation and Development*, pp. 259–72.

10. F. Barth (ed.), *Ethnic Groups and Boundaries* (Little, Brown & Co./Allen & Unwin, oston/London, 1969), p. 14.

11. Ibid., p. 37.

12. F. Barth, *Sohar, Culture and Society in an Omani Town* (Johns Hopkins Univer-ity Press, Baltimore and London, 1983).

13. R.P. Shaw, *Mobilizing Human Resources in the Arab World*, (Kegan Paul Inter-ational, London, 1983), p. 175.

14. Al-Moosa and McLachlan, *Immigrant Labour in Kuwait*, p. 122.

15. Ibid.

16. Helga Graham, *Arabian Time Machine: Self Portrait of an Oil State*, (Heinemann, ondon, 1978), p. 6.

17. Abeer Abu Saud, *Qatari Women Past and Present*, (Longman, London, 1978), p. 33.

18. Ibid., and Graham, *Arabian Time Machine*, Part Three.

19. MEED, 28 September 1985, p. 25.

14 Language Development in the Gulf: Lexical Interference of English in the Gulf Dialects

J.R. Smart

The object of this short essay will be first of all to review the prese state of our knowledge of the subject and secondly to make a few gener observations and suggestions for future research. That lexical interferenc — or, in plain man's language, borrowing words — should have take place is no surprise, given:

(i) the commercial/political history of the area over the past centurie

(ii) the oil exploration and later production activities since 1932, agai English-language based, and

(iii) the rapid development and commercial expansion consequent upo oil wealth.

The English language involved is of three varieties: British, America and Indian. The last has a long history which continues into the presen being (along with Hindi) the *lingua franca* used among the large numbe of workers from the Indian subcontinent who came from a multitud of linguistic backgrounds, and (exclusively) between these and virtuall all other foreigners and the local Arab inhabitants.

On the Arabic side, we are not concerned here with the writte language, Standard Arabic (SA), which is affected by interference fro English no more in the Gulf than it is in many other areas of the Ara world, but what we shall call Gulf dialects defined as the Arabi vernaculars spoken between Arabs on the Gulf Coast and adjace territories from Kuwait to the Sultanate of Oman. This is not to say th we are dealing with a single dialect or even a group of dialects,[1] b the only divergences which concern us here are a few distinct phoneti realisations.[2]

Gulf dialect Arabic is comparatively rarely written down and as suc confined to the local theatre[3] and radio/TV productions, the dialogu in at least one Gulf novel,[4] local colloquial poetry when published,[5] an perhaps other literature of a regional nature.

The phenomenon of the infiltration of foreign words in Arabic ha been discussed since classical times,[6] but modern literature specificall referring to the Gulf area and its dialects starts with Jayakar's article published in 1889[7] and Reinhardt's descriptive work of 1894,[8] both concerning Oman. These are the only two real pre-oil works and as such can be dealt with separately and briefly. Jayakar's list, containing some 600-odd entries with etymologies has only one reference to English, and that indirect, when he derives *tanak*[9] ('tin') from Hindustani (the same word) 'from English tin' (p. 873). Reinhardt (p. 126) devotes a special section to *Fremdwörter* and gives 11 words from English along with others from Hindustani (6), Persian (12), Portuguese (2) and Swahili (1).[10] All the English borrowings are, unsurprisingly, of a maritime/commercial nature: *shitti*[11] ('*Zettel*'), *manwār* ('*Kriegsschiff*'), *angar* ('*Anker*'), *inginīr* ('*Ingenieur*'), *bōn* ('Pfund Sterling'), *bōrd* ('bord') (*sic*, presumably nautical 'board'), *shīt* ('sheet') (*sic*, presumably the English word and the nautical variety), *mēl* ('mail') (ditto, and presumably the vessel), *manifesht* (*sic*, with the German spelling '-sch' which does not appear in his phonetic guide on p. 1 ff) ('manifest'), *bamba* ('*Pompe*'), *fīf* ('pipe') (the barrel, not the tube; this word is still in use, at least in Oman, for oil-drums and similar containers).[12]

For about the next 50 years, although the oil exploration activities, which as we shall see prompted the flood of later borrowings, started in Bahrain in 1932, there seems to be a gap in the literature. However, this comes to an end with the only comprehensive scientific work specifically devoted to linguistic borrowing in Eastern Arabia, B. Hunter Smeaton's *Lexical Expansion due to Technical Change*[13] which, although not published until 1973, is based on material gathered in Ḥasā during the years 1945–49 (see p. xiii). The principal value of this document lies in the fact that it caught the influx of English terms (mainly technical) into the Gulf dialects very near its inception, but as a consequence of this — and no fault of the author's — it must also be said to suffer from two main defects. These are lack of material and simultaneous interference from other Arabic dialects whose influence can now be seen to have subsequently died out. Smeaton can muster only 86 borrowings from English (not counting loan translations) alongside 13 from Persian, nine from Hindustani, three from Turkish and one from Portuguese.

All of these are, however, modern borrowings from the age of (oil) technology and its related activities, and very different from Reinhardt's offerings cited above. Thus we have items like *sbana*[14] ('spanner'), *rigg* ('rig'), *swīch* ('switch') from the technical field and *hāwzin*[15] ('housing') (the ARAMCO administrative Housing Division), and *brūsh* ('brush') from non-technical but company-related activities. He is also the first to put on record verbal (form II) formations with *fannash* ('to fire, discharge'),[16] *dabbal* ('to double de-clutch') (when changing gear in heavy vehicles without syncromesh gearboxes) and *sallaf* ('to step on the starter') (from 'self' in self-starter). The first of these is still in common use, the second with a more general meaning,[17] but the third seems to have disappeared, leaving only the noun *silf* ('starter'). This may be due to the existence of the identical Arabic *sallaf* ('to lend').

Smeaton's etymologies are sensible in the main. As far as I know, he is the only source to ascribe (albeit tentatively, see, p. 64) the word *trīk*, which is glossed as various kinds of lights, lamps, torches in other sources and derived from English elec*tric*, to Swedish *trycklampa* ('pressure lamp') (the meaning he gives). This is not, of course, to suggest a Swedish influence in the area other than that an imported Swedish lamp may have had the word printed on it. This is by no means an unlikely path of entry into the language. The trade acronym DELCO for Delaware Electric Company who manufactured vehicle electrical components has given *dēlku* or *dilku* for 'distributor' or 'ignition system', still in use although it was almost certainly never uttered by an English speaker.[18]

The interference from other dialects of Arabic mentioned stemmed from the Ḥijāzī workmen who were recruited into the company. The influence here is the mainly French-based Cairene technical terminology whose effect on Ḥijāzī Arabic Smeaton explains in a note on pp. 146–7. Unlike Smeaton, who recognises the problem, many later writers have fallen into the trap of making such unlikely derivations as *baṭṭāriyya* from English 'battery' and *shokōlāṭa* from 'chocolate',[19] when the Gulf dialects exhibit the obviously direct borrowings *batri, bētri* (various forms) and *chaklēt*.[20] It is usually easy enough to spot Egyptian/Syrian infiltrations, but Iraqi Arabic contains more direct English borrowings and it is not always a simple matter to ascertain whether Gulf versions came in direct or through that dialect. A similar problem exists in the area of Anglo-Indian borrowings.

After Smeaton come the three ARAMCO handbooks of around 1956–57,[21] entitled *Spoken Arabic, Basic Arabic* and *Conversational Arabic*, again relating to Ḥasā in Saudi Arabia. These are, of course, nothing more than elementary teaching books designed for American company employees, but their study reveals some 80 words of English provenance which we must assume to have been firmly enough established, at least in the oil sector of the local community, to make them worth learning. These are again obviously oil company words and include some interesting developments such as *migraza* ('grease gun'), a noun of instrument from the English 'root' g-r-z ('grease') which also produces the verb *yigarriz*. There is also the *British* English (I presume since Smeaton, p. 66, cannot find a 'plausible explanation . . . for such a borrowing') *kafar* (*Basic Arabic*, p. 123) for 'tyre' alongside the more current *tāyir* (ibid., p. 133). This, of course, derives from the now somewhat outmoded 'cover' for the *outer* tyre as opposed to the *inner* tube.[22]

Dating from 1958 we have Everdene de Jong's *Spoken Arabic of the Arabian Gulf*,[23] based on Kuwait, but with a separately duplicated 'Oman Supplement'. This is another basic teaching book which nevertheless yields about 20 lexical items from English, mostly again technical despite the work's missionary origins. Two of the more domestic items, *krēb* and *wēl* (p. 150) for the materials 'crêpe' and 'voile' I have not come across elsewhere and perhaps reflect the lady author's less oily interests. In 1964 came the publication of Johnstone and Muir's specialised article 'Some Nautical Terms in the Kuwaiti Dialect of Arabic'[24] which includes five English borrowings, including *burd* ('board') and *anyar/anjar* ('anchor') which we have already seen.

In the same year appeared the first dictionary of a Gulf dialect, Shaykh Jalāl al-Ḥanafī's *Mu'jam al-Alfāẓ al-Kuwaytiyya*[25] which, apart from anything else, is an important source of comparison between Kuwaiti and Baghdadi Arabic as the author makes constant cross-references.[26] This contains about 60 English items and some shaky etymologies. For instance, he derives *wanēt* ('pick-up') from (non-existent) English 'vanette',[27] but on the other hand he ascribes correctly to Hindi *kankari* ('small stones used in building') which many confuse with English 'concrete'.

Also published in the same year was the Shell Company of Qatar's three-volume *Glossary: English-Spoken Arabic*[28] which adds a further dimension to the subject by giving triple entries, English, Qatari and what it calls 'Northern Arabic'. The last are distinctly Syro-Palestinian, and presumably there for the benefit of oil company staff from that area. Thus Gulf Arabic *lēsan*, plural *layāsin* ('driving licence') is sternly accompanied by *rukhṣa/rukhaṣ* (vol. 2, p. 191). Whether these Northern entries are also inspired by a purist or reformatory zeal I cannot say, but I know that my (Palestinian) predecessor as Arabic Instructor to Petroleum Development (Oman) Ltd in the late 1960s was doing his best to spread culture and enlightenment by teaching the European staff *shu biddak* ('What do you want?'), which phrase, when tried out on Omanis, produced only blank stares.[29]

On going through unpublished notes made during my period in the above position (1967–68) I find that I listed upwards of 250 items borrowed from English, most of which had appeared independently previously or have appeared since. I can, however, claim the unique plural *gilṣān* for *glāṣ* ('drinking glass'), usual pl. *glāṣāt*; the verb *yifayyil* ('to file', of papers, documents) and the distinction *qāṭ/ghāṭ*[30] for '*coat of paint*' as opposed to the universally quoted *kōt*, pl. *akwāt* ('coat, jacket').

The late Professor T.M. Johnstone's *Eastern Arabian Dialect Studies*,[31] published in 1967, is a comparative study of the Gulf dialects as a whole and with separate attention to Kuwaiti, Bahraini, Qatari and the vernaculars of the then Trucial Coast (actually Dubai and Abu Dhabi). A sample of 11 borrowings from English is given on pp. 57–8, but a reading of the texts at the end of the book yields about another 50. These include surprising examples such as *ṣārdin* ('sardines') (p. 228) — surprising because these are extensively fished in the area and there are two perfectly good local words, *ṣīma* and *'ūma*.[32] There is also (p. 214) an interesting juxtaposition of *trafik* (Eng. '*traffic* department') with the SA equivalent *qalam al-murūr* and (same page) SA (local pronunciation) *sā'ig* with *drēwir*.[33]

Another dictionary in Arabic of local terms, this time in the United Arab Emirates, is Fāliḥ Ḥanẓal's *Mu'jam al-Alfāẓ al-'Āmmiyya fī Dawlat al-Imārāt al-Muttaḥida*[34] published in 1977. This contains at least 60 entries given English etymologies, some with accompanying quotations from local colloquial (*nabaṭī*) poetry. For instance under *taym* — from English 'time' but in Gulf usage usually referring to 'time of work', 'office hours'[35] — we find

ṣawārim ḥīn al-waghā mā la-hā tyūm
'swords which in time of war keep to no limited working hours'[36]

Another folkloric entry under *ring* ('rim (of a wheel)')[37] describes the use of a bicycle wheel-rim pushed along by a child with a stick in the game of hoops.

In 1978 another specialised academic study of the problem appeared, this time by M.R. Zughoul whose article 'Lexical Interference of English in Eastern Province Saudi Arabia'[38] offers a brief and somewhat superficial treatment from the historical, cultural, phonetic and semantic points of view. After a potted history of the oil company's activities in the area, he then divides the data he has collected[39] into ten categories of reference such as modern inventions, sports and recreations, food, professions and so on. He finds, not surprisingly, that about 45 per cent of the data are technology-related (p. 217), the bulk of them connected with motor vehicles.[40] The rest of Zughoul's categories are, as expected, much smaller, ranging from 22 items under 'Food and Food-Related' to three under 'Finance and Banking'. He then gives a section on the range of usage of these words which reveals an underlying defect in his approach, that is, the inclusion of what he calls (p. 220) words 'used throughout Saudi Arabia and other parts of the Arabic-speaking world'. In fact, many of these terms (he gives, for instance, *talafōn, kilogrām*) are, if not SA like these two,[41] certainly in use far beyond the area covered by the Gulf dialects and therefore, I would suggest, nothing *particularly* to do with them. These — and I would also include the names of specific models of cars (pp. 217–18) and the English football terminology (p. 128) — should be excluded from such a study. Zughoul's other ranges of usage become more and more restrictive, starting with all Saudi Arabia (e.g. *stēshin* ('station' — usually from the present author's experience 'a taxi stand'), then its Eastern province (*sikrāb* ('scrap'), *kumisry* ('commissary') — oil company terms), then 'a restricted but very large group of people in the Eastern Province' (p. 220). By this he means those employed in or directly associated with oil activities (*blānt* ('mechanical *plant*'), *tarmīdha* ('Intermediate Staff')). After a vague reference to Bloomfield's theories in an attempt to define the nature of the linguistic situation (pp. 220–1), he goes on to give a sketch of the phonetic changes affecting English words entering Arabic. This had already been touched on by Smeaton (pp. 167–73) and was to be the main concern of Linda Thornberg's article discussed below. The remainder of Zughoul's paper contains some remarks on morphology and semantics, neither dealt with in any great depth.

Hamdi A. Qafisheh has produced three books on Gulf Arabic,[42] and the glossary in *Gulf Arabic: Intermediate Level* (1979)[43] is a rich source of importations from English. Again Qafisheh's books are teaching/reference works, not particularly concerned with linguistic borrowings, so there is little discussion of the problem and few etymologies are given. There are, however, in excess of 150 items, including the puzzling non-English *trāy* for 'driving test' (already noted in Johnstone's *Eastern Arabian Dialect Studies*, p. 214). The term in this sense is certainly not current in British or American English, and I suspect it may have stemmed from a confusion of the verb and the noun in some such sentence as 'Try your driving test' uttered perhaps by an English-speaking driving instructor.[44]

Linda Thornberg's 1980 article[45] is concerned with the formulation of phonological 'borrowing rules' (p. 523) based on current linguistic theory, and her data comprise 283 words elicited from a Ḥasāwī informant, written down by him in Arabic script, tape-recorded, then transcribed in the International Phonetic Alphabet (pp. 527–8). There is no room here to discuss in detail the results of this research, but they appear to constitute a significant contribution to a very complex facet of the subject, obscured as it is by dialectal and even idiolectal variations, the temptation to superimpose (irrelevant) SA phonology and morphology and other obstacles. As already stated, Smeaton and Zughoul have made contributions in this direction but, while Thornberg brings things right up to date, there still remains much work to be done. She must also be taken to task for including educated/SA items (e.g. encyclopaedia, propaganda, opera) and for at least two faulty etymologies. *Ambēr* (p. 530) is from '*ampere* gauge' not 'pointer' (p. 538), (see Smeaton, p. 61), although this may now be the meaning, and *barasti* neither means nor comes from 'barracks'; (the etymology is doubtful, but the meaning is a 'hut made of palm leaves'; see Ḥanẓal, *Mu'jam*, p. 77).

The remaining two books with which we shall conclude this review are both concerned with Bahrain Arabic. *Language and Linguistic Origins in Bahrain* by Mahdi Tajir[46] is a descriptive study of the 'Bahārnah speech forms' (p. xxiii, i.e. as opposed to the 'Anazī ones, though this is unlikely to make much difference in connection with borrowings), and discusses loan-words on p. 133 ff. 'Specimen borrowings' from English are given (p. 135) along with a concise but informative historical introduction (pp. 133–4). The section headed 'Notes on Hindustani loan words' (p. 134) also contains useful information on early borrowings of presumably Anglo-Indian commercial origin such as *bīma* (from the — obsolete? — commercial insurance term 'bailment' and well testified in the present material both as the noun and the verb *yibayyim* ('to insure')).[47] An interesting etymology (this time under Persian borrowings, p. 138) is *būk*, said to be from *buqča* (correctly *bughche*). Ḥanẓal[48] is the only other source to give this, but derives it from English 'pocket book'. The Persian (actually originally Turkish) word is in wider circulation as *bughsha* ('envelope').[49]

Clive Holes's 1984 *Colloquial Arabic of the Gulf and Saudi Arabia*,[50] another practical handbook based on data collected in Bahrain (p. 2), contains more than 50 English borrowings scattered throughout the vocabularies, texts and exercises. There is an interesting little passage (pp. 224–5) which sounds authentic though he does not state its origin, where some of the English terms in context stick out rather as quotations from the European language than integrated borrowings from it. For instance, would *il-kāwnts* ('accounts department') be generally understood out of context? Perhaps so. Even though it is not attested elsewhere, it shows a degree of integration in the substitution of the

Arabic definite article for the first syllable.[51] Another, and this time definitely authentic, passage taken from a local radio play (see pp. 264 and 267) includes the English *nōṭ* ('banknote') and the soccer term probably not restricted to the Gulf, but here used in an extended, non-sport related sense, *yifawwil* ('to foul'): *'lā tifawwil 'alayya'* ('don't diddle/cheat me').

Such then, is the 'state of the art'.

As has been mentioned, the total number of borrowings from English so far recorded in printed sources and the present writer's own notes is in the region of 400, after exclusion of SA words and proper or trade names unless they are used in transferred or extended senses. These data do, however, span a period of at least 40 years (the two nineteenth-century sources being ignored) and a check needs to be made in the field to see how much of this vocabulary is still active. This would represent the extent of social or cultural integration of these lexical items, something which, at least on the surface of it, could only be affected by their replacement with native Arabic words as has happened in some of the northern dialects, though only to a very limited extent.

Purely linguistic integration is an entirely different matter and, apart from specifically phonological concerns as dealt with by Zughoul and Thornberg, it might prove fruitful to carry on along the lines suggested by Smeaton, who divides his data into three degrees of naturalisation 'on the basis primarily of *morphological* integration' (p. 61; his italics) according to various criteria. It seems an intuitively safe assumption that a word like *yirēwis* ('to reverse (a vehicle)'), which operates as a fully conjugated verb (verbal noun *rēwasa*), or a noun like *sakrūb* (which has a broken plural *sakārīb*), or perhaps even *chaklēt*, for which one source gives the relative adjective *chaklēti* ('chocolate-coloured')[52] have achieved a greater degree of penetration into the fabric of the language than, say, *lēt* whose only other manifestation is the external plural *lētāt*. But is there a process of change in action which will give us eventually **alyāt*, or even **yilayyit*? After all we already have *rēl/aryāl* ('rail') (Smeaton, p. 74) and *yichayyik* ('to check' (everywhere)), but these appear to have entered the language in these forms in the first place.

I leave the reader with the sentence, perhaps apocryphal:

flittēt in-nakhl wa-fakaft . . .[53]

Notes

1. See T.M. Johnstone, *Eastern Arabian Dialect Studies*, (Oxford University Press, London, 1967) especially p. 1 ff.

2. Mainly that of the English *j* as *j, y* (many areas) or *g* (Oman, certain dialects); the realisation in loan words of English consonants not found in Arabic, for instance *p* as *b* (mainly), *f* or *p* (occasionally) has merely been reproduced as heard personally or recorded by others.

3. Active initially in Kuwait and Bahrain, but now also in the Emirates. For further information, see Muḥammad Ḥasan 'Abdullāh, *al-Ḥaraka al-Adabiyya wa'l-Fikriyya fī'l-Kuwayt*, (Rābiṭat al-Udabā', Kuwait, 1973) p. 251 ff, and 'Alī al-Rā'ī, *al-Masraḥ fī'l-Waṭan al-'Arabī*, ('Ālam al-Ma'rifa Series, Kuwait, 1980), especially pp. 394–449.

4. *Mudun al-Milḥ* by 'Abd al-Raḥmān Munīf, discussed elsewhere in this volume by my colleague Dr Rasheed El-Enany to whom I am grateful for the information.

5. For instance the *dīwāns* mentioned below, note 36.

6. E.g. al-Jawālīqī, *al-Mu'arrab min al-Kalām al-A'jamī*, 2nd edn., ed. by Aḥmad Muḥammad Shākir, (Dār al-Kutub, Cairo, 1969).

7. A.S. Jayakar, 'The O'manee Dialect of Arabic', *Journal of the Royal Asiatic Society*, (1889), pp. 649–87 and 811–89. It is the second part, the vocabulary, which will concern us here.

8. C. Reinhardt, *Ein Arabischer Dialect gesprochen in 'Omān und Zanzibar*, (Lehrbücher des Seminars für orientalische Sprachen zu Berlin, 13, Stuttgart-Berlin, 1894).

9. Citations of words printed in the Arabic alphabet, such as this one, will be given in the transliteration system uniform throughout this volume. It should be borne in mind, however, that the diphthongs rendered *aw* and *ay* should be pronounced long *o* (as in German *Not*) and long *e* (Ger. *Mehl*) respectively. The consonants *ch* (church), *g* (gag), *v* and *p* will be transliterated as such when expressed in the Arabic texts by means of Persian letters.

10. It is not the intention in this essay to deal with borrowings from languages other than English, if only because such loans, with perhaps one or two exceptions, appear to have come to a stop with the oil/technical age. There are still, however, many words from Persian, Hindi, Turkish in daily use; see, for instance, Johnstone, *Eastern Arabian Dialect Studies*, pp. 55–8, Mahdi Tajir, *Language and Linguistic Origins in Bahrain*, (Kegan Paul International, London, 1982), pp. 133–8.

11. Since this volume is not principally aimed at linguists, it was, after considerable deliberation, decided to standardise the spelling of Arabic words from transcribed sources. This will involve some inaccuracy but phonetics concern us here only marginally, and the standardisation will spare the reader mastering over 20 different systems from as many sources. The same principles will be applied as outlined in note 9 above, with the exception that the two diphthongs referred to will be written *o* and *e* respectively.

12. The examples translated in German refer, of course, to Anglo-Indian 'chitty', 'chit'; 'anchor', 'engineer'; 'pound' and presumably 'pump' (modern German 'Pumpe').

13. Indiana University, Bloomington, 1973.

14. p. 67. Interesting as a pre-American borrowing presumably from Bahrain, the US term for the tool being 'wrench'. Smeaton gives it with a short medial vowel, but most later sources have a long one.

15. The diphthong *āw*, relating to English *ou* in 'housing', sometimes occurs and is thus transcribed. The related *āy* representing the medial sound in English 'wire', 'tight', 'time' etc. sometimes appears (often followed by an anaptyctic *i* as in *wāyir* ('wire') but is more often reduced to *ē* (*tēt, tēm*). This needs more research.

16. This occurs in practically all the sources cited below and is now both transitive 'to dismiss' and intransitive 'to resign'. It derives, of course, from English 'finish'.

17. Hamdi A. Qafisheh, *Gulf Arabic: Intermediate Level*, (University of Arizona Press, Tucson, 1979), p. 254 gives 'to double s.th.'.

18. See Smeaton, *Lexical Expansion*, p. 62. The present author noted it in Oman in 1967 in the shape of *dīrgu*.

19. M.R. Zughoul, ('Lexical Interference of English in Eastern Province Saudi Arabia', *Anthropological Linguistics*, vol. 20 (1978), pp. 214–25) has both: see pp. 217 and 218 respectively. They are, of course, from Italian.

20. E.g. Daud Atiyeh Abdo (comp.), *Glossary: English-Spoken Arabic*, (3 vols., Shell Company of Qatar Ltd., Training Centre, Qatar, 1964), and Qafisheh, *Gulf Arabic: Intermediate Level*, and many more.

21. *Spoken Arabic*, (ARAMCO, Dhahran, 1956); *Basic Arabic*, (ARAMCO, Dhahran, n.d.), and *Conversational Arabic* (ARAMCO, Dhahran, n.d.). Johnstone, *Eastern Arabian Dialect Studies*, p. 252, dates the second 1957. It may be as well to mention here that I have been unable to consult a potentially important source also cited by Johnstone: BAPCO, *Handbook of the Spoken Arabic of Bahrain* (BAPCO, Bahrain, n.d. but possibly from this period or earlier).

22. Interestingly enough, Fāliḥ Ḥanẓal's *Mu'jam al-Alfāẓ al-'Āmmiyya fī Dawlat al-Imārāt al-Muttaḥida*, (Ministry of Information and Culture, UAE, 1977) picks up the slightly different *kawar*, which he glosses as 'cover' in general, or 'the cover of the engine of a car', i.e. bonnet.

23. American Press, Beirut, 1958.

24. *Bulletin of School of Oriental and African Studies*, vol. XXVII, no. 2 (1964), pp. 299–332.

25. As'ad Press, Baghdad, 1964.

26. He had previously written *Mu'jam al-Lugha al-'Āmmiyya al-Baghdādiyya*; see back cover of the volume cited in the previous note.

27. The correct etymology is probably that suggested by Zughoul, ('Lexical Interference', p. 225 note 1), viz. 'one eight' — though probably a model rather than a registration number as he seems to suggest. I have been unable to trace the exact vehicle type, though Qafisheh's entry, (*Gulf Arabic: Intermediate Level*, p. 280) *siziki*: 'Suzuki (kind of small Japanese pick-up)' may give a clue.

28. See note 20 for full bibliographical details.

29. The true Omani equivalent of the time was *mū bāghi*, now giving way to the more general *ēsh trīd*.

30. The variant pronunciation *gh* for *q/g* is common in the Gulf dialects. See for instance Tajir, *Language and Linguistic Origins*, p. 48; Johnstone, *Eastern Arabian Dialect Studies*, p. 20.

31. See note 1 for bibliographical details.

32. Johnstone, p. 250, note 10 has *'ūm*.

33. There are, in fact three possibilities here, the third being the general dialect *sawwāg* from the same SA root. The passage cited does, however, seem to imply that *drēwir* is a *professional* driver. More common in this English borrowing is the substitution of *l* for the *r*, *drēwil*, plural *drēwiliyya*.

34. See note 22 for bibliographical details.

35. Cf. Clive Holes, *Colloquial Arabic of the Gulf and Saudi Arabia*, (Routledge & Kegan Paul, London, 1984), p. 225.

36. The same author is responsible for the publication of five *dīwāns* of *nabaṭī* poetry with SA commentary. There is no space to mention these individually here, but they yield more than 20 English words, illustrating not only, like the example in the text, the mere *use* of these borrowed terms but their deeper penetration to the roots of folk culture. For instance, the poet al-Ẓāhirī (*Dīwān*, ed. F. Ḥanẓal, (Dār al-Fikr, UAE, 1984)) complains that love has affected him like the bite of a poisonous snake, his limbs cannot carry him and

wa-ḥattā 'l-mafāṣil jayyaman jām
'even the joints jammed a jamming (jammed up)' (p. 141).

37. The word must come from 'ring'; (indeed Tajir, *Language and Linguistic Origins*, p. 134 gives this meaning), but it is more often used in this specific sense. Cf. also Persian *rang* ('colour') in common use.

38. See note 19 for bibliographical details.

39. It is somewhat difficult to count the number of borrowings as he tends to make double or even treble entries if a word can be ascribed to more than one category, but there appear to be about 200 in all.

40. This had already been noted earlier on by Smeaton, (*Lexical Expansion*, p. x), and a preliminary survey of about 400 Gulf Arabic words by the present writer yielded 49 per cent in the three categories of general technology, oil technology and automotive technology.

41. I would suggest as a criterion their presence in Wehr's dictionary: see Hans Wehr, *A Dictionary of Modern Written Arabic*, 4th edn, ed. by J. Milton Cowan, (Otto Harrassowitz, Wiesbaden, 1979).

42. *A Basic Course in Gulf Arabic*, (University of Arizona Press/Librarie du Liban, Tucson/Beirut, 1975); *A Short Reference Grammar of Gulf Arabic*, (University of Arizona Press, Tucson, 1977); and *Gulf Arabic: Intermediate Level* (University of Arizona Press, Tucson, 1979).

43. He says this 'contains the vocabulary items in the *Basic Course*, those in the *Reference Grammar* and some more items of high frequency'. (p. xiv).

44. Cf. Smeaton, (*Lexical Expansion*, p. 62) on *dabalgēr* ('double gear'), another term not used in English. It still exists in the Gulf dialects in the shortened form *dabal* used for any or all parts of the four-wheel drive mechanism in cross-country vehicles.

45. 'Arabic Loan Phonology: the Assimilation of English Lexical Items', *Linguistics*, vol. 18 (1980), pp. 523–42.

46. See note 10 for bibliographical details.

47. Eg. in colloquial poetry (*Dīwān al-Ẓāhirī*, p. 161, v. 18); Abdo (comp.), *Glossary: English-Spoken Arabic*, vol. 2, p. 173, (noun and verb, s.v. insurance, insure); Qafisheh, *Gulf Arabic: Intermediate Level*, (s.v. *bayyam, biima*).

48. *Mu'jam*, p. 96.

49. See, for instance, Abdo (comp.), *Glossary: English-Spoken Arabic*, vol. 1, p. 109; Johnstone, *Eastern Arabian Dialect Studies*, p. 20.

50. See note 35 for bibliographical details.

51. This interesting and not at all rare phenomenon needs attention from the phonologists/morphologists. Well attested, for instance, are *slētar* ('accelerator'), *fēnri* ('refinery'), which in definite use would presumably give *is-slētar* and *il-fēnri* respectively.

52. Tajir, *Language and Linguistic Origins*, p. 136.

53. The *isnād* of this quotation is: *ḥaddathanā* John Mattock of Glasgow University *'an* David Jackson of St Andrews *'an* Douglas Galloway who heard it in Oman!

15 *Cities of Salt*: A Literary View of the Theme of Oil and Change in the Gulf

Rasheed El-Enany

The moment the drilling rigs first struck oil in the Arabian Peninsula can in retrospect rightly be compared to the first bite from the apple of the Tree of Knowledge. For the discovery of oil in Arabia has brought with it all the pain and suffering attendant on a state of knowledge or experience. It has also brought, though only for some and not for all, many of the pleasures that go with such a state. Or this is at least what 'Abd al-Raḥmān Munīf seems to purport in his colossal novel *Cities of Salt*.[1]

Many a study has been written both in Arabic and other languages on the subject of the discovery of oil in Arabia and the enormous changes, political, economic and social, that it brought about. Indeed the present volume is one more such work to join a huge body of writing. Surprising though it may seem, no Arab novelist — for a subject on such a scale lends itself naturally to fictional treatment — has attempted to record, in the words of Jabrā Ibrāhīm Jabrā, 'the arduous and painful move from nomadic existence to oil'.[2] No novelist, that is, until Munīf and his *Cities of Salt* published only in 1984 and 1985 and as yet incomplete.

It appears a most felicitous coincidence that the novelist who eventually undertook such a massive task is also, by qualification and, for a period of his life, profession, an oil economist.[3] And as though this were not enough, he was born in Saudi Arabia[4] in 1933 on the very day the Concession Agreement was signed[5] between the Saudi Government and the then California Arabian Standard Oil Company (later, in 1944, ARAMCO).[6] Munīf must have had the theme of *Mudun al-Milḥ* on his mind for a number of years before he actually sat down to write it. For as early as 1979 he speaks in an interview about the relationship between his profession as an oil economist and his 'hobby' as a novelist. He says that the world of oil 'may help in exploring some of the fictional possibilities in modern Arab life . . .' and remarks that the effects of oil on Arab reality 'have not been dealt with [in fiction] . . .'[7] Within five years Munīf undertook himself the task he had hinted at in that interview.

Mudun al-Milḥ will probably eventually take its place in histories of Arabic fiction as the greatest novel of epic dimensions since the publication by Najīb Maḥfūẓ of his *Trilogy* in 1956/7. And in the same way as Arab posterity will always feel indebted to Maḥfūẓ for recording in his *magnum opus* a period of Egypt's modern social history that otherwise would have been lost, so it will always be held in Munīf's debt for documenting in his latest novel[8] a phase of Saudi Arabia's life (and, by analogy, that of most Arabian oil states), the traces of which are already difficult to discern today. It is interesting, though, that in the odd 1,200 pages of the novel so far published not once is the name of Saudi Arabia, or any of its cities, towns, or past or present rulers mentioned. However, internal evidence is ample and far too obvious for anyone with the slightest knowledge of the region and its modern history and geography not to realise long before he is half-way through *al-Tīh* that he is reading a novel about Saudi Arabia from 1933 onwards (no dates are given either). Once this discovery is made, the intelligent reader does not find it particularly hard to read fact behind fiction where relevant. Thus the fictitious Ḥarrān is soon established to be none other than the famous Dhahran and the puzzling inland oasis Wādī al-'Uyūn of the first page is safely construed on page 427 to be 'Ayn Dār.[9] Similarly in volume two, *al-Ukhdūd*, Mūrān is almost immediately read for what it is: Riyadh. It is also used to refer to the entire Kingdom (in the novel a mere Sultanate), while Sulṭān Khuraybit is obviously Ibn Su'ūd (d. 1953), founder of the Kingdom, Khaz'al is Su'ūd, his son and first successor on the throne (1953–64), and Finar is Fayṣal (1964–75) who took over from Su'ūd. This is a time-honoured technique of Munīf's: in the seven novels he published before *Mudun al-Milḥ*, he has written, among other things, about political repression supposedly in Iraq (*East of the Mediterranean*), the Arab defeat in 1967 in the war with Israel (*When We Abandoned the Bridge*), and the Muṣaddiq period (1951–53) in Iran (*The Marathon*),[10] all without naming names or specifying dates. For the reader it is all guesswork, sometimes easy, sometimes difficult. Munīf himself has an explanation for his consistent technique of disguise. He confesses to an interviewer that the Arab novelist is unable to make a historical pronouncement in a direct and candid manner. He therefore 'hides away, opting for safety and often taking extra care to give a testimony open to more than one interpretation'.[11] In addition to that, one might add that the novelist's concealment of factual details serves in effect to widen the scope to which his testimony relates. For political repression is a phenomenon common to many Arab, and indeed non-Arab, countries. Similarly, the effects of oil, good and bad, on bedouin society are not confined to Saudi Arabia, but are typical of several other oil states in the region. Thus the disguise, while giving the author the 'safety' he needs, seems to be artistically beneficial as well.

To a large extent the novelist dons, in *Mudun al-Milḥ*, the mantle of the chronicler. *Al-Tīh* spans a period of some 17 years of the life of the Kingdom from 1933 to 1950,[12] while *al-Ukhdūd* covers a period of just over ten years beginning in 1953 with the demise of Ibn Su'ūd and ending with the deposition in 1964 of his successor King Su'ūd and the assumption of power by the latter's brother, Fayṣal. Thus between them the two volumes stretch across the first 30 years or so of Saudi Arabia's oil life. However, one must establish from the beginning that *Mudun al-Milḥ* is no annalistic account of Saudi Arabia. It is a documentary novel only in the sense that Tolstoy's *War and Peace* in its account of Russia during the Napoleonic invasion, or Maḥfūẓ's *Trilogy* in its survey of the Egyptian society between the two world wars, are such. It has a life and a vision of its own. Indeed, rather than being a historical account, it is an interpretation of history through the medium of fiction which in good hands can capture in the life of a community what no history book can. In the words of the novelist, writing a historical novel is 'a reshaping of history within a particular intellectual framework . . . [It is] the social and psychological reshaping of an environment with the aim of discovering the deep, internal movement of history'.[13]

Al-Tīh opens with a lyrical description of life at Wādī al-'Uyūn, an inland oasis where the bedouin live in peace and harmony if often in hardship. They grow their own food and raise their own cattle and trade with passing caravans, with which their sons sometimes leave for distant lands to return after a long time with a small fortune with which to begin a family. The scene depicted breathes an air of timelessness; there is no reason to suspect that life was any different hundreds of years earlier or that it will be hundreds of years into the future. On the other hand, the novel ends with scenes of industrial action met with coercion and bloodshed in Ḥarrān. The odd 500 pages between the two scenes are a lamentation for a society's sad fall from grace — a fall brought about, paradoxical as this may seem, by the arrival of the Americans and the discovery of oil.

In his interview with *al-Waṭan*, Munīf sums up very neatly what he set out to do in *Mudun al-Milḥ*:[14]

In the first volume of the novel I tried to record the features of two

> stages. Since the beginning of time and up to the thirties of this century, life had always gone on in the same way: a group of people living in an oasis on a caravan route. They are always waiting for one thing or another: their returning sons, rain or caravans . . . I tried to record [all this] in quick vignettes. As for life after oil, [things] became very different . . . The self-same oasis turned into a city of glass, iron and stone, and hordes of adventurers and entrepreneurs swarmed in. Thus patterns of behaviour, relationships and interests very different from the existing ones began to form. In the midst of all this mutation, the indigenous inhabitants were unable to adjust to the new fast rhythm and the new relationships, and in their search for a new identity they became distorted.

The mutation that Munīf speaks about has spared no aspect of the bedouin's life. It engulfed their entire system of values: social, economic, political and technological. In the following pages we shall attempt to examine the presentation of these changes in the novel under discussion.

'Merchants are devils dressed up like men . . . How can you compare a man who works all the year round to earn a living with one who makes the most money in a single moment?'.[15] These words put the economic value system of bedouin society in a nutshell. To them economic gain is the result of human toil and is not divorced from morality. This simple value system was to give way to one based on the qualities of speculation, manipulation and enterprise. The discovery of oil quickly created the need for labour, construction, transportation, urban expansion, services etc. These conditions inevitably gave rise to a class of entrepreneurs, both from within and outside the community. Two classic examples in the novel of the bedouin turned entrepreneur are the characters of Ibn al-Rāshid and al-Dabbāsī. The first leaves his native Wādī al-'Uyūn for Ḥarrān where he is sub-contracted by the oil company to supply labourers from all over the place, a task which he fulfills largely by making false promises to the men to entice them out of the desert to the rapidly growing Ḥarrān. Once they arrive, he buys off their camels (thereby guaranteeing their stay) which he then invests by hiring them to the company to transport the stones which the men cut.[16] Another entrepreneurial venture that he engages in is the purchase from naive and unsuspecting local bedouin of land whose value he knows is going to double and redouble in no time because of the rapid economic and urban growth.[17] As for the other character, al-Dabbāsī, he is a somewhat more sophisticated version of Ibn al-Rāshid, having travelled around a bit and worked in trade. He returns to his native Ḥarrān only after it has come up in the world. He resettles there and enters into a fierce competition with Ibn al-Rāshid which culminates in the latter's utter destruction.

The tension created by these conditions builds up over the years and results in social unrest which takes the form of a strike by natives working for the American company in response to the sacking of a number of their fellow-workers. But the sackings were only the event which triggered the strike. Underlying them were long-harboured grievances. In a passage which reflects the collective stream of thought of the workers and shows how the traditional ills of capitalism at its worst have been transplanted into the previously bedouin society, the author states the workers' grievances:[18]

> No one knew if they would remain alive or if tomorrow they would find food. True the company paid them, but what they received today was spent on the following day. Prices kept rising from day to day and money was accumulating in a few hands. As for the promises of houses and a comfortable life which Ibn al-Rāshid had made them years ago as he herded them from 'Ajra and other places, they had vanished even before Ibn al-Rāshid himself. And as for the promises of the personnel office in the company to build houses for the workers to enable them to bring their families over and return home in the evening to wife and children, years had passed without a single house being built.

The social upheaval which came in the wake of oil was no less than the economic one. Entire communities were forcibly uprooted from the land where they had lived for generations to allow exploration to take place and buildings and installations to rise. The agony which unavoidably accompanied this process is described in the novel at length and with great affection, but nowhere is it more powerful and more touching than in the symbolic scene where the trees of Wādī al-'Uyūn are cut down to clear the ground for work. The scene takes place in front of the eyes of the people who are shortly to be evacuated:[19]

> That move was a true herald of the end which came damned and maddening. If anyone remembered those distant days, the days when there existed a place called Wādī al-'Uyūn, a man called Mut'ib al-Hadhdhāl,[20] a spring and trees, and men of a certain nature — if there is still anyone who remembers, here are the strongest memories which still make the heart ache when the mind goes back and

> recollects: the tractors as they charged the trees like hungry wolves and began to tear them apart and knock them down one by one . . . Then having finished with one cluster they would attack another with the same ferocity. As they bent and staggered and before they fell, the trees screamed and shouted, wailed and raved — they made one last painful plea. And when they finally neared the ground, they fell prostrate, as though in prayer — as though wanting again to unite with the soil, to sprout anew.

The anthropomorphising of the trees in this passage is not without significance. In the following chapters of the novel, the uprooting of the community of Wādī al-'Uyūn is shown to have been no less ruthless an experience.

As time goes by, the effects of the emerging discordant society begin to show on the individual and on human relationships. Gone is the old simplicity and communal harmony:[21]

> In the hubbub of daily life and its stresses which increased and grew more complicated day after day, people were engulfed by their cares. In spite of the abundance of people and the incessant and limitless growth of their numbers, each man became his own closed world. And dealing with other people who came from various, and sometimes incompatible, backgrounds became a matter for caution and even fear.

The values of communal solidarity and spontaneous co-operation which were to be ousted by those of material gain are best illustrated in the novel by the two extremes of Mufḍī al-Jad'ān and Ṣubḥī al-Maḥmaljī. The first is the native herbal doctor of Ḥarrān who despised money and was incensed whenever he was offered a fee for his services, while the second is the qualified doctor who came from Lebanon to seek his fortune in the oil *El Dorado*, and who, by contrast, is an opportunist profiteer who would see a patient dead before treating him for nothing.[22] Thus technical superiority is shown in a way to have brought with it moral degeneration.

There is probably nothing in the novel so amusing as the scenes in which the author portrays the early bedouin's puzzlement and shock on encountering the machinery and technology of the twentieth century as they arrive in a desert that has existed for hundreds of years hardly aware of the outside world and the progress that has been made. The novelist assumes the viewpoint of the bedouin and recreates with loving tenderness the confused feelings of these simple people:[23]

> When animal noises began to fill the air at sunset, that machine roared again with a sound that frightened everyone. This time its roaring was accompanied by glaring lights which dazzled the eyes, and in a little while scores of small bright suns shone above. The place was filled with a light that no man could imagine or endure. Men and children drew back and looked again at the lights to make sure that they still saw them. They glanced at each other in fear and wonder.

The amazing machine described above is obviously nothing but an electric generator. The book abounds with such accounts, sometimes touching, sometimes hilarious, which go to underline the cruel suddenness with which oil flung these people across the centuries into modern life.

In *al-Ukhdūd* the growth of oil wealth is shown to widen progressively the gulf between the rich and the poor:[24]

> The rich, whose wealth inflated day after day, were afraid, and their fear increased proportionately with their fortune, while the poor, who knew how to make ends meet in the old days, found the new life too cunning for them. It flung them about and they did not know where next it would push them or where their graves would be.

The novel is very much concerned with the way in which the simple bedouin society, with its closely knit relationships where every individual in the community mattered and where barriers between governor and governed did not exist, developed (retrogressed would be the word suggested by the spirit of the novel) thanks to oil, into a repressive State. Towards the end of *al-Tīh* the grievances of the striking workers are not listened to and investigated but are met with force, which results in the murder of several workers. Ḥarrān sees for the first time the set-up of such an alien concept to the desert as a police force who are trained to treat the bedouin with brutality: 'I want you to teach them [the bedouin] what red death is like. Smash their bones. Curse their fathers and take no mercy on them'; thus the chief of the force educates his men.[25] With the police also comes the first prison in the township, and into the prison are hurled those who say the wrong thing, on such incongruous charges as 'vagrancy'; and when imprisonment proves an insufficient deterrent, a beating good enough to lead to death will do.[26]

Al-Ukhdūd sees the establishment and the sprawling all over Mūrān of a powerful intelligence service. The native chief of the service is patiently initiated into the arts of his new profession by his American adviser. 'Money and force', he is told, are the secrets of the game:[27]

> Money for persons and sections [of society] which consider the *status quo* to suit them best because through it they can make profit, gain power and secure their interests; and force for the other persons and sections, the mutinous ones, who are satisfied with nothing.

If anything the tenor of *Mudun al-Milḥ* is pessimistic. The novel idealises the past, resents the present and, at least in the two volumes so far published, seems to see no hope for the future. The very title of the trilogy *Mudun al-Milḥ* (*Cities of Salt*) betrays the author's gloomy vision: this oil-based civilisation is not real; it is as though its cities are built of salt and one day (i.e. when the oil dries out) they are bound to crumble or melt away.[28] The author's unequivocal purport is that the discovery of oil in Arabia came not as a blessing but as a curse. The message he dresses up as fiction is spelt out in a newspaper interview which merits being quoted at some length:[29]

> The tragedy is not in our having the oil, but in the way we use the wealth it has created and in the future awaiting us after it has run out. Trees were cut down, people uprooted from their land, the earth dug up and oil finally pumped out only to turn people into a crowd of open mouths waiting for charity or a crowd of arms fighting over a piece of bread and building an illusory future. In developed countries like Britain or Norway, the oil 'whim' . . . brings a new strength to the community, but in underdeveloped societies, and in the manner that it has been exploited . . . oil becomes a damnation, a ceiling that screens the future from view. In twenty or thirty years' time we shall discover that oil has been a real tragedy for the Arabs, and these giant cities built in the desert will find no-one to live in them and their hundreds of thousands of inhabitants will have to begin again their quest after the unknown. Oil could have been a road to the future; it could have made possible a natural and continuous progress from nomadic life to civilisation . . . but what actually happens is nothing like that. As a result we shall again have to face a sense of loss and estrangement, this time in complete poverty . . .

In another interview he defines the plight of oil societies which he tries to illustrate in his novel in terms of consumerist extravagance which means 'the ability to buy everything without being able to produce anything, scorning work and dependence on others for securing the simplest needs of life . . .'; a condition, he goes on to say, which is of necessity provisional and doomed to end in tragedy.[30]

The author's sombre view of the future is voiced more poetically by one of his characters, viz. Najma al-Mithqāl, an old woman who dies during the forcible rehabilitation of the Wādī al-'Uyūn community. Before her death the old woman erupts intermittently into a series of prophecies which people remembered and circulated for a long time afterwards. In a style reminiscent of the rhyming prophecies of the ancient Arabian soothsayers, she says:[31]

> From the valley of Janāḥ up to Ḍāli', and from Sāriḥa up to Maṭāliq, every day of the days to come will count as a year of these our days. In the beginning plenty will prevail in the land, and in the end locusts shall be the food of men. In the beginning there shall be rain and inundation, and in the end rulers without discrimination. In the beginning there shall be grain and brocade, and in the end darnel and swirling sand. Gold and Silver shall people worship, and to Phallus and Vulva shall they make their holy pilgrimage. The rich shall rob the poor, and the strong oppress the weak, and each shall his own deliverance seek.

Notes

1. The Arabic title is *Mudun al-Milḥ*, (al-Mu'assasa al-'Arabiyya li 'l-Dirāsāt wa 'l-Nashr, Beirut, 1984). The novel is a trilogy of epic length. At the time of writing only volumes one and two had been published with the sub-titles *al-Tīh* (The Wilderness) and *al-Ukhdūd* (The Trench) respectively, to be followed at an unspecified date by the third and last volume whose advertised title is *Taqāsīm al-Layl wa 'l-Nahār* (The Divisions of Day and Night).

2. See back cover of *al-Tīh*.

3. Munīf studied for his doctorate in oil economics in Egypt and at one time was editor-in-chief in Baghdad of the magazine *Oil and Development*. See *UR: The International Magazine of Arab Culture*, vol. 1, (1982), p. 56. He also seems to have worked for some time at OPEC. See 'Abd al-Raḥmān Majīd al-Rubay'ī, *Aṣwāt wa Khuṭuwāt: Maqālāt fī 'l-Qiṣṣa al-'Arabiyya*, (Al-Mu'assasa al-'Arabiyya li 'l-Dirāsāt wa 'l-Nashr, Beirut, 1984), p. 252.

4. Some vagueness surrounds the question of Munīf's national identity. Though Saudi-born, he is thought to be of Iraqi nationality. One gets the feeling that the novelist deliberately mystifies or avoids this issue in his pronouncements, just as he disguises the names of places and historical figures in his fiction. In both cases the reasons can only be political. See al-Rubay'ī, *Aṣwāt wa Khuṭuwāt*, p. 252.

5. See the interview with Munīf in *al-Waṭan* supplement, (Kuwait, 10 September 1985), p. 2.

6. The Agreement was signed in Jidda on 29 May 1933 and made effective on 14 July by publication in the official journal of the Saudi Arabian Government. See *Aramco*

Handbook, (ARAMCO, 1960), p. 133.

7. 'Ḥiwār ma'a 'Abd al-Raḥmān Munīf', *al-Ma'rifa*, No. 204, (Damascus, February 1979), pp. 188–9.

8. *Mudun al-Milḥ* is Munīf's eighth novel. His first, *al-Ashjār wa Ightiyāl Marzūq* (The Trees and the Assassination of Marzūq) was written in 1971 and published in 1973. See Jūrj Ṭarābīshī, *Sharq wa Gharb, Rujūla wa Unūtha*, 3rd reprint, (Dār al-Ṭalī'a, Beirut, 1982), p. 187.

9. At this point the novel talks about a pipeline being extended between Ḥarrān (i.e. Dhahran) and Wādī al-'Uyūn. Historically a pipeline between Dhahran and 'Ayn Dār was completed in 1950. See *Aramco Handbook*, p. 150.

10. The Arabic titles are *Sharq al-Mutawassiṭ*, *Ḥīna Taraknā al-Jisr* and *Sibāq al-Masāfāt al-Ṭawīla* respectively.

11. *Al-Ma'rifa*, p. 198. See Note 7.

12. No dates are stated in the novel, but these can be established from the fact that it begins with the arrival of the Americans in the desert to make their early geological surveys for oil, and ends with the celebration of the completion of the Trans-Arabian pipeline.

13. See interview in *al-Waṭan*, 10 September 1985.

14. Ibid.

15. *Mudun al-Milḥ: al-Tīh*, pp. 13–14.

16. Ibid., pp. 226, 230.

17. This point is taken up again in Volume Two (*al-Ukhdūd*) and members of the royal family are shown to take a lively interest in the practice. See pp. 239 and 264.

18. *Al-Tīh*, p. 552.

19. Ibid., p. 105.

20. A key figure in *al-Tīh*. Suspicious from the beginning of the arrival of the Americans and disconsolate at the changes around him which he cannot comprehend, he reaches breaking-point at the sight of the trees which have been cut down. He picks up his gun, mounts his camel and silently rides into the desert never to appear again. He is later rumoured to have formed a gang of men to attack and sabotage company installations and pipelines. Gradually he turns into a legendary figure and becomes part of the folklore of the people.

21. *Al-Tīh*, p. 235.

22. Ibid., p. 508 ff. The character of Dr Ṣubḥī al-Maḥmaljī is taken up and further developed in Volume Two of the novel, *al-Ukhdūd*, where he plays a central part. There is ample evidence in the novel that the doctor's character is based on the person of Dr Rashād Fir'awn (Rashad Pharaoun), the Syrian physician who arrived in Riyadh in 1936 to serve King Ibn Su'ūd in a medical capacity. Later he was to serve as senior adviser to Kings Su'ūd, Fayṣal and Khālid in succession. However, as there are, in places, considerable differences between the histories of the fictitious doctor and the real one, it becomes obvious that the novelist did not so much intend to recreate the historical character as to paint a picture of the corrupt, scheming, opportunist courtier. For facts about Rashad Pharaoun see D. Holden and R. Johns, *The House of Saud*, (Sidgwick & Jackson, London, 1981), *passim*. See also Robert Lacey, *The Kingdom*, (Hutchinson, London, 1981), *passim*.

23. *Al-Tīh*, p. 70.

24. *Al-Ukhdūd*, p. 453.

25. See p. 541.

26. See the incident of Mufḍī al-Jad'ān in the last few chapters of *al-Tīh*.

27. *Al-Ukhdūd*, p. 452.

28. Ibid., p. 236 (for the interpretation of the title).

29. See *al-Khalīj* (published in UAE, 21 November 1984), p. 10.

30. See interview in *al-Waṭan*, 10 September 1985.

31. *Al-Tīh*, p. 158.

16 Oil: Current Trends and Future Prospects

Walid Khadduri

Since the early 1970s, the international oil industry has undergone more critical changes than any other sector of the world economy. Within a short period of time oil supply and demand patterns changed dramatically and the centres of the decision-making process moved upstream, while forecasting future developments — particularly in the long term — became hazardous.

The oil market has become highly competitive and volatile, and has failed to evolve a modern structure to deal with the new problems. Institutional relations organised around long-term contracts between companies and between companies and producing countries have now given way to short-term arrangements among an unprecedented number of players, many of them not directly involved with the oil industry. World demand for oil outside the Communist countries has fallen from more than 51 million barrels a day (mn b/d) in 1979 to around 45 mn b/d in 1985, with energy demand in the Western industrialised countries declining by an estimated 1–2 per cent annually.

As a result of these rapid developments, both producers and consumers face an agonising period of reassessment. The OPEC producers have become acutely aware that they do not have firm control over the market under present conditions. The breakdown of the traditional supply networks controlled by the majors both upstream and downstream, along with declining demand for oil, has made it difficult for the OPEC states to maintain their control of supplies or to preserve harmony within their ranks. They know that the present situation is a direct result of their own actions, of the rapid increase in oil prices during the 1970s, particularly in 1979, and of rising expectations in their own countries. They also appreciate that concerted action by the industrialised countries has led to conservation and the rational utilisation of energy, as well as to an unprecedented effort to discover petroleum outside the OPEC states, and particularly outside the Arab region. Yet the future does not look so bleak for OPEC as some might want to picture it, since the member states still possess the major part of world oil reserves. Furthermore, their economic needs, if planned rationally, could be comfortably met with much lower rates of crude oil production than those prevailing during the 1970s.

The consumers, on the other hand, have within a decade turned the tables in the world oil market. They established the International Energy Agency (IEA) to co-ordinate policies in times of emergency and, more importantly, to undercut OPEC's role in world markets. At the same time, a media campaign was launched in the West to portray OPEC and the Arabs as solely responsible for the economic malaise of the Western world, the purpose of this campaign being to emphasise the need to reduce dependence on imported OPEC oil. These measures were coupled with well-planned and effective policies to conserve oil and to find alternative energy sources.

While most of these actions on the part of the industrial states have met with a large degree of success, a basic problem remains: how long can these policies be implemented successfully? No giant oil fields have been discovered recently, conservation has almost reached its zenith, the Western economies are gradually recovering, there is growing social opposition to nuclear energy, and cheaper oil could delay the development of alternatives. Current forecasts are again warning of oil shortages in the mid-1990s.

Throughout this decade of profound changes there has been no genuine attempt to co-operate on a long-term basis for the mutual benefit of all parties concerned. The short-term interests of both sides, along with internal rivalries within each group, have aborted several attempts at co-operation between oil producers and consumers. An effective formula for co-operation remains of paramount importance if the world is to pass securely through the transitional period from the oil era to the next. Such a formula would help the OPEC states to plan the future of their societies despite the finite nature of their oil resources.

Changes in the Market and its Structure

The decision in August 1960 by the major oil companies to reduce oil prices caused five oil-exporting countries (Saudi Arabia, Venezuela, Iraq, Iran and Kuwait) to meet in Baghdad on 14 September and establish the Organisation of Petroleum Exporting Countries (OPEC). OPEC was completely ignored during the 1960s by the seven sisters (Exxon, Texaco, Standard Oil of California, Mobil, Gulf, BP and Royal Dutch/Shell), who refused to discuss substantive issues with it collectively and insisted on dealing with individual producing countries. A similar attitude was adopted by the industrialised countries. Both groups did realise, however, the potential threat OPEC represented to their dominant position in the production, transportation, refining and sale of oil in the international market. OPEC, while not achieving much in practical terms during the 1960s, was able nevertheless to consolidate its unity, strengthen the political and diplomatic links among its members, and pave the way for recruiting other Third World oil-producing countries such as Qatar, Indonesia, Libya, Algeria, the United Arab Emirates, Nigeria, Ecuador and Gabon. The Organisation was also able to draw up a Declaratory Statement of Petroleum Policy in 1968 which laid the foundation for many of the changes that have occurred since. The Statement incorporated the principles of direct exploitation of oil resources by the state, participation in the ownership of the operating companies, relinquishment of areas not developed by the companies, and conservation of oil resources. It also affirmed that posted prices should be determined by the producer governments themselves and that these prices should be linked to the prices of imported goods in order to prevent the erosion of the purchasing power of oil revenues.

Conditions in the world oil market changed in the early 1970s. First individually and later collectively, OPEC member states began taking the initiative in obtaining better treatment in their relations with the concessionary companies. Prices were increased, foreign companies were nationalised, and conservation laws were legislated in several member states. In this the OPEC countries were assisted by several external factors, among them the increasing dependence of the industrial countries on cheap OPEC oil and the failure to discover comparable reserves elsewhere. OPEC was also helped by the lack of co-ordination between the Western oil companies, particularly between the majors, the independents and the national oil companies of the industrial states.

The turning point came in October 1973, when two separate decisions were taken which changed the course of the international oil industry and eventually had a major impact upon the Arab states and the world as a whole. The first of these was OPEC's decision to set oil prices and production unilaterally, independent of the oil companies. The second was the resolution adopted by the Arab Oil Ministers meeting in Kuwait to reduce supplies to those states that were aiding Israel in the war with Egypt and Syria. Coming at the same time these two decisions sent shock waves through the international oil industry. The fact that the two decisions were undertaken under the auspices and planning of Saudi Arabia gave them a credibility and strength they would otherwise have lacked.

As a result of these developments the OPEC states regained sovereignty over their most important asset, with upstream oil no longer forming part of the integrated system of the major companies. Instead of 80–90 per cent of crude oil being lifted by a few major companies, scores of new customers emerged, including former concession-holders, independents (American, European and Japanese), Third World state oil companies, refiners and traders. At the same time, however, the disintegration of the international oil industry contained the seeds of instability. Whereas prior to 1973, under the control of the majors, prices were administered to serve largely fiscal purposes (mainly taxes and royalties paid to the host governments), after 1973–74 prices were determined on a short-term basis reflecting a perceived balance between the OPEC members' domestic requirements and concern over the international economy. There was little co-ordination between these sovereign states in downstream operations.[1]

The assumption of new powers by the OPEC producers was accompanied by a significant rise in prices, production and revenues. In the Arab oil-exporting countries high rates of economic growth were achieved, especially in the less-populated countries, where particular attention was paid to infrastructural projects, education and health. Imports increased as a result, as did the inflow of foreign labour. Several countries were able to build large investment portfolios overseas and much private wealth was accumulated as a result of the sudden and massive increase in oil revenues.

Despite the positive contribution of this influx of wealth to the economic development of the oil-exporting countries, much unnecessary spending — both private and public — resulted in lost social and economic opportunities and the waste of an unrenewable natural resource. In a major study of the evolution of the Arab oil economies during the 1970s, the noted Arab economist, Yusif A. Sayigh, wrote:[2]

> The record of the 1970s reveals areas of over-use and misuse of financial resources, whether in the adoption of excessive consumer-oriented styles of living, or in permissiveness in the design and costing of development works . . . In addition to 'high consumption' (in the Rostovian terminology), which threatens to arrive before the stage of 'high production' or 'high development' and which leads to high importation owing to the weak and limited productive capacity of the region, there is over-spending on development projects; but more significantly we witness the building of projects of a very low degree of urgency. Cases of 'conspicuous investment' or showy development

are abundant enough, in almost every country, to justify special condemnation.

Expenditures in the Arab oil-exporting countries during the 1970s were based on the premise that either production or prices would continue to increase indefinitely. But the increase in oil prices in 1979–80, at a time when the market basically favoured the buyers, eroded OPEC's capacity to administer prices and eventually production. The official price of Arabian Light, the OPEC marker crude, fell from $34 a barrel in 1982 to $29/B in March 1983 and to $28/B in January 1985. Demand for OPEC crude oil production also decreased, from 30.9mn b/d in 1979 to 16.3mn b/d in 1984 (the lowest rate since 1967), while for the first time since OPEC was founded its member countries' revenues from oil decined for three successive years (see Tables 16.1 and 16.2).

The industrialised countries did not take favourably to the success of a Third World economic organisation, and a large part of OPEC's problems in the 1980s can be attributed to policies adopted individually and collectively by the member states of the Organisation of Economic Co-operation and Development (OECD). The principal forum determining these policies was the International Energy Agency (IEA), which was established in February 1974. The IEA used market forces and government policies to influence patterns of energy production and consumption. Measures were adopted to curtail the consumption of oil, particularly OPEC oil, through intensive exploration in non-OPEC areas, conservation and increasing reliance on other energy sources. New high levels of stockpiling, both strategic and commercial, were made mandatory in order to manipulate the market and counteract any sudden shortfall of supplies. A joint-sharing plan was also adopted in case of emergencies. Finally, any attempt to enter into a meaningful dialogue with OPEC was postponed until structural changes in the international oil industry brought about a more favourable situation for the consumer countries.[3]

The effective implementation of energy policies by the member countries of the IEA, coupled with a prolonged economic recession and a basic structural change in the Western economies away from energy-intensive industries, has had a critical impact upon the world oil market during the 1980s. Oil consumption in the 24 OECD member countries fell by more than five per cent annually between 1980 and 1983, while the share of oil in total energy consumption, which had already been reduced from 54 per cent in 1973 to 51 per cent in 1979, declined to 45 per cent in 1983. Furthermore, the overall use of energy per unit

Table 16.1: Crude oil production in OPEC member countries, 1973–84 (Thousand Barrels per Day)

	1973	1977	1979	1980	1981	1982	1983	1984
Algeria	1,097.3	1,152.3	1,153.8	1,019.9	797.8	704.5	660.9	695.0
Ecuador	208.8	183.4	214.2	204.9	211.0	198.3	237.5	256.1
Gabon	150.2	222.0	203.4	174.5	151.4	155.1	155.4	157.4
Indonesia	1,338.5	1,686.1	1,590.8	1,575.7	1,604.2	1,324.8	1,245.3	1,280.1
Iran	5,860.9	5,662.8	3,167.9	1,467.3	1,315.9	2,391.3	2,441.7	2,032.4
Iraq	2,018.1	2,348.2	3,476.9	2,646.4	897.4	1,012.1	1,098.8	1,221.3
Kuwait	3,020.4	1,969.0	2,500.3	1,663.7	1,129.7	824.3	1,054.1	1,053.4
Libya	2,174.9	2,063.4	2,091.7	1,830.0	1,217.8	1,136.0	1,104.9	1,077.9
Nigeria	2,054.3	2,085.1	2,302.0	2,058.0	1,439.6	1,287.0	1,235.5	1,388.0
Qatar	570.3	444.6	508.1	471.4	415.2	332.0	269.0	325.3
Saudi Arabia	7,596.2	9,199.9	9,532.6	9,900.5	9,808.0	6,483.0	4,539.4	4,079.1
United Arab Emirates	1,532.6	1,998.7	1,830.7	1,701.9	1,502.3	1,248.8	1,149.0	1,069.0
Venezuela	3,366.0	2,237.9	2,356.4	2,165.0	2,108.3	1,895.0	1,800.8	1,695.5
Total OPEC	30,988.5	31,253.4	30,928.8	26,879.2	22,598.6	18,992.2	16,992.3	16,330.5

Source: *OPEC Annual Statistical Bulletin 1984*, (OPEC, Vienna, 1985), Table 13, p. 14.

Table 16.2: OPEC member countries' revenues from oil, 1973–84 (US $mn)

	1973	1977	1979	1980	1981	1982	1983	1984
Algeria	988	4,254	7,513	12,500	10,700	8,500	9,700	9,700
Ecuador	129	499	800	1,394	1,560	1,184	1,100	1,600
Gabon	29	600	900	1,800	1,600	1,500	1,500	1,400
Indonesia	688	4,692	8,100	12,859	14,393	12,703	9,660	10,400
Iran	4,399	21,210	20,500	13,500	9,300	17,600	20,000	16,700
Iraq	1,843	9,631	21,291	26,100	10,400	9,500	8,400	10,400
Kuwait	1,735	7,615	16,863	17,900	14,900	9,477	9,900	10,800
Libya	2,223	8,850	15,223	22,600	15,600	14,000	11,200	10,400
Nigeria	2,048	9,600	15,900	23,405	16,713	13,086	10,100	12,400
Qatar	463	1,994	3,082	4,795	4,722	3,145	3,000	4,400
Saudi Arabia	4,340	36,540	57,522	102,212	113,200	76,000	46,100	43,700
United Arab Emirates	900	9,030	12,862	19,500	18.700	16,000	12,800	13,000
Venezuela	3,029	8,106	11,956	16,344	17,401	13,543	13,500	13,700
Total OPEC	22,813	122,621	192,512	274,909	249,189	196,238	156,960	158,600

Source: Ibid., Table 33, p. 34.

of output decreased at an annual average rate of 3.5 per cent during 1980–83, and the consumption of oil per unit of Gross National Product (GNP) fell by 1983 to less than two-thirds of its level in 1973.[4]

In 1984, despite the fact that economic growth in the OECD member countries averaged about five per cent, oil consumption grew by around two per cent (0.7mn b/d), with some of the growth, which took place during the first half of the year, being attributable to the UK coal-miners' strike (0.3mn b/d). On the supply side, the IEA estimates that world production outside the Centrally Planned Economies (CPEs), plus net exports by the CPEs increased by some 1.4mn b/d between 1983 and 1984. Most of this increase was attributed to non-OPEC sources: the North Sea (0.3mn b/d), North America (0.3mn b/d), the developing countries (0.6mn b/d) and the CPEs (0.2mn b/d). OPEC's share of non-Communist world (NCW) supplies decreased from 59 per cent in 1979 to 40 per cent in 1984, while the non-OPEC share increased from 41 per cent to 60 per cent during the same period (see Table 16.3).

Table 16.3: World oil supply and demand, 1979–84 (mn b/d)

	1979	1980	1981	1982	1983	1984
NCW consumption	52.4	49.7	47.7	46.0	45.2	46.1
NCW supply (includes net imports from CPEs)	53.7	50.4	47.0	44.9	44.6	46.0
OPEC supply (crude oil and NGL)	31.6	27.6	23.5	19.8	18.4	18.5
Non-OPEC supply (includes net imports from CPEs)	22.1	22.8	23.5	25.1	26.2	27.5
OPEC % share of NCW supply	59	55	50	44	41	40
Non-OPEC % share of NCW supply	41	45	50	56	59	60

Source: International Energy Agency, *Annual Oil Market Report, 1984*, (IEA, Paris, 1985), Table A4, pp. 36–7.

These signals, and many others, have been quite clear to the OPEC member states for some time. But differences of opinion arising from divergent national interests and political orientations have weakened the ability of the Organisation to confront the situation. There are wide demographic, social and economic differences between the member states (see Table 16.4), not to speak of security and development needs, that occasion legitimate differences of opinion over short- and long-term policies on pricing and production.

The overwhelming bulk of OPEC's proved reserves are in the least

Table 16.4: Population, GNP per capita and proven oil reserves in OPEC member countries, 1984

	Population (Thousands)	GNP per capita (US $)	Proven crude oil reserves (mn barrels)
Algeria	21,140	2,521	9,000
Ecuador	9,550	1,243	1,181
Gabon	1,150	2,887	518
Indonesia	158,130	494	8,650
Iran	43,360	2,650	58,874
Iraq	15,190	2,185	65,000
Kuwait	1,780	18,517	92,710
Libya	3,500	7,771	21,000
Nigeria	96,594	801	16,650
Qatar	290	26,207	4,500
Saudi Arabia	10,840	9,121	171,710
United Arab Emirates	1,290	22,434	32.490
Venezuela	16,840	2,939	25,845
Total OPEC	379,654	Average 1,625	Total OPEC 508,228 % of World 68.3

Source: *OPEC Annual Statistical Bulletin 1984*, (OPEC, Vienna, 1985), Tables 2, 3 and 34, pp. 1, 2 and 36.

densely populated states of the Arabian Gulf. Other states are much more highly populated and with low reserves, while a third group is moderately populated and with large reserves. Security and development policies also come into play at different times, causing further complications. All these factors play an important role in determining a country's short- and long-term needs and hence the orientation of its oil policy.

None the less, attempts have been made to deal with the issues at hand. A Long-Term Strategy was drawn up in 1980 and a Summit of the OPEC Heads of States was to convene in the same year, on the twentieth anniversary of the Organisation, to discuss the future course of action. Both these initiatives came to nothing because of the war between two of the founding members, Iraq and Iran. A lack of decisiveness has characterised OPEC since then, and unless there is a negotiated settlement to end this conflict political problems will continue to preoccupy OPEC proceedings and prevent it from taking effective action.

It took months of public controversy and several frustrating Ministerial Conferences before OPEC was able to put its house in order and face up to the instability of the world oil market. The assumption at the time was that price cuts, production programming and co-operation on the part of non-OPEC producers would do the trick.

The first shot was called at Ṣalāla, Oman, on 14 October 1982 by the Oil Ministers of the Gulf Co-operation Council (GCC), who issued a declaration warning oil exporters, both inside and outside OPEC, in no uncertain terms that the GCC states would not shoulder the responsibilities of other oil producers and that if these others 'continue in their misguided actions they will not be protected by the member countries of the GCC from the consequences of these actions'. This was followed by the OPEC London Agreement of 14 March 1983 at which the OPEC Oil Ministers, for the first time in the history of the Organisation, agreed to reduce the price of the marker crude, from $34/B to $29/B. A production programme of 17.5mn b/d was also approved, with individual quotas being allocated to member countries. Saudi Arabia was to act as the swing producer, meaning in effect that it would supply the balancing volume to meet market requirements within the overall ceiling. The Oil Ministers also pledged, among other things, not to give discounts, not to dump products on the world oil market, and not to sell on the spot market, either directly or indirectly. Non-OPEC producers were asked to do their share to stabilise the market.

After the London Agreement the market remained stable for about 15 months. However, the slow growth of the world economy and the continuing increase in non-OPEC oil production caused a further reduction in demand for OPEC oil and in OPEC's share of the market. In October 1984 the Oil Ministers agreed to reduce the production quota further to 16mn b/d. This was followed in December 1984 and January 1985 by an agreement to monitor the member states' production levels more closely, to narrow price differentials, and to realign official crude oil prices through a further reduction in the price of the Arabian Light marker crude to $28/B.

As a result of these measures the average oil export price, in nominal dollar terms, was reduced by 20 per cent from the peak reached during the first quarter of 1981. OPEC's share of the market declined to its lowest level ever and the majority of the OPEC members were obliged to abandon term contracts at Government Selling Price (GSP) and convert to market-related contracts, netback deals, barter, countertrade, discounts, spot sales, etc.

The dilemma facing OPEC members during the first half of the 1980s was that, as they reduced their production in order to stabilise the market, the volumes withdrawn from the market were immediately replaced by non-OPEC oil. The resulting loss of markets and decline in the role of oil in global energy demand, along with the loss of revenue — which caused considerable domestic pressures and anxieties — forced OPEC to take a second look at its earlier policies and to adopt an alternative strategy.

The official communiqué of the OPEC Ministerial Conference of 7–9 December 1985 stated clearly that the purpose of the new policy is 'to secure and defend for OPEC a fair share of the world oil market consistent with the necessary income for member countries' development'. What this means in effect is that OPEC has abandoned its production ceiling of 16mn b/d and its official price structure. This radical departure from traditional policies was not surprising, particularly since Saudi Arabia had warned earlier in the summer of its impatience with the price-cutting tactics of a majority of the OPEC member states and stated its resolution to regain its share of the market. The first step in this direction was the signing of netback-related contracts in August–September 1985, which resulted in Saudi production rising from 2mn b/d in August to near the quota level of 4.3mn b/d in December. Further steps are also contemplated if the non-OPEC exporters do not modify their production policies.

All the indications are that the non-OPEC producers will not respond positively to OPEC's new policy. OPEC, for its part, is determined to pursue its new objectives. This means in effect that it will no longer assume the role of the world's swing producer. This significant change in policy was made clear in a speech in November 1985 by Fadhil al-Chalabi, Deputy Secretary General of OPEC:[5]

> OPEC will, of course, continue to make every effort to stabilise the market and prevent a price collapse. However, the process of replacing OPEC oil in world supply by other producers should be stopped. If there is no co-operation from the other producers/sellers, this could mean that OPEC may cease to play the role of residual supplier. With the very low production levels and the increasing financial difficulties for its member countries, the concept of OPEC as the residual supplier is already breaking down. Perhaps a possible alternative would be that OPEC should set for itself a minimum production level and market share that could be defended in order to optimise the relationship between OPEC's financial requirements for development and world market stability. This would ultimately mean that, contrary to its past policy of rigid price defense at the expense of volume, OPEC may consider the possibility of shifting to defending a minimum market share in addition to the price. This may mean that OPEC will abandon its role as the world's swing producer of oil.

Challenging Times Ahead

While there is an overwhelming consensus among oil officials and observers that prices will continue their downward drift in the short term, opinions differ sharply as to the future course of the oil market in the long term. In the short term, forecasts differ only on the speed and extent of the decline in prices. There are very few specialists who think otherwise on the subject, in view of the surplus production capacity available, slow world economic growth, stagnant demand for oil, intensive competition from other sources of energy, and the conflicting interests of the various oil producers.

What is more important, however, are long-term prospects. Most forecasts (OPEC, IEA, IMF, Chevron and Conoco) point towards a growth in oil demand for the next decade of around one per cent annually, although this could be higher if the impact of conservation and substitution is reduced by the soft short-term market. By the year 2000, the IEA estimates that world demand, excluding the Centrally Planned Economies, could reach about 53.8mn b/d, as compared with 46.3mn b/d in 1984. The OECD member countries expect a decrease in their oil demand from 34.8mn b/d in 1984 to 33.8mn b/d in 2000, whereas in other countries (excluding the CPEs) demand is expected to rise from 11.5mn b/d in 1984 to 20mn b/d in 2000.[6]

But it is on the supply side of the picture that major changes are likely to occur. The real cost of finding new hydrocarbon resources is becoming more expensive all the time. And despite technological advances the average discovery is becoming smaller. The drive to find oil outside OPEC has been very costly for the international oil companies during the past few years, according to OPEC experts Nordine Ait-Laousine and Francisco R. Parra:[7]

> In the decade from 1963 to 1973, world production (excluding the CPEs) increased by 25.5mn b/d (mainly from the Middle East) at a capital cost of $76.2bn, or almost $3,000 per barrel per day of incremental production (although of course much of the capital cost is in fact spent on maintaining existing capacity and some of it on finding and developing gas). From 1973 to 1982, an estimated $420bn was spent, outside the OPEC area, for a gain of slightly less than 6mn b/d, a capital cost of $70,000 per barrel per day of incremental production.

Nor is the outlook for supply in the non-OPEC producing countries very bright either. If present trends continue, with two-thirds of world oil production originating from countries with one-third of the world's reserves, then the rate of depletion in these countries will drastically shorten the lifespan of their reserves and, assuming a one per cent growth in world demand for oil, their reserve-to-output ratio will fall to 5.5 years in 1995. Replacing this oil and finding new reserves, particularly in more difficult areas and in much smaller quantities, will be very costly. Meanwhile the cost of finding a new barrel of oil in the Middle East is still less than $1, compared to an average of around $8 worldwide. Furthermore, the reserve-to-production ratio of the Arab oil-producing countries, because of the recent fall in production, has risen from 47 years in 1973 to 113 years in 1984, while the lifespan of OPEC oil reserves has increased from 37 years at the 1973 rate of production to 85 years at the present rate.[8]

The above analysis, however, is not shared by all. There are those who argue that while it is true that no giant oilfields have been discovered lately, the smaller discoveries which have been made have resulted in annual increases in non-OPEC production of between 600,000–700,000 b/d over the past three years. Furthermore, the cost of finding new oil has been reduced by technological advances, particularly offshore. It is also argued that discovery cost is no longer the sole relevant factor in finding new oil, and that other factors such as taxation levels, national security, foreign exchange savings and employment prospects must also be considered.[9] Finally, the share of the alternative sources in the overall energy basket has grown significantly during the past decade and projections are that in coal and nuclear energy this trend will continue. The IEA countries expect coal production to rise by 230 million tons of oil equivalent (mtoe), or 28.2 per cent between 1983 and 1990, and by a further 301 mtoe, to 1,346 mtoe, in 2000. The contribution of nuclear power is expected to grow from the thermal equivalent of 156.8 mtoe in 1983 to 318 mtoe in 1990 and 460 mtoe in 2000. Its share of future electric power generation could increase from 13 per cent in 1983 to 21 per cent in 1990 and 25 per cent in 2000.[10]

Whatever might emerge in the future (and energy forecasts have not been known for their accuracy during the past decade), the prospects facing OPEC do not look as bleak as some might wish. Much will depend on how the Organisation and its member states face the challenges ahead.

Foremost among these is putting their own house in order through rationalising and diversifying their economies. The total dependence of these states upon oil revenues simply postpones the day of reckoning. And without a fundamental change in economic and social orientation from a one-resource economy to a more diversified one they will remain at the mercy of a volatile international commodity whose future prospects are not very stable.

A second objective should be co-ordination and co-operation among the OPEC member states during both bad and good market cycles. OPEC has now to wage a long-delayed battle to secure and protect its market share. A free-for-all on production and pricing by the member states could deal a fatal blow to the whole concept of the Organisation. And as long as the Iraq-Iran war is not settled on a negotiated basis leading to a comprehensive peace, OPEC will be plagued by indecision and indecisiveness.

A third objective is mutually beneficial co-operation on energy matters between the producing and industrialised consuming countries. Past experience of international negotiations and dialogue leaves much to be desired in this regard. Joint research to identify long-term developments in the energy and oil markets could help define more precisely the position of the countries concerned, their aspirations, and possible new areas for trade and co-operation.

Finally, a more serious attempt should be made by the OPEC states to tap the markets of the Third World countries, since it is here that oil demand is expected to grow most quickly. The level of economic activity in many of these states is still relatively low, meaning that there are wide opportunities to expand trade and service agreements to the mutual benefit of both parties concerned.

Notes

1. Major reference works on the history of OPEC during the 1960s and 1970s, include: Fadhil J. Al-Chalabi, *OPEC and the International Oil Industry: A Changing Structure*, (Oxford University Press, Oxford, 1980) and Ian Seymour, *OPEC: Instrument of Change*, (Macmillan, London, 1980).

2. Yusif A. Sayigh, *Arab Oil Policies in the 1970s*, (Croom Helm, London, 1983), pp. 184–6.

3. Henry Kissinger, 'Energy: The Necessity of Decision' in *US International Energy Policy, October 1973–November 1975* (US State Department Selected Documents, Washington, DC, 1975), pp. 29–30.

4. International Monetary Fund, 'World Oil Situation', supplement note 4 in *World Economic Outlook*, (IMF, Washington, DC, April 1985), p. 142.

5. Fadhil J. Al-Chalabi, 'The Role of OPEC in Market Stabilization', *MEES*, 25 November 1985.

6. International Energy Agency, *Energy Policies and Programmes of IEA Countries, 1984 Review* (IEA, Paris, June 1985).

7. Nordine Ait-Laousine and Francisco R. Parra, 'The Development of Oil Supplies during the Energy Crisis of the Past Decade and some Questions for the Future', *MEES*,

Supplement, 14 June 1985.

8. Fadhil J. Al-Chalabi, 'Cooperation between Oil Exporting and Importing Countries', *MEES*, 20 May 1985.

9. 'Will Non-OPEC Oil Reserves Last Longer than Anticipated?', *Oil and Energy Trends*, 20 September 1985.

10. IEA, *Energy Policies and Programmes*.

17 Women and the Law in the United Arab Emirates

Doreen Hinchcliffe

Rarely can an area of the world have undergone such a rapid change as did the Shaykhdoms of the Arabian Gulf when in the mid-1960s oil was discovered in large deposits beneath their deserts and their territorial waters. Before this phenomenon the Gulf Shaykhdoms were of little interest to the outside world and reckoned something of a nuisance by the Raj. The area contained only one settled town of any size, Dubai, which because of its geographical location at the mouth of a navigable creek, was a natural harbour and a centre for trading (and smuggling) with Iran and the subcontinent of India. The transcendental law of the Shaykhdoms was the *Sharī'a*, although for certain subjects legislation had been imposed by the British, who were the overlords of the Shaykhdoms by virtue of a treaty relationship. The Trucial States, as they were then known, were administered mainly from Bombay with the aid of a handful of Resident Officers. The discovery of oil and the resulting wealth from the oil revenues found the Emirates with an almost total lack of law, either statutory or customary, which could deal with the increasingly complex problems which resulted.

Accordingly, the period from the mid-1960s until the present day has seen the enactment of a large body of statutory law, both Federal (UAE) and for each Emirate. However, no legislation, Federal or Emiri, has been enacted which affects the law of personal status, and so the law relating to marriage, divorce, guardianship of children and succession on death is still the Sharī'a, the law which Muslims believe was given by God for the guidance of His people and, being God-given, was not susceptible to change by man, However, despite the doctrine of the immutability of the Sharī'a the majority of the countries of the Middle East have effected legislation to alter those aspects of the traditional law which are not in keeping with the twentieth century. These changes have been brought about without abandoning any principles of the Sharī'a itself but in accordance with a doctrine of the Sharī'a known as *siyāsa*, whereby the ruler of the Islamic community has the right to confine and define the jurisdiction of his courts, provided always that in so doing no principle of the Sharī'a is violated. Therefore the changes were brought about by adopting the principles of a school other than that prevalent in the area; by adopting the views of an individual jurist which had not become the prevailing doctrine of his school; by combining the views of different jurists; and finally, as in the case of Tunisia, by reinterpreting certain verses of the Qur'ān itself.

In the Emirates, however, and in the other countries of the Gulf area including Saudi Arabia itself, no changes have taken place in the law relating to the family, with a single exception in Kuwait, where a law allowing an orphaned grandchild to inherit has been promulgated. Although obviously the law of personal status applies equally to men and to women, it is beyond question women who are most adversely affected by its provisions. Thus at the present time the women of the Gulf are in the anomalous position of enjoying one of the highest standards of living in the world and yet being subject to a law which was developed over a thousand years ago, with the result that their status in law is often inferior to that enjoyed by their own servants.

There are four schools of law in Sunnī Islam: the Ḥanafī, which is the largest of the schools, the Mālikī, the Shāfi'ī and the Ḥanbalī. In the Emirates of Dubai and Abu Dhabi the law applied is that of the Mālikī school and in the remaining smaller Emirates that of the Ḥanbalī school.

All the schools of law recognise child marriage, but throughout the major part of the Muslim world restrictions have been placed on this practice so that in some cases penal sanctions are incurred by adults who purport to contract children in marriage and in others the marriage of children below a certain age is held to be invalid. In the Emirates, however, the traditional law continues to be applied and therefore children of either sex may be contracted in marriage, without their consent, by their marriage guardian, usually their father. In the case of a male child, however, he can, on reaching puberty, which is equated with the age of majority in Islamic law, or at any time thereafter, seek to terminate the marriage at will if it does not prove satisfactory. This remedy is not, however, available to a female child. Moreover, according to the Mālikī and Ḥanbalī schools, even an adult woman, provided she has not previously been married, can be compulsorily contracted in marriage by her marriage guardian. The law does not require a woman to give her consent to her marriage and, indeed, denies her the right to conclude her own marriage contract. The Ḥanafī law, on the other hand, gives women, on attaining majority, complete contractual capacity including the right to conclude their own marriage contracts.

Once a marriage has been concluded, Islamic law imposes certain duties and grants rights to the parties which are of a reciprocal nature. Thus, upon marriage the wife acquires the right to a dower. The dower is an integral part of every Muslim marriage contract and even where no dower is stipulated in the contract, or even when it is expressly stipulated that no dower shall be paid, the wife is entitled to receive a dower which is calculated taking account of certain factors, such as the age and beauty of the wife, whether she has previously been married and the amount of dower received by other members of her family.

It is common practice for the dower to be divided into two parts. The first part, the 'prompt' dower, is paid immediately on the contract, and the second part, the 'deferred' dower is to become payable on the termination of the marriage, thus in theory providing a deterrent to a husband's wilful use of his right to divorce or to supplement the small amount she would receive from her husband's estate as his widow. Until the wife receives payment of the prompt dower, she can refuse to consummate the marriage and such refusal will not constitute disobedience to her husband, but if she allows consummation to take place she cannot thereafter refuse to have sexual relations with her husband without being held to be disobedient.

It has been argued by some jurists that the presence of dower in the Islamic marriage contract equates that contract to a contract of sale. There is no doubt that, before the coming of Islam, a marriage contract was in effect a contract of sale with the father of the wife receiving from the husband the bride price and, in return, handing over his daughter to the husband. One of the reforms introduced by the Qur'ān itself was that henceforth women were to be given their dower. Nevertheless, it is sometimes argued that the elements of sale are still present in the marriage contract although the wife is no longer being 'sold', but is herself selling the right to have intercourse with her.

Once a marriage has duly taken place, whatever the financial position of either party may be, the husband bears the sole responsibility for the maintenance of his wife. The most important aspect of maintenance is the provision of a home or dwelling, which conforms to the strict requirements of the Sharī'a in being not only safe for her person, but which is free from the presence of all members of the husband's family, with the exception of infant children of a previous marriage. Until such a dwelling is provided the wife has the right to refuse to begin cohabitation. Of course, many wives in the Emirates are unaware of this right which the law accords them and, perhaps more importantly, are unperturbed by the prospect of living with her husband's family, including, in some instances, their husband's other wives.

The husband must also provide the day-to-day maintenance for his wife. He must feed her and clothe her, providing, according to traditional law, a new outfit each spring and another each winter. Obviously present-day practice does not accord with this traditional doctrine and nor does it accord with the doctrine of traditional law, which absolves a husband from paying his wife's medical expenses. The reason for this curious provision is that the wife's right to maintenance continues only while she remains obedient to her husband and submits to his control. If she is ill, however, and, as a result, unable to fulfil all the duties the law imposes on her, she forfeits the right to maintenance. Of course, the more usual cause for the wife forfeiting her maintenance is her wilful disobedience. Islamic law, as applied by all the schools, subjects the wife to the complete control of her husband and if she disobeys him in any way by, for example, leaving her home when he has forbidden it, or buying something against his express command, she not only loses her right to maintenance until she once more submits herself to his control, but she may also be chastised by her husband who may beat her provided only, the law says, he does not do it to excess, as for example, by breaking any bones!

The women of the Emirates which follow the Ḥanbalī school have an advantage over their Mālikī sisters, for the Ḥanbalīs, taking the legal maxim, ascribed to Muḥammad, 'Muslims must abide by their stipulations' as the basis for the law of contract, allow the normal rights and duties which flow from a contract of marriage to be varied by the parties to the contract, provided that no fundamental principle of the contract of marriage is breached. Thus the parties to a Ḥanbalī contract of marriage may insert stipulations that the wife may leave the matrimonial home without the husband's consent, or work outside the home, or that the husband will not take a second wife.

Most of the countries of the Islamic world have attempted to place restrictions on the husband's right under traditional Islamic law to marry polygamously. Tunisia, indeed, abolished polygamy in 1957, justifying the reform by a reinterpretation of the Qur'anic verse which deals with polygamy — Sūra iv verse 3.

In the Gulf States, however, the traditional law remains unchanged and a husband may marry up to four wives at any time, and the consent of the existing wife or wives is not required. Even if a woman from one of the Emirates where Ḥanbalī law applies, exercises her right to insert a stipulation against polygamy in her marriage contract, she cannot go to the court to seek an injunction restraining him from taking a second wife if he announces his intention to do so. If her husband, contrary to the express stipulation takes another wife, her remedy is to seek a judicial divorce on the grounds that, as her husband has broken the marriage contract, she is no longer bound by it.

Strict law requires a husband with more than one wife to divide his time equally between them. The texts draw up complicated rules to ensure that more time is not spent in the company of one wife than another, and provide for the application of special provisions if the husband goes on a journey and elects to take one wife only, and allow him to spend an extra period of time with a new wife without having to make up the time with his existing wives. Needless to say, these rules would be impossible to implement and, like other infringements of the Sharī'a, the sanction is not to be found in the court, but in the hereafter!

The women of the Emirates are in a much more favourable position than their Ḥanafī sisters regarding their right to obtain a dissolution of their marriage, for traditional Ḥanafī law allows a woman to obtain a divorce only on the grounds of her husband's failure to consummate the marriage. The Ḥanbalī law, on the other hand, allows a woman to petition the court for a dissolution of her marriage on several grounds: certain physical and mental defects in the husband such as insanity and impotence, failure to provide maintenance, desertion without cause for more than six months, and breaking a stipulation in the contract of marriage.

The position of the Mālikī women is even more favourable for the law recognises not only physical and mental defects, desertion and failure to maintain as grounds for dissolution but also ill-treatment (*ḍarar*), although the texts of the school make it clear that neither taking a second wife nor chastising a wife constitutes ḍarar for this purpose!

Once a wife petitions the court pleading ḍarar, even if the judge does not find the ill-treatment proved, he must set up an arbitration council consisting of two arbitrators, one chosen from the family of the husband and one from the family of the wife. The arbitrators must first try to effect a reconciliation. If they fail they must then establish which of the two parties is responsible for the breakdown of the marriage. If they find that the husband is to blame they will pronounce an irrevocable repudiation (*ṭalāq*) but if they find that the wife is to blame they can refuse to dissolve the union or they can pronounce a repudiation and order the wife to make a payment to her husband, usually the return of the dower or the foregoing of the dower-debt.

If, however, a husband wishes to terminate his marriage he need have no recourse to the court. The husband, in all schools and sects of Islam, has the right to divorce his wife at will, without giving a cause and without petitioning the court, merely by pronouncing the formula of repudiation (the ṭalāq). Although the Qur'ān prescribes this method of effecting a divorce, by pronouncing a single repudiation when the wife is in a period of purity, that is in a period after menstruation when no intercourse has taken place, or by pronouncing a single repudiation in three successive periods of purity, the most common method employed by husbands is the ṭalāq of innovation (*Ṭalāq al-bid'a*), whereby three ṭalāqs are pronounced at the same time. Although this method is regarded as sinful, all the schools of Sunnī Islam recognise it as being legally valid.

Many countries of the Middle East have enacted legislation giving the triple ṭalāq the effect only of a single ṭalāq, which means that it becomes a ṭalāq of a revocable nature so that the husband, if he has second thoughts, can revoke it while the wife is observing the *'idda* period. The 'idda is the period during which the law forbids all divorced women to remarry. It lasts for three menstrual cycles and its purpose is to determine the paternity of any child with which she may be pregnant.

In the Emirates up to the present time, however, no restrictions have been placed on the triple ṭalāq which remains the most common method by which divorces are effected.

A divorced woman is not entitled to any alimony and her husband's duty to maintain her ceases once she has completed her 'idda period. After this time the duty of maintaining an indigent wife falls on her father or other kinsmen.

Following divorce, the women of Dubai and Abu Dhabi, the Emirates which follow the Mālikī doctrine, are entitled in accordance with the law of the prevalent school, to the custody of their children until puberty in the case of boys, and until marriage in the case of girls. In the other Emirates which adhere to the Ḥanbalī school, female children remain with their mothers until marriage, but once boys have reached the so-called age of reason, that is, seven or eight, they have the choice of remaining with their mother or going to their father. However, in all schools even where the mother has custody of the children, the father remains the guardian of the person of the child and it is he alone who has overall control of the child. He may even contract the child in marriage against the wishes not only of the child but of the mother.

If the marriage is terminated by death rather than by divorce the widow again becomes entitled to the outstanding amount of the dower. She is not, however, held to be a secured creditor and the dower debt ranks along with any other of her husband's unsecured debts. She is also one of her husband's heirs, her share of his estate being one-quarter if he dies survived by no descendants. If, however, he leaves descendants her share is reduced to one-eighth, even if the husband's children are from another wife. If there are several wives, they share the one-quarter or the one-eighth equally between them so that it is possible for the share of a widow to be as little as one-thirty-second.

Although the shares of other heirs may, in certain circumstances, be increased in those Emirates where the Ḥanbalī law applies, the entitlement of the widow may never exceed one-quarter of the estate. Moreover, the law does not allow a bequest to be made to an heir, so the husband cannot legally make further provision for his wife by making a legacy in her favour. However, although the position of a woman under the law of personal status is clearly that of an inferior, her legal position otherwise is that of an equal, certainly under the Ḥanbalī doctrine.

In Ḥanbalī law a woman, once she has obtained her majority, which is equated with the onset of physical puberty or at the age of fifteen whichever is earlier, although she cannot contract her own marriage has otherwise complete contractual capacity. She can buy, sell or lease, give or be given security, act as a guarantor or herself be guaranteed.

In Mālikī law a woman acquires the same rights not on puberty but on marriage. Islamic law has never recognised the doctrine of coverture and, unlike the position in English law until the passing of the Married Women's Property Act in 1882, a married woman has always had the same rights over her property as a single woman.

Today a substantial amount of real estate in the Emirates is owned by women although transactions in respect of it are for the most part undertaken by agents. A few women are also working outside the home, not only as nurses and teachers but also in commercial offices and banking. With the increase in education for both men and women, however, more and more women will wish to take their place as full and responsible citizens of the Federation.

This growth in the workforce will surely be for the benefit of the United Arab Emirates, for with such a small indigenous population the young Federation cannot afford to allow the talent of half its people to lie dormant.

Brief Biographies of Contributors

Mr Michael Adams
Worked as Middle East correspondent for *The (Manchester) Guardian* from 1956 to 1962. He has been a Research Fellow in the Centre for Arab Gulf Studies, University of Exeter, since 1984. His publications include *Chaos or Rebirth: the Arab Outlook*, (BBC Publications, London, 1968), and *The Middle East: a Handbook* (ed.), (Anthony Blond, London, 1971). He was also editor of *Middle East International* from 1971 to 1981 and is still a contributing editor to that journal.

Mr Paul Auchterlonie
Has been subject librarian for Arabic and Islamic Studies at the University of Exeter since 1981, having previously held a similar position at the University of Lancaster. He is Secretary of the Middle East Libraries Committee and author of numerous articles and books in the field of Middle Eastern bibliography and librarianship, including *Union Catalogue of Arabic Serials and Newspapers in British Libraries*, (Mansell, London, 1977, with Y.H. Safadi) and *Arabic Biographical Dictionaries: A Summary Guide and Introduction*, (MELCOM, Durham, 1986).

Professor Aziz al-Azmeh
Is the Sharjah Professor of Islamic Studies in the University of Exeter. He is the author of *Ibn Khaldūn in Modern Scholarship*, (Third World Centre for Research and Publishing, London, 1981), *Ibn Khaldūn: An Essay in Reinterpretation*, (Frank Cass, London, 1982), *Historical Writing and Historical Knowledge: Principles of Arab Historical Writing* (in Arabic), (Dār al-Ṭalī'a, Beirut, 1983) and *Arabic Thought and Islamic Societies*, (Croom Helm, London, 1986).

Mr Glen Balfour-Paul
Ex-diplomat, serving latterly as H.M. Ambassador in Iraq, Jordan and Tunisia. He then spent two years as Director General of the Middle East Association in London before joining Exeter University's Centre for Arab Gulf Studies as a Research Fellow in 1979.

Dr Rasheed El-Enany
A Lecturer in the Department of Arabic and Islamic Studies at Exeter

University where he has taught since 1978. He did his BA in English at Cairo University where he taught until 1977. His doctorate, done at the University of Exeter, was on Naguib Mahfouz, the Egyptian author, of whose novels he has translated *Respected Sir* due to be published late in 1986.

Dr Doreen Hinchcliffe

A practising barrister who has been a Research Fellow in the Centre for Arab Gulf Studies, Exeter University, since 1982. Prior to that she was a Lecturer in Islamic Law at the Institute of Advanced Legal Studies, London University (1979–82) and a Lecturer in Law at the School of Oriental and African Studies and the Institute of Advanced Legal Studies (1967–79). She has edited many volumes of *Business Laws of the Middle East*.

Dr Richard Hitchcock

Born in 1940, he spent his childhood in Cornwall, and studied in the University of St Andrews where he was taught by Professors A.M. Honeyman, M.A. Ghul and C.E. Bosworth. He wrote a thesis on the Mozarabs in the Iberian Peninsula, and is at present Senior Lecturer in Spanish in the University of Exeter. His major research area is Hispano-Arabic history and literature, and he has published papers on aspects of Mozarabism, and on the *kharjas*, an abiding preoccupation.

Dr Hugh Kennedy

Spent a year at the Middle East Centre for Arabic Studies in Shemlan, Lebanon, before reading Arabic, Persian and History at Pembroke College, Cambridge. He is now a Lecturer in Medieval History at the University of St Andrews in Scotland. He is the author of *The Early Abbasid Caliphate: a Political History*, (Croom Helm, London, 1981) and *The Prophet and the Age of the Caliphates*, (volume 1 of the Longman History of the Near East, to be published early in 1986).

Dr Walid Khadduri

Executive Editor of the *Middle East Economic Survey* (MEES). He was formerly Director of Information and International Relations at the Organisation of Arab Petroleum Exporting Countries (OAPEC), Instructor in Political Science at Kuwait University, and Director of Research at the Institute of Palestine Studies, Beirut.

Dr Keith McLachlan
Senior Lecturer in Geography with reference to the Near and Middle East at the School of Oriental and African Studies, University of London. His published works include *Immigrant Labour in Kuwait*, (Croom Helm, London, 1985 with A.A. Al-Moosa), *The Gulf War*, (Economist Publications, London, 1985 with E.G.H. Joffe) and *Agricultural Development in the Middle East*, (John Wiley, Chichester, 1985, ed. with Peter Beaumont).

Dr Ian Richard Netton
A Lecturer in the Department of Arabic and Islamic Studies at Exeter University, specialising in medieval Islamic Philosophy and Theology, but also keenly interested in medieval Arab travellers. He is the author of *Muslim Neoplatonists*, (Allen & Unwin, London, 1982) and *Middle East Materials* (Library Association Publishing, London, 1983). He succeeded Professor M.A. Shaban as Head of the Department of Arabic and Islamic Studies in 1985.

Sir Anthony Parsons
Retired diplomat, now part-time Research Fellow, Centre for Arab Gulf Studies, and Lecturer, Department of Arabic and Islamic Studies, University of Exeter. He served in British Embassies in Baghdad, Ankara, Amman, Cairo and Khartoum, and was Political Agent, Bahrain 1965–69 and British Ambassador to Iran 1974–79. His last posts were as UK Permanent Representative to the UN 1979–82 and Foreign Affairs Adviser to the Prime Minister 1982–83. He is an Honorary Fellow of Balliol College, Oxford and author of *The Pride and the Fall (Iran 1974–79)*, (Jonathan Cape, London, 1984) and *They Say the Lion (Britain's Legacy to the Arabs)*, (Jonathan Cape, London, 1986).

Professor the Rev. Canon J.R. Porter
After holding a Fellowship at Oriel College, Oxford from 1949 to 1962, he was appointed Professor and Head of the Department of Theology at Exeter University, from which posts he retired in 1985/86. He is a Canon of Chichester Cathedral and his numerous publications include the Cambridge Bible Commentary on *Leviticus*, (Cambridge University Press, Cambridge, 1976).

Mr B.R. Pridham
Was in the Army and the Foreign Office (later HM Diplomatic Service) from 1952 to 1981, and served in many Arab and other countries,

including Muscat and Oman, and was Director of the Middle East Centre for Arab Studies (MECAS) in Lebanon 1975–76. He has been at the University of Exeter since 1981 where he succeeded Professor M.A. Shaban as Director of the Centre for Arab Gulf Studies in 1985. He is also a Lecturer in the University's Department of Arabic and Islamic Studies.

Mr J.R. Smart

Has taught Arabic in the Universities of St Andrews, Cambridge, Edinburgh and Exeter where he currently holds a Lectureship. He has spent long periods in Egypt where he worked on the dialect and folk-literature of the Western Desert bedouin, and the Arabian Gulf where he taught local dialect Arabic to the employees of an oil company. He is the author of various articles and the new edition of *Teach Yourself Arabic*, (Hodder & Stoughton, London, 1986).

Dr Roger Webster

Born in Qatar in 1955. After studying Arabic at SOAS he worked in Saudi Arabia and Oman. He has carried out field work among bedouin and rural communities in Saudi Arabia, Qatar and Oman, and also done doctoral research at the University of Exeter and development consultancy.

Index

In this index the Arabic definite article 'al-' has been omitted from proper names at the *beginning* of an entry. 'B.' and 'ibn' both appear as 'b.' in the *middle* of a name.